THE BLUE GUIDES

Austria
Belgium and Luxembourg
China
Cyprus
Czechoslovakia
Denmark
Egypt

FRANCE
France
Paris and Versailles
Burgundy
Normandy
Corsica

GREECE
Greece
Athens and environs
Crete

HOLLAND
Holland
Amsterdam

Hungary

ITALY
Northern Italy
Southern Italy
Florence
Rome and environs
Venice
Tuscany
Umbria
Sicily

Jerusalem
Malta and Gozo

Moscow and Leningrad
Morocco
Portugal

SPAIN
Spain
Barcelona

Switzerland

TURKEY
Turkey: the Aegean
   and Mediterranean Coasts
Istanbul

UK
England
Ireland
Scotland
Wales
London
Museums and Galleries
   of London
Oxford and Cambridge
Gardens of England
Literary Britain and Ireland
Victorian Architecture in Britain
Churches and Chapels
   of Northern Engalnd
Churches and Chapels
   of Southern England
Channel Islands

USA
New York
Boston and Cambridge

Yugoslavia

Detail of the façade of San Salvatore at Campi in the Valnido

BLUE GUIDE

Umbria

Alta Macadam

Maps and plans by John Flower

A & C Black
London

WW Norton
New York

First edition 1993

Published by A & C Black (Publishers) Limited
35 Bedford Row, London WC1R 4JH

A CIP catalogue record of this book
is available from the British Library.

ISBN 0–7136–3705–6

Published in the United States of America by
WW Norton and Company, Inc
500 Fifth Avenue, New York, NY 10110

Published simultaneously in Canada by
Penguin Books Canada Limited
2801 John Street, Markham, Ontario L3R 1B4

ISBN 0–393–30990–8 USA

The author and the publishers have done their best to ensure the accuracy of all the information in Blue Guide Umbria; however, they can accept no responsibility for any loss, injury or inconvenience sustained by any traveller as a result of information or advice contained in the guide.

Alta Macadam has been a writer of Blue Guides since 1970. She lives in Florence with her family (the painter Francesco Colacicchi, and their son Giovanni). Combined with work on writing the guides she has also been associated in Florence with the Bargello Museum and the Alinari photo archive. She is now involved in work for Harvard University at the Villa I Tatti in Florence. As author of the Blue Guides to Northern Italy, Rome, Venice, Sicily, Florence, Tuscany, and Umbria she travels extensively in Italy every year in order to revise new editions of the books.

For permission to reproduce the photographs in this guide, the publishers would like to thank **Joe Cornish** (pages 2, 40, 44, 58, 62, 79, 80, 82, 89, 101, 108, 111, 119, 145, 159), the Comune di Bevagna (page 129), the Associazione Pro-Todi: Foto Benigni (page 138), Armando Gregori (page 166), and the APT of Cascia, Norcia e Valnerina (page 176).

Printed and bound in Great Britain by
Butler & Tanner Ltd, Frome and London

CONTENTS

ACKNOWLEDGEMENTS

I am particularly indebted to **Roberto Colacicchi** and **Raffaella Trabalza** for their generous help to me in the preparation of this guide. Their expert knowledge on many different aspects of Umbrian life, its landscape, and its art, was invaluable to me.

Paul Langridge encouraged this guide from the start, and made many useful suggestions. I am also very grateful to Nicolai Rubinstein for his help. I would like to thank Dr John Law for his excellent article on the history of Umbria.

Signora Gigliola Lantini of the ENIT press office in Rome kindly offered assistance where possible. The local 'APT' offices in Umbria gave help to me on the spot, particularly those in Castiglione del Lago, Gubbio, Todi, Orvieto, Amelia, Spoleto, and Cascia. The 'Pro-Loco' offices of Spello and Gualdo Tadino, and the Associazione 'Pro-Todi' also went out of their way to be helpful. Signora Anna Maria Tirimagni of the 'Pro-Loco' of Montone was particularly welcoming. In Assisi, Maurizio Zubboli gave advice about the town, and Antonio Lanari, librarian of the comune of Bevagna, offered invaluable help. At Avigliano Umbro Zefferino Cerquaglia was very kind and helpful. My thanks are also due to Armando Gregori of Spoleto.

A NOTE ON BLUE GUIDES

The Blue Guide series began in 1915 when Muirhead Guide-Books Limited published 'Blue Guide London and its Environs'. Finlay and James Muirhead already had extensive experience of guidebook publishing: before the First World War they had been the editors of the English editions of the German Baedekers, and by 1915 they had acquired the copyright of most of the famous 'Red' Handbooks from John Murray.

An agreement made with the French publishing house Hachette et Cie in 1917 led to the translation of Muirhead's London guide, which became the first 'Guide Bleu'—Hachette had previously published the blue-covered 'Guides Joannes'. Subsequently, Hachette's 'Guide Bleu Paris et ses Environs' was adapted and published in London by Muirhead. The collaboration between the two publishing houses continued until 1933.

In 1933 Ernest Benn Limited took over the Blue Guides, appointing Russell Muirhead, Finlay Muirhead's son, editor in 1934. The Muirhead's connection with the Blue Guides ended in 1963 when Stuart Rossiter, who had been working on the Guides since 1954, became house editor, revising and compiling several of the books himself.

The Blue Guides are now published by A & C Black, who acquired Ernest Benn in 1984, so continuing the tradition of guidebook publishing which began in 1826 with 'Black's Economical Tourist of Scotland'. The Blue Guide series continues to grow: there are now more than 50 titles in print with revised editions appearing regularly and many new Blue Guides in preparation.

'Blue Guides' is a registered trade mark.

EXPLANATIONS

TYPE. The main routes are described in large type. Smaller type is used for branch-routes and excursions, for historical and preliminary paragraphs, and (generally speaking) for descriptions of greater detail or minor importance.

ASTERISKS indicate points of special interest or excellence.

DISTANCES are given cumulatively from the starting-point of the route or sub-route in kilometres. Mountain heights have been given in the text and on the map of Umbria in metres.

HOTELS. A small selection of hotels has been given in the text, with their official star rating in order to give an indication of price. In making the choice for inclusion, small hotels have been favoured, and those in the centre of towns, or in particularly beautiful positions in the countryside. For further information, see under Accommodation in the Practical Information section.

RESTAURANTS. A small selection of restaurants has been given in the text. They have been divided into three categories which reflect price ranges in 1992: 'LUXURY-CLASS' where the prices are likely to over Lire 60,000 a head (and sometimes well over Lire 100,000 a head). These are the most famous restaurants in Umbria and they usually offer international cuisine. '1ST-CLASS RESTAURANTS' where the prices range from Lire 35,000 and above. These are generally comfortable, with good service, but are not cheap. The third category, called 'SIMPLE TRATTORIE AND PIZZERIE' indicates places where you can eat for around Lire 25,000 a head, or even less. Although simple, the food in this category is usually the best value.
For further information, see under Eating in Italy in the Practical Information section.

MAIN ROADS are designated in the text by their official number. Autostrade (motor-ways) always carry 'A' before their number.

POPULATIONS (approximated to the nearest hundred) have been given from the latest official figures. They refer to the size of the Comune or administrative area, which is often much larger than the central urban area.

PLANS. Double-page town plans are gridded with numbered squares referred to in the text thus: (Pl. 1–16). On the ground plans of museums and churches figures or letters have been given to correspond with the descriptions which appear in the text.

ABBREVIATIONS. In addition to generally accepted and self-explanatory abbreviations, the following occur in the guide:

ACI   Automobile Club Italiano
Adm. admission
APT Azienda di Promozione Turistica (official local tourist office)
CAI Club Alpino Italiano
CIT Compagnia Italiana Turismo
ENIT Ente Nazionale per il Turismo
fest. *festa*, or festival (i.e. holiday)
fl. floruit (flourished)
FS Ferrovie dello Stato (Italian State Railways)
IAT Information office of 'APT'
Pl. plan
RAC Royal Automobile Club
Rte Route
TCI Touring Club Italiano

UMBRIA

Umbria, one of the twenty regions of Italy, lies at the very heart of the country. It is the only region on the peninsula without a sea coast. Although less well-known to foreigners than its famous neighbour Tuscany, it has some of the most beautiful landscape to be found in the country, as well as some of its most interesting towns. Its capital is Perugia, a city of great antiquity with numerous works of art. Gubbio, Spello, Todi, and Spoleto remain among the most attractive and best preserved small medieval towns in Italy. Orvieto, with its magnificent cathedral, has perhaps the most spectacular position of all the hill towns. Assisi is world famous as the birthplace of St Francis. Smaller, less well-known towns of the greatest interest include Bevagna, Montefalco, Trevi, Norcia, Amelia, and Narni.

With an area of 8456 square kilometres, Umbria has only 850,000 inhabitants. The landscape is characterised by hills covered with small silver olive trees, chestnut woods, and vineyards. The soil of Umbria is not particularly rich and so farmers have to cultivate with care the fields of their smallholdings. At the crossroads of country lanes, often marked by cypresses, numerous little tabernacles (locally known as 'maestà'), with a devotional image, survive. A special feature of Umbria is Lake Trasimene, the fourth largest lake in Italy, with its reedy shores and lovely islands. The Tiber river traverses most of the region: in its upper reaches tobacco is cultivated, while S of Perugia its valley widens out and passes beneath the town of Todi, often covered by a blueish mist off the river. In the SW corner of Umbria, between the Tiber and Nera rivers, are isolated castles and villages amidst chestnut woods and farming country. Farther E are the Monti Martani, pretty wooded hills dotted with villages and country churches. The exceptionally wide alluvial plain SE of Perugia, known as the 'Valle Umbra' is watered by numerous small rivers and is overlooked by the compact little hill towns of Trevi, Spello, and Assisi. Here the beautiful Monte Subasio (1290m) is a protected area. In the SE corner of Umbria is the lesser known Valnerina which follows the Nera river from its source in the high Monti Sibillini in the Marches down a pretty wooded valley on the slopes of which are small villages and churches, towards Terni and the spectacular Marmore waterfalls. Nearby is the delightful Lago di Piediluco. Above Norcia is a remarkable solitary upland plain (1300m) known as the Piano Grande di Castelluccio, a protected area of great interest to naturalists.

Umbria takes its name from the 'Umbri', called 'gens antiquissima Italiae' by Pliny the Elder. Of Indo-european origin, they inhabited an area considerably larger than present-day Umbria (including Romagna and part of the Marches). They settled here in prehistoric times, and reached their moment of greatest cultural importance around the 5–4C BC. The seven bronze 'Eugubian tables' still preserved in Gubbio include the most important known examples of the Umbrian language.

Umbria has a great variety of monuments from all periods of Italian history. Impressive Etruscan remains survive in Perugia, including the Arco d'Augusto, Porta Marzia, and the Ipogeo dei Volumni. The walls of Amelia date from around the 5C BC. Prehistoric, Etruscan, and Roman finds are displayed in the archaeological museums of Perugia and Orvieto. Some of the most remarkable Roman monuments N of Rome are to be found in Umbria. These can be seen at Assisi (Temple of Minerva), Narni (the Ponte d'Augusto), Bevagna (a mosaic, temple, and part of a theatre), Spello (several gateways and an amphitheatre), Todi, and Spoleto. The ruined

Roman towns of Carsulae and Ocriculum are archaeological sites of the greatest interest. Paleochristian churches include San Salvatore in Spoleto and Sant'Angelo in Perugia, as well as the unusual little Tempietto di Clitunno.

The Gothic and Romanesque period is expressed in churches, castles, town halls, and abbeys all over Umbria, as well as in frescoes and sculptural works. The great Gothic cathedral of Orvieto is one of the most memorable sights in Italy, and the interior of San Fortunato in Todi, and the upper church of San Francesco in Assisi are important examples of Italian Gothic architecture. 12C and 13C Romanesque churches include San Silvestro in Bevagna, San Pietro and Santa Chiara in Assisi, and Sant'Eufemia in Spoleto. Lesser known churches which also represent this period include the Collegiata of Lugnano in Teverina and San Felice di Narco, and the pievi in the Monti Martani, as well as the abbeys of San Pietro in Valle (where the 12C frescoes are among the most important works in Italy of this date) and San Eutizio. Splendid sculptured 12C façades include those of San Rufino in Assisi and San Pietro in Spoleto.

Of all the civic buildings erected in Umbria in the Middle Ages, the most impressive is Palazzo dei Consoli in Gubbio, begun in 1332, and attributed to Gattapone, perhaps the most ingenious Umbrian architect (who is also thought to have built the Ponte delle Torri in Spoleto). Other fine town halls are to be found in Orvieto (Palazzo del Popolo) and in Perugia (Palazzo dei Priori). Fine examples of military architecture include the 13C castle at Castiglione del Lago, and the splendid fortresses of Assisi, Spoleto and Narni, built for Cardinal Albornoz in the 14C.

The frescoes in the upper and lower churches of San Francesco in Assisi painted in the late 13C and early 14C to celebrate St Francis, by the greatest Italian painters of the time (Cimabue, Giotto, Simone Martini, and Pietro Lorenzetti) deserve a place apart in the history of art. These churches also contain some of the best stained glass windows to be found in Italy. Church treasuries of the greatest interest are preserved in Assisi (San Francesco) and Città di Castello (Museo Capitolare).

The Renaissance produced isolated masterpieces in Umbria, such as the frescoes by Filippo Lippi in the Duomo of Spoleto, and the frescoes by Luca Signorelli in the chapel of San Brizio in Orvieto cathedral. Numerous frescoes and paintings by Perugino, the greatest Umbrian painter (1446–1523), and master of Raphael, can be seen in Perugia (notably the Collegio del Cambio), Città della Pieve, and other towns. His pupils included Pinturicchio, who frescoed a chapel in Santa Maria Maggiore in Spello. Montefalco preserves some fine frescoes by Benozzo Gozzoli.

Gifted 15–16C artists of the Umbrian school of painting, whose work can be seen almost exclusively in Umbria, include Pier Antonio Mezzastris, Nicolò di Alunno, Matteo da Gualdo, Francesco Melanzio, Tiberio d'Assisi, and Bartolomeo di Tommaso of Foligno. The best comprehensive view of Umbrian painting is provided by the Pinacoteca Nazionale in Perugia.

Umbria also produced skilled woodworkers whose carvings can be seen in numerous churches all over the region. Agostino di Duccio carried out beautiful sculptural work on the façade of the Oratorio di San Bernardino in Perugia. One of the most remarkable Renaissance buildings in Umbria is the domed centrally planned church of Santa Maria della Consolazione in Todi.

Sixteenth and seventeenth century architecture, sculpture, and painting can be seen in Santa Maria degli Angeli outside Assisi. The 17C and 18C in Umbria is perhaps best represented by the palaces of Foligno which contain pictorial decorations by Pietro da Cortona, Marcello Leopardi, and Coccetti. Local architects of the 19C include Giovanni Santini. The region is particularly rich in late-18C and early-19C theatres, many of which have recently been restored; these can be found in Terni, Narni, Amelia, Spoleto, Norcia, Monteleone di Spoleto, Montecastello di Vibio, Orvieto, Trevi, Todi, Panicale, Città della Pieve, and Bevagna.

An attempt has been made in this guide to include small and lesser-known places of interest in order to give as comprehensive a picture as possible of the art and architecture of Umbria. These places will generally not be visited by those with little time at their disposal, but will be of interest to the more leisurely travellers. A comprehensive index of artists has also been provided to help scholars in their exploration of Umbria.

Umbria is now very well equipped with hotels and restaurants of all categories. Local transport by bus or train is generally excellent. As in the rest of Italy, the best time to visit Umbria is in early spring or autumn. At Easter and in summer the more famous sights can be uncomfortably crowded. Assisi totally changes character out of season: in winter it remains one of the most fascinating and beautiful towns in Italy.

UMBRIA: AN HISTORICAL INTRODUCTION

John Law

Umbria for long remained one of the regions of Italy little explored by foreign travellers, even in the age of the Grand Tour, and despite expanding tourism in the 19C. In the main, it lay off the principal routes chosen by pilgrims, antiquarians and connoisseurs heading for Rome and further south. Its rich heritage of medieval art and architecture was largely unacknowledged as long as taste was dominated by the classical: the legacies of Rome and the Renaissance.

Within the Papal States, the cities of Umbria acquired a provincial character; the aspirations of its larger cities for wide autonomy or statehood had ceased with the Renaissance, and the absence of the society and patronage associated with court life had encouraged noble families, intellectuals and artists to gravitate to major or capital cities like Rome or Florence. Protestants, liberals and supporters of Italian Unification viewed papal government with hostility, as reactionary and oppressive, dependent on *bastille*-type prison citadels in cities like Perugia, Narni and Spoleto. They also criticised the papal regime on social and economic grounds, in terms of absentee, grasping landlords, backward industries and an absence of exports other than a steady migration of people in search of better opportunities elsewhere in Italy or abroad. Umbria had to await Italian Unification (1860) before its railways were built. This retarded its economic growth and with it the development of the hotels and spas attendant on expanding tourism.

However, tastes and interests were changing even before the overthrow of papal rule and the expansion of the rail network. More adventurous and discerning travellers could see Umbria in sympathetic and even romantic terms. Off the beaten track, it was purer, more natural, more spiritual, more medieval than centres of long-acclaimed importance and growing popularity like Florence, Venice or Rome. A pioneer in this respect was Thomas Trollope (1810–93) who published an account of his journey under the title *Travels in Central Italy or a Lenten Journey* in 1862. Unbridled and emotional enthusiasm for Umbria was expressed by Edward Hutton (1875–1969) in his *Cities of Umbria* first published in 1905 before running into many subsequent editions. Hutton's work was beautifully illustrated, as was another early guide for the discerning English-speaking public, Ada Harrison's *Some Umbrian Cities* (1925).

But it would be a mistake to see the greater knowledge and enthusiasm that the growing literature on Umbria represents in terms only of a reaction to the more frequented resorts and cities of Italy. The legacy and shrine of St Francis of Assisi (1181–1226) had an increasing impact on travellers, Protestant and Catholic alike, who saw the saint and his immediate followers as representatives of a purer, revitalised Christianity. At the same time, appreciation grew for the art and architecture of the region, as perceived in such cities as Perguia, Assisi and Orvieto. The influence of John Ruskin (1819–1900) and the pre-Raphaelites insured that the medieval period was no longer dismissed as primitive, superstitious, naive or quaint. Medieval sculptors, masons and painters became admired, not only for their craftsmanship, but also for their ability to express Christian belief in a pure and direct form. To such sympathetic eyes, even the Umbrian countryside, with its many shrines, hermitages and monasteries, could be viewed in spiritual terms: the 'Italia mystica' of Edward Hutton. Indeed Hutton expressed the fear that the special heritage, character and 'secret' of Umbria were under threat from a modernising, industrialising and secular Italy.

However, Hutton's enthusiasm for an unspoiled, timeless Umbria did not lead him to suggest that the region had been by-passed or unmarked by history. It has suffered from natural disasters in the forms of earthquake, plague and disease. The flourishing Roman *municipium* of Carsulae on the Via Flaminia was abandoned after a serious earthquake. The whole region was hit by the Black Death (1348) and its successive outbreaks; Todi lost around half its population from plague in 1523. Malaria has only recently been eradicated, but depopulation continues, draining the inhabitants from the farms and smaller communities of the countryside. Man-made disasters came in the form of wars and invasions. Terni's history is punctuated by moments of destruction: by Totila (546), by Frederick I Hohenstaufen (1174), by Allied bombardment (1944).

Not only could the region be caught up in wider events; its internal history was also frequently agitated and violent. This helps to explain why the present boundaries were stabilised only in the 20C. Moreover, the name 'Umbria' was not in continuous use to denote the area. It was adopted by the Romans, and re-emerged in the works of local antiquarians in the 16C. The name derives from the Umbri, an Italic tribe whose principal area of settlement stretched from the Tiber to the Adriatic, and therefore did not correspond with the present region. Their neighbours to the west, who occupied most of what is now Umbria, were the Etruscans whose civilisation was at its most influential from the 8C to the 5C BC.

By the 3C BC both peoples had succumbed to Roman hegemony. This was marked by military defeat (the destruction of Etruscan Orvieto in 265 BC); colonisation (Spoleto, 241 BC); some redistribution of land; some instances of rebellion (Perugia, 40 BC). However, on balance Romanisation should not be seen in terms of wars of conquest and military rule. Neither the Umbrians nor the Etruscans were organised into centralised, unified states, and the advance of Roman influence and authority was piecemeal, with some cities like Gubbio first becoming allies of Rome. Many cities showed their loyalty in the dark days of the Second Punic War and Hannibal's crushing defeat of Rome at Lake Trasimene (217 BC). Rome recognised Umbrian communities as self-governing *municipia* and extended its citizenship to their inhabitants. There was religious and cultural toleration; indeed Roman civilisation and religion were heavily indebted to the Etruscans. The whole process was expressed and encouraged by the construction of a network of roads, principally the Via Flaminia (220 BC). Under Augustus (29 BC–8 AD) Umbria emerges for the first time as an administrative region—later it was joined to Tuscany under Diocletian (285–305). This eliminated a border which the absence of clear, natural frontiers remained hard to draw throughout history.

Whatever its frontiers, Roman provincial organisation collapsed with the Roman Empire and the massive invasions of the Visigoths (5C) and the Ostrogoths (early 6C). On the road to Rome, central Italy became a battleground between the invaders and the Byzantine empire whose emperors claimed the Roman succession and tried to uphold its authority and defend its territories in the west. Byzantine-led resistance was not without success. The emperor Justinian (527–65) sent armies under Belisarius and Narses to fight the Ostrogoths; in 552 Totila, king of the Ostrogoths, was defeated and killed. However the Byzantines were less able to withstand the invasion of the Lombards later in the century; they captured Umbria and established a Lombard duchy at Spoleto (570). Their ascendancy lasted to the late 8C when the Franks intervened in Italy under Pepin III (714–68) and Charlemagne (742–814). Frankish rule over the ducy of Spoleto dates from 789.

Frankish intervention had been solicited by the papacy which tried to secure their loyalty by crowning Charlemagne as emperor in Rome in 800; the papacy also sought Frankish recognition of papal lordship over central Italy. This claim, to govern as secular rulers what came to be called the Lands of St Peter or the Papal States, was criticised and contested by lawyers, reformers, political thinkers and opponents of the papacy from the early Middle Ages to the 20C. As the claim has considerable bearing on the history of Umbria, it merits some attention. In the first place, the papacy was anxious to secure itself from attack and political pressure. The popes also sought to control the agricultural land, the ports, the trade and pilgrim routes necessary to sustain the city of Rome. They were also anxious to establish their authority over other wealthy and influential churches and monasteries in central Italy. Lastly, the popes saw themselves as legitimate heirs to the temporal authority of the Roman emperors.

To strengthen its position, the papacy secured recognition of its claims from Frankish rulers, Pepin in 756 and Charlemagne in 774, 781 and 787. It also resorted to invention and forgery in the Donation of Constantine, an 8C document which purported to be the cession of temporal authority in the west to the papacy by the emperor Constantine (306–27) in recognition of his conversion to Christianity and his miraculous recovery from illness. The validity of the grant was attacked in the Middle Ages by Roman lawyers hostile to papal pretensions, and its authenticity was demolished in the 15C by the humanist Lorenzo Valla (1407–57).

However, papal authority in the States of the Church for long remained stronger in theory than in practice. It was only with Innocent III (1198–1216) that an attempt was made to realise papal lordship, but for centuries after that papal rule remained intermittent. For example, in 1353 Innocent VI made the Spanish cardinal Albornoz his representative in Italy, and a series of military and political successes appeared crowned by the issue of a constitution in 1357. That remained on the statute book until the 19C; its implementation proved much more difficult.

There are various reasons for the weakness of papal rule in the later Middle Ages: breaks in the succession (e.g. 1292–94); a prolonged absence from Italy (1305–76); schism within the Papal States (1378–1418); challenges to papal authority from Church councils (e.g. the Council of Basle, 1431–49). Threats to papal rule also came from secular rulers. They included: the Hohenstaufen emperors Frederick I (1152–90) and Frederick II (1212–50); the Florentine Republic; Ladislas of Naples (1386–1414), Giangaleazzo Visconti, lord then duke of Milan (1378–1402). Papal rule in Umbria was also weakened by lords from within the Papal States, some of whom were also mercenary military leaders, or *condottieri*, and all of whom were anxious to defend and extend their lands. Some were native to Umbria like the Trinci of Foligno who ruled that and neighbouring cities from c 1300 to 1439 or Braccio da Montone (1368–1424) who established an ascendancy over Perugia in 1416. Others came from other papal provinces like the

Montefeltro of Urbino who ruled Gubbio from 1387 to 1508 or Francesco Sforza who held Amelia briefly from 1434 to 1435.

A major reason why Umbria attracted the ambitions of foreign and native rulers, and a further reason for the intermittent nature of papal rule was the development of towns in political, economic and military terms. As cities like Perugia, Spoleto, Todi and Orvieto still bear witness—even to the non-archaeologist—the urban life of Umbria predates the Roman period by centuries. The Etruscans and the Umbrians most often chose hill sites for reasons of security, health, availability of building stone and the economical use of agricultural land. Other cities owed their origin and development to river crossings or the road system (Foligno, Terni). As throughout the Roman Empire, city life was equated with civilisation (*civis* means citizen). If the majority of the population worked the land and if agriculture remained the major engine of the economy, towns were the centres of political, cultural and religious activity. The spread of Christianity from the 2C was closely linked to the road system and the towns along it. The barbarian invasions damaged rather than destroyed the situation, but the collapse of central authority as represented by pope or emperor did not in the longer term prevent the revival of the towns in the 10C and 11C, in most cases on Etruscan, Umbrian or Roman sites. Gradually the towns recovered in terms of population and economic activity as local and then regional markets, and as centres of industry (construction, textiles, pottery).

Such developments fuelled growing political and military muscle which in turn led the individual towns and cities of Umbria to form themselves into associations or communes, to increase their privileges and seek greater self-government in the 11C and 12C. This period saw the communes of Umbria gradually extending their authority over the surrounding *contado* (county or jurisdiction) at the expense of lay and ecclesiastical landlords and smaller communities. Distant overlords, the emperors in particular, could challenge but not reverse this trend. For example, contemporary and later authorities probably exaggerate when they describe periods of Hohenstaufen rule in towns like Montefalco in the 12C and 13C in terms of devastation.

Historians once enthused over the communes as early bourgeois republics, if not as democracies, which destroyed the power of local bishops and feudatories and which developed the economy beyond a dependence on agriculture into trade and industry. Nowadays the communes tend to be viewed in a much more critical light. They were jealous of their own authority in matters of territory, jurisdiction and trade routes. The history of medieval Umbria is full of internecine disputes; the young Francis of Assisi (1181–1226) was captured when fighting for his city against its neighbour and arch-rival Perugia in 1202; later that city's acceptance of his preaching and his cult was grudging. The freedoms and privileges the cities enjoyed were not extended to subject communities and the rural population. Nor were the communes themselves in any sense democracies. Full political, legal and economic rights remained in the hands of an oligarchy of the longer established families. When the *popolo* (the people) acquired a share in government in the 13C, they did not represent a democratic revolution, as their party name might suggest, but the arrival of new wealth.

The communes of medieval Umbria were small; the largest, Perugia, possibly reached 28,000 inhabitants at the peak of the population curve, c 1300. None was a major financial, industrial or manufacturing centre; the bulk of the population drew its wealth and support from the land. Moreover the feudal lords had not been destroyed as a class; magnate families resided in the cities often behind private fortifications. They built up networks of clients and dependents. Their more aristocractic life-style appealed to aspiring members of the bourgeoisie, and their power and influence were sources of political and social instability. Indeed, faction stalked the internal history of the communes. There was no sense of legitimate opposition, and political and family rivalry could explode in street-fighting, murder and exile, as between the Oddi and the Baglioni of Perugia c 1500. Faction could also reflect and feed off conflicts on a larger scale, most notoriously between the pro-papal Guelfs and the pro-imperial Ghibellines, in 14C Oriveto for example. Finally, the record of instability helps to explain why many of the communes of Umbria succumbed in the late medieval period to the hegemony or formal lordship (*signoria*) of prominent local families, like the Baglioni in Perugia or the Trinci in Foligno.

However, it would be wrong to conclude that the communal period was one of disaster and failure; after all, this was the period that largely shaped the towns and cities of Umbria as they appear today. The communes defended themselves with circuits of walls. Hostile regimes and unruly families were punished by the reduction of their fortresses. Legislation was passed to stimulate the economy and protect the environment; for example, legislation was passed to try to prevent the erosion of the cliffs on which Orvieto was built. The common interest, the public good was expressed in books of statutes and more obviously in the public buildings (*palazzi*) that housed the communal courts, council halls, treasuries and archives. The public interest was also served by the paving of streets and squares, the construction of bridges and roads, the provision of markets and the installation of wells and fountains—prized engineering marvels in the hill towns. In the religious sphere, the community was served and expressed by the construction, enlargement and embellishment of churches. The cathedral tended to take pride of place, but the churches associated with religious orders (especially the friars), parishes and local cults were also of importance to the community. In Perugia a university was founded in the 13C which soon acquired a formidable reputation for law.

But, however considerable and abiding their achievements, the communes of Umbria failed to retain the status of independent city states for long. Many of the reasons for this have been suggested above, but none of the communes had the resources to resist papal authority, set out in the Middle Ages but enforced in the Renaissance. Architecture can again prove very revealing. The great fortresses built by Albornoz, for example at Spoleto or Narni, signal an early attempt to secure papal rule. When Perugia rebelled against papal taxation in 1540, the forces of Paul III took the city, reduced its privileges, levelled the houses of the prominent Baglioni dynasty and began work on a citadel, the *Rocca Paolina*. The fortress lasted until 1860, and increasingly became a means and a symbol of oppression. When Thomas Trollope visited the city after its liberation from papal rule, he rejoiced at the destruction of that *bastille*-type structure.

However, to see Umbria's history within the Papal States entirely in terms of oppression would be misleading on two counts. The spread of papal authority, particularly from the 15C, could be represented in terms of liberty and good government; when the warrior cardinal Giovanni Vitelleschi overthrew the Trinci of Foligno in 1439 this was justified as bringing an end to tyranny. The despotic reputation of papal rule itself emerged late, in the 18C and 19C. Unrest and criticism were encouraged by the experiments and changes brought about by the Revolutionary and Napoleonic wars, when the continuity of papal government was interrupted. Only with the

19C is there evidence of active sedition and revolt (1831, 1848, 1859). Some concessions were made to reform, as in the early years of the pontificate of Pius IX (1846–78). More generally, papal government was distant and inefficient. Communes preserved their sense of identity and a degree of autonomy. Leading families, like the Geraldini of Amelia, could be flattered and advanced by papal favours and service. The construction of a large number of civic theatres in the 18C and early 19C suggests that social and cultural life was far from dead.

Secondly—and much more positively—Umbria was of great significance to the Roman Catholic Church in religious terms. It was converted early, and its saints and martyrs have remained closely associated with its towns and cities. Moreover, the region long remained a breeding-ground for religious revival. St Benedict (480–550), the founder of western monasticism, was born at Norcia. His example later influenced St Francis, the reluctant founder of one of the principal mendicant orders of friars. And the saints of Umbria were by no means always male. An early disciple of Benedict was his sister, St Scholastica. The reputation of the Franciscan movement was spread thanks to the example of a close follower of Francis, St Clare of Assisi, founder of the order of Poor Clares (1194–1253). Ideas central to the Catholic faith were strengthened in Umbria. St Francis and his followers elaborated the Nativity story, giving it its abiding appeal. The feast of Corpus Domini was inaugurated at Orvieto in 1264 after a local miracle concerning the Eucharist. Both events led to the foundation of the magnificent cathedral (1290).

But not all religious activity supported the official Church. Orvieto was also associated with the Cathar heresy in the 13C. In 1260, Perugia was a starting point for the penitential Flagellants whose extremism and anti-clericalism alarmed the Church. The mystical Franciscan poet, Jacopone da Todi (1230–1306) is venerated now for his hymns, or lauds, to the Virgin, among them the Stabat Mater. From 1298 to 1303 he was imprisoned for attacking the corruption of the papacy. In the late 19C, count Enrico Campello from near Spoleto led a movement to reform the Catholic Church which drew inspiration and support from the Protestant world; he was later persuaded to recant. Although he has a fine tomb at Campello, there is no cult attached to his memory.

The plethora of Umbrian saints and religious figures still attract both an international and a local following. St Benedict was declared patron saint of Europe in 1964 and Assisi has ecumenical appeal, but small towns like Montefalco proudly preserve shrines—like that to St Clare (1268–1308)—that still attract the devout. And such cults can also be seen as manifestations of an urban-orientated society that pre-dates Christianity. To this day, local patriotism, or *campanilismo*, can easily be detected, finding expression in such ceremonies as the Corsa dei Ceri at Gubbio. This part-religious, part-sporting event is held on 15 May in honour of St Ubaldo (1100–60), a local bishop who allegedly saved the city from Frederick I Hohenstaufen. But the origins of the ritual may well be much older, like the city of Gubbio itself.

Further Reading

J. Bentley, *Umbria* (London, 1989).

J. Bentley, *Italy: the Hill Towns* (London, 1990).

G. Fauré, *The Land of St Francis of Assisi* (London, 1924).

A. Harrison, *Some Umbrian Cities* (London, 1925).

D. Hay (ed.), *The Longman History of Italy* (London, 1980–).

H. Hearder and D.P. Waley (eds.), *A Short History of Italy* (Cambridge, 1962).

H. Hearder, *Italy: A Short History* (Cambridge, 1990).

W. Heywood, *A History of Perugia* (London, 1910).

E. Hutton, *The Cities of Umbria* (London, 1905).

P. Partner, *The Lands of St Peter* (London, 1972).

J. Pemble, *The Mediterranean Passion* (Oxford, 1988).

T. Trollope, *Travels in Central Italy or a Lenten Journey* (London, 1862).

D.P. Waley, *The Italian City Republics* (London, 1978).

Place names in Italian towns and cities

Many of the place names in Italian towns and cities have ancient origins; the names assigned to public buildings, market places, towers, bridges, gates and fountains frequently date to the Middle Ages. But the practice of formally naming all streets and squares began in the 19C. Frequently local—even parochial—patriotism determines the choice as the community celebrates its own history and its own political, literary, religious and scientific figures, as well as famous foreign visitors.

But the choice of place names can reflect wider issues, and events and figures from Italian national history are prominently represented. Thus a united republican Italy can be celebrated in terms of concepts (e.g. Via della Repubblica, della Libertà, della Vittoria), events (e.g. Via del Plebiscito recalling the vote that preceeded a region uniting with the Kingdom of Italy in the 19C), or by drawing on the gazetteer of Italian rivers, mountains, seas and cities.

Broadly speaking the national figures and events chosen tend to be representative of four phases in recent Italian history. Probably the most emotive and frequently commemorated is the Risorgimento (the Resurgence), the movement that led to the unification and independence of Italy in the 19C; among the battles commemorated are: Custoza, Lissa, Solferino, Magenta, Montebello, Mentana. For some historians, Italy's entry to the First World War represents the final phase in the pursuit of national unity; the battles and campaigns between Italy, and her allies, and the Central Powers are also frequently recorded in place names: the Isonzo; Monte Pasubio; Caporetto; Monte Grappa; the Piave; Vittorio Veneto. Opposition to Fascism and the ending of the Second World War are also commemorated in this way, as are the statesmen and events associated with the country's reconstruction, economic development and membership of the EC. Casualties in Italy's successful struggle against political terroism (Aldo Moro, murdered by the Red Brigades in 1978) and the less successful war with organised crime (Alberto della Chiesa, killed by the Mafia in 1982) are also being honoured.

Largely censored and deleted from the record are the events and personalities closely linked to Fascism, Italy's empire and the reigns of the last two members of the House of Savoy, Vittorio Emanuele III (1900–46) and Umberto II (1946). However, the keen-eyed observer might be able to identify traces of Fascist insignia and the Fascist system of dating (1922, when Mussolini was inivited to lead the government, is year 1) on public buildings and monuments, and some street names still recall territories once ruled from Rome (e.g. Istria, Dalmazia, Albania, Libia).

Below are listed a selection of the more prominent figures and events from recent Italian history the traveller is likely to encounter time and again.

People

Vittorio ALFIERI (1749–1803), poet and dramatist.

Cesare BATTISTI, Italian patriot executed by the Habsburg regime in Trent, 12 July 1916.

Giosuè CARDUCCI (1835–1907), patriotic poet and literary critic.

Camille CAVOUR (1810–61), statesman and cautious architect of Italian unification.

Francesco CRISPI (1818–1901), statesman.

Ugo FOSCOLO (1778–1827), poet and patriot.

Giuseppe GARIBALDI (1807–82), inspirational political and military leader in the Risorgimento.

Antonio GRAMSCI (1891–1937), political thinker, Marxist, opponent of Fascism.

Daniele MANIN (1804–57), Venetian patriot and statesman, defender of that city against Habsburg forces, 1848–49.

Guglielmo MARCONI (1874–37), electrical engineer and radio pioneer.

MARGHERITA of Savoy (1851–1926), wife of King Umberto I, noted for her piety, good works and cultural patronage.

MARTIRI DELLA RESISTENZA (or DELLA LIBERTÀ), opponents of Fascism and German occupation, 1943–45.

Giacomo MATTEOTTI (1885–1924), socialist politician, assassinated by Fascists.

Guiseppe MAZZINI (1805–82), leading republican figure of the Risorgimento.

Guglielmo OBERDAN (1858–82), Italian patriot, executed by the Habsburg regime in Trieste.

Bettino RICASOLI (1809–80), Florentine statesman, instrumental in securing Tuscany's adherence to the Kingdom of Italy in 1860.

Aurelio SAFFI (1819–1890), man of letters and hero of the Risorgimento.

UMBERTO I of Savoy, King of Italy, 1878–1900.

GIUSEPPE VERDI (1813–1901), prolific opera composer whose output was often associated with the cause of a united Italy. This surname could be read as the initials of 'Vittorio Emanuele Re d'Italia'.

VITTORIO EMANUELE II of Savoy, King of Sardinia-Piedmont from 1849, King of Italy 1861–78.

Events

XI FEBBRAIO: 11 February 1929, formal reconciliation between the papacy and the kingdom of Italy.

XXIX MARZO: 29 March 1943, armistice between Italy and the Allies.

XXVII APRILE: 27 April 1945, Benito Mussolini captured in northern Italy. The Fascist leader was quickly tried and executed on 28 April.

XI MAGGIO: 11 May 1860, Garibaldi landed with 1000 men at Marsala (Sicily), launching the military campaign that led to the Unification of Italy.

XXIV MAGGIO: 24 May 1915, Italy enters the First World War.

II GIUGNO: 2 June 1946, referendum designed to favour a republican constitution.

XX GIUGNO: 20 June 1859, papal forces and their supporters violently suppressed a pro-Unification rising in Perugia.

XIV SETTEMBRE: 14 September 1860, the forces of the Kingdom of Italy entered Perugia.

XX SETTEMBRE: 20 September 1870, Italian forces enter Rome, overthrowing papal rule.

IV NOVEMBRE: 4 November 1918, proclamation of the armistice between Italy and Austria.

PRACTICAL INFORMATION

Approaches to Italy

Direct air services (scheduled flights as well as charter flights) operate between London (Heathrow, Gatwick, and Stansted) and Italy. Pisa, Florence, Bologna, and Rome are the nearest airports to Umbria. There are direct rail services from Calais and Boulogne via Paris to Florence and Rome. The easiest approaches by road are the motorways through the Mont Blanc, St Bernard, or Monte Cenis tunnels, over the Brenner pass, or along the coast from the south of France.

Among the numerous **Tour Operators** who organise inclusive tours and charter trips to Italy are: Citalia, Martin Randall Travel, Fine Art Courses Ltd., Nadfas Tours, Pilgrim Air, Prospect Music and Art Tours, Serenissima Travel, Swan Hellenic, Italian Escapades and Italiatour. Chapter Travel Ltd, 102 St John's Wood Terrace, London NW8 6PL, Tel. 071/722 9560, specialise in holidays to Italy.

Air Services between London and Italy are operated by British Airways (Tel. 081/897 4000), Alitalia (Tel. 071/602 7111), and (Florence only) Air UK (Tel. 0345 666777) and Meridiana (Tel. 071/839 2222). Charter flights (often much cheaper) are also now run to most of the main cities in Italy; the fare often includes hotel accommodation. All scheduled services have a monthly excursion fare, and a limited number of special reduced fares (usually only available if booked well in advance). The airline companies offer a 25 per cent reduction of the return fare to full-time students (12–26 years old) and young people between the ages of 12 and 21. Car hire schemes in conjunction with flights can also be arranged.

Rail Services. The most direct routes from Calais and Boulogne via Paris and Dijon (with sleeping compartments) are via Modane to Turin, Genoa, and Pisa or via Lausanne and Domodossola to Milan, Bologna, and Florence. A service from London Victoria via Dover, Calais, Basel, and Chiasso runs to Milan, Florence, and Rome. Information on the Italian State Railways (and tickets and seat reservations) may be obtained in London from Citalia, Marco Polo House, 3–5 Lansdowne Road, Croydon, Surrey CR9 1LL (Tel. 081/686 0677), and Wasteels Travel, 121 Wilton Road, London, SW1V 1J2 (Tel. 071/834 7066).

Bus Service. A bus service operates in two days between London (Victoria Coach Station) and Rome (Piazza della Repubblica) via Dover, Paris, Mont Blanc, Aosta, Turin, Genoa, Milan, Bologna, and Florence, daily from June to September, and once or twice a week for the rest of the year. Reduction for students. Information in London from the National Express office at Victoria Coach Station, from local National Express Agents, and in Italy from SITA offices.

By Car. British drivers taking their own cars by any of the routes across France, Belgium, Luxembourg, Switzerland, Germany, and Austria need the vehicle registration book, a valid national driving licence (accompanied by a translation, issued free by the RAC, AA, and ENIT offices), insurance cover, and a nationality plate attached to the car. If you are not the owner of the vehicle, you must have the owner's permission for its use abroad. A Swiss Motorway Pass is needed for Switzerland, and can be obtained from the RAC, the AA or at the Swiss border.

The continental rule of the road is to drive on the right and overtake on the left. The provisions of the respective highway codes in the countries of transit, though similar, have important variations, especially with regard to priority, speed limits, and pedestrian crossings. Membership of the 'Automobile Association' (Tel. 0256 20123), or the 'Royal Automobile Club' (membership enquiries and insurance, Tel. 0345 3331133; route information Tel. 0345 333222) entitles you to many of the facilities of affiliated societies on the Continent. They are represented at most of the sea and air ports.

Motorway routes to Italy from Europe. The main routes from France, Switzerland, and Austria are summarised below.

A. The direct motorway route from France, by-passing Geneva, enters Italy through the **Mont Blanc Tunnel**. The road from Courmayeur to Aosta has not yet been improved. At Aosta the A5 motorway begins: it follows the Val d'Aosta. Just beyond Ivrea is the junction with the A4/5 motorway: the A5 continues S to Turin, while the A4/5 diverges E. At Santhia the A4 motorway from Turin is joined for Milan via Novara, or the A26/4 can be followed S via Alessandria, reaching the coast at Voltri, just outside Genoa. For Umbria there is a choice between the 'Autostrada del Sole' (A1) from Milan or the Florence–Pisa motorway from Genoa. The latter route avoids the Apennine pass between Bologna and Florence which carries very heavy traffic and can be subject to delays.

B. The most direct approach to Turin from France is through the **Monte Cenis Tunnel** from Modane in France to Bardonecchia. A road continues to Oulx where a motorway is under construction via Susa to Turin parallel to the old road. From Turin a motorway (A6) descends direct to the coast at Savona, or the motorway (A21, A26) via Asti and Alessandria leads to Genoa; either one joins directly the coastal motorway for Pisa and Florence. Alternatively, the A4 motorway leads from Turin E to Milan for the 'Autostrada del Sole'.

C. The **Coastal route from the South of France** follows the A10 motorway through the foothills with frequent long tunnels to enter Italy just before Ventimiglia. The motorway continues past Alassio, Albenga, and Savona (where the motorway from Turin comes in), to Voltri (where the A26 motorway from Alessandria comes in) and Genoa (with the junction of the the A7 motorway from Milan). The coastal motorway continues beyond Rapallo and La Spezia past the resorts of Versilia, and at Viareggio divides. The left branch (A11) continues via Lucca to Florence (and the 'Autostrada del Sole'), while the coastal branch (A12) continues to Pisa and Livorno.

D. The approach to Italy from Switzerland (Lausanne) is usually through the **Great St Bernard Tunnel** (or by the pass in summer) which only becomes motorway at Aosta (see A, above).

E. Another motorway route from Switzerland is via the **St Gotthard Tunnel** (opened in 1980) and Lugano. The motorway (A9) enters Italy at Como and continues to Milan where the 'Autostrada del Sole' (A1) begins for central Italy.

F. From Germany and Austria (Innsbruck) the direct approach to Italy is by the motorway over the **Brenner Pass**. The motorway (A22) continues down the Isarco valley to Bolzano and the Adige valley via Trento to Verona. Here motorways diverge W for Brescia and Milan, or E for Vicenza and Venice, or continue S via Mantua to join the A1 motorway just W of Modena for Florence and central Italy.

Car sleeper train services operate from Boulogne and Paris, Hamburg, Vienna, and Munich to Milan, Bologna, Rome, etc.

Passports are necessary for all British travellers entering Italy; American travellers must carry passports. British passports valid for ten years are issued at the Passport Office, Clive House, Petty France, London SW1, or may be obtained for an additional fee through any travel agent. A 'British Visitor's Passport' (valid one year) can be purchased at post offices in Britain. You are strongly advised to carry some means of identity with you at all times while in Italy, since you can be held at a police station if you are stopped and found to be without a document of identity. A stolen or lost passport can be replaced with little trouble by the British or US embassy in Rome, or the British or US consulate in Florence.

Money. The monetary unit is the Italian lira (plural; lire). The current exchange value is approximately 2200 lire to the £ sterling (1200 lire to the US dollar). There are coins of 10, 20, 50, 100, 200 and 500 lire, and notes of 1000, 2000, 5000, 10,000, 50,000, and 100,000 lire. Travellers' cheques and Eurocheques are the safest way of carrying money while travelling, and most credit cards are now generally accepted in shops and restaurants (but rarely at petrol stations). The commission on cashing travellers' cheques can be quite high. For banking hours, see under 'General Information', below. Money can be changed at exchange offices ('cambio') in travel agencies, some post offices, and main stations. Exchange offices are usually open seven days a week at airports and some main railway stations. At some hotels, restaurants, and shops money can be exchanged (but usually at a lower rate).

Police Registration is formally required within three days of entering Italy. If you are staying at a hotel the management takes care of this. The permit lasts three months, but can be extended on application.

Information Offices

Italian Tourist Boards. General information can be obtained abroad from the 'Italian State Tourist Office' (ENIT; Ente Nazionale Italiano per il Turismo'), who distribute free an excellent 'Traveller's handbook' (revised about every year), and provide detailed information about Italy.

In London their office is at 1 Princes Street, WIR 8AY (Tel. 071/4081254); in New York at 630 Fifth Avenue, Suite 1565 (Tel. 2454822); and in Chicago at 500 North Michigan Avenue, Suite 1046 (Tel. 6440990).

In Umbria the Regional State Tourist office is in Perugia: 'Assessorato al Turismo della Regione dell'Umbria', 30 Corso Vannucci, Tel. 075/5041. Umbria is divided into sectors, each with a local tourist information office, the 'Azienda di Promozione Turistica' ('APT') which provides invaluable help to travellers on arrival: they supply a free list of accommodation (revised annually), including hotels, youth hostels, and camping sites; up-to-date information on museum opening times and annual events; and information about local transport. They also usually distribute, free of charge, illustrated pamphlets about each town, sometimes with a good plan, etc. The headquarters are normally open Monday–Saturday 8–14.00, but in the towns of particular interest there is sometimes a separate 'APT' information office, which is also often open in the afternoon.

The 'APT' of Umbria are as follows:

'APT di Perugia', 21 Via Mazzini, Perugia (Tel. 075/25341); Information Office, 3 Piazza IV Novembre (Tel. 075/23327).

'APT del Ternano' (for Narni, Terni, etc.), 5 Viale Battisti, Terni (Tel. 0744/43047). Information Office, 7A Viale Battisti, Tel. 0744/43047).

'APT di Assisi', 12 Piazza del Comune (Tel. 075/812450). Information Office, Piazza del Comune (Tel. 075/812534).

'APT della Valnerina-Cascia' (also for Norcia), 2 Via Da Chiavano, Cascia (Tel. 0743/71401). Information Office, 1 Piazza Garibaldi (Tel. 0743/71147).

'APT dell'Alta Valle del Tevere' (for Città di Castello), 2B Via Raffaele di Cesare, Città di Castello (Tel. 075/8554817).

'APT del Folignate-Nocera Umbra' (for Bevagna, Foligno, Montefalco, Spello, and Trevi), 12 Piazza Garibaldi, Foligno (Tel. 0742/350493). Information Office, Porta Romana (Tel. 0742/60459).

'APT di Gubbio', 6 Piazza Oderisi, Gubbio (Tel. 075/9220693).

'APT di Spoleto', 7 Piazza della Libertà, Spoleto (Tel. 0743/49890). Information Office (Tel. 0743/220311).

'APT dell'Orvietano', 24 Piazza Duomo, Orvieto (Tel. 0763/41772).

'APT del Trasimeno' (for Castiglione del Lago, Città della Pieve, Passignano, etc.), 10 Piazza Mazzini, Castiglione del Lago (Tel. 075/9652484).

'APT del Tuderte' (for Todi, Monti Martani, etc.), 6 Piazza Umberto I, Todi (Tel. 075/8943395). Information Office, 38 Piazza del Popolo (Tel. 075/8943062).

'APT del Amerino' (for Amelia and environs), 1 Via Orvieto, Amelia (Tel. 0744/981453).

Approaches to Umbria from the rest of Italy

By Air. The nearest international airports to Umbria are at Pisa (230km NW of Perugia), and at Rome (210km SW of Perugia). There is a daily bus service (by 'SULGA') from Rome airport (Fiumicino) to and from Perugia (in 3½hrs). From Pisa airport there is a train to Florence, and from there trains on the main line to Rome (change at Terontola for Perugia). There is a small airport at Sant'Egidio, 12km from Perugia, with flights from Milan (Tel. 075/6929447).

By Train. The main line between Florence and Rome has a station at Terontola (slow trains only) on the branch line to Lake Trasimene, Perugia, Assisi, Spello and Foligno. From the S, the main line between Rome and Florence has a station at Orte, for the line to Narni, Terni, Spoleto, Trevi, and Foligno. Orvieto is on the main line between Florence and Rome (slow trains only). From the Adriatic coast there is a line from Ancona to Foligno, Spoleto, and Terni.

By Bus. There are long-distance bus services from Florence to Perugia and Assisi, and from Rome to Perugia.

By car. The A1 motorway from Milan and Florence has exits for Umbria at 'Valdichiana' (connecting with the 'superstrada' for Perugia), and 'Chiusi-Chianciano Terme'. The A1 motorway from Rome has exits at 'Orte', 'Attigliano', 'Orvieto', and 'Fabro'. The A14 motorway down the Adriatic coast of Italy has exits at Cesena (for the E7 superstrada to Città di Castello and Perugia.

Umbria is often visited **from Tuscany**, which adjoins it to the N (see 'Blue Guide Tuscany'). By car the quickest approach is by the A1 motorway to the 'Valdichiana' exit, where a 'superstrada' begins which enters Umbria at Lake Trasimene and continues to Perugia. By this route, Perugia can be reached in under 2 hours from Florence. There is also a road from Cortona, just across the border in Tuscany. Another beautiful approach from Tuscany can be made from Pienza, Montepulciano, and Chiusi, a short distance to the W of Lake Trasimene.

Driving in Italy

Temporary membership of the 'Automobile Club d'Italia' (ACI) can be taken out on the frontier or in Italy. The headquarters of ACI are at 8 Via Marsala, Rome, with branch offices in all the main towns. They provide a breakdown service ('Soccorso ACI', Tel. 116).

Rules of the road. Italian law requires that you carry a valid driving licence when travelling. It is obligatory to keep a red triangle in the car in case of accident or breakdown. This serves as a warning to other traffic when placed on the road at a distance of 50 metres from the stationary car. It can be hired from ACI for a minimal charge, and returned at the frontier. It is now compulsory to wear seat-belts in the front seat of cars in Italy. Driving in Italy is generally faster (and often more agressive) than driving in Britain or America. Road signs are now more or less standardised to the international codes, but certain habits differ radically from those in Britain or America. If a driver flashes his headlights, it means he is proceeding and not giving you precedence. In towns, Italian drivers are very lax about changing lanes without much warning. Unless otherwise indicated, cars entering a road from the right are given precedence. Italian drivers tend to ignore pedestrian crossings. In towns beware of motorbikes, mopeds, and Vespas, the drivers of which seem to consider that they always have the right of way.

Motorways ('Autostrade'). Italy probably has the finest motorways in

Europe, although in the last ten years or so too many have been constructed to the detriment of the countryside. Tolls are charged according to the rating of the vehicle and the distance covered. There are service areas on all autostrade (open 24 hours), and, generally speaking, the 'FINI' cafés and restaurants are usually the best. Most autostrade have SOS points every 2km. Unlike in France, motorways are indicated by green signs (and normal roads by blue signs). At the entrance to motorways, the two directions are indicated by the name of the most important town (and not by the nearest town). This can be momentarily confusing: from Florence the motorway towards Umbria is signposted 'Roma' (as opposed to 'Milano'). The only motorway in Umbria is the AI motorway from Florence to Rome which skirts its western border, with exits at 'Valdichiana', 'Chiusi', 'Fabro', 'Orvieto', 'Attigliano', and 'Orte'.

'**Superstrade**' are dual carriageway fast roads which do not charge tolls. They do not usually have service stations, SOS points, or emergency lanes. They are also usually indicated by green signs. In Umbria a 'superstrada' (N75bis) connects the 'Valdichiana' exit from the AI motorway to Lake Trasimene and Perugia. The 'superstrada' (E7; formerly N3bis) from Cesena in Emilia-Romagna to Orte in Lazio runs through the centre of Umbria past Città di Castello, Perugia, Todi, Terni, and Narni. Another fast road (N75 and N3), dual carriageway in places, connects Perugia to Foligno and Spoleto.

Petrol stations are open 24 hours on motorways, but otherwise their opening times are: 7–12, 15–20; winter 7.30–12.30, 14.30–19.30. There are now quite a number of self-service petrol stations open 24hrs operated by bank notes (Lire 10,000), usually near the larger towns. Unleaded petrol has become easy to find in the last few years. Petrol in Italy costs more than in England, and a lot more than in America.

Car Parking. Not all towns have solved their traffic problems as successfully as Perugia, where several car parks have been built below the old town, and connected to the centre by a series of escalators. However, now almost every town in Umbria (as in the rest of Italy) has taken the wise step of closing its historic centre to traffic (except for residents) which makes them much more pleasant to visit on foot. Access is allowed to hotels and for the disabled. It is always advisable to leave your car well outside the centre (places to park are usually indicated), and details have been given in the text below. Some car parks are free, while others charge an hourly tariff. In some towns mini-bus services connect car parks with the centre. With a bit of effort it is almost always possible to find a place to leave your car free of charge, away from the town centre. It is forbidden to park in front of a gate or doorway marked with a 'passo carrabile' (blue and red) sign. Always lock your car when parked, and never leave anything of value inside it.

Car Hire is available in most Italian cities. Arrangements for the hire of cars in Italy can be made through Alitalia or British Airways (at specially advantageous rates in conjunction with their flights) or through any of the principal car-hire firms (the best known include Maggiore, Avis, and Hertz).

Roads in Umbria. Umbria has an excellent network of roads, and drivers are strongly advised to avoid motorways and 'superstrade' and use the secondary roads which are usually well engineered and provide fine views of the countryside. Buildings of historic interest are often indicated by yellow signposts (although there are long-term plans to change the colour to brown). White road signs sometimes indicate entry into a 'comune' which is (confusingly) often a long way from the town of the same name. In autumn, winter, and spring many of the roads in Umbria (especially between Perugia and Spoleto) can be covered with thick fog in the early morning or late afternoon.

Maps

Although detailed town plans have been included in this book, it has not been possible, because of the format, to provide an atlas of Umbria adequate for those travelling by car. The maps at the end of the book are only intended to be used when planning an itinerary. The Italian Touring Club publishes several sets of excellent maps: these are constantly updated and are indispensable to anyone travelling by car in Italy. They include the 'Grande Carta Stradale d'Italia' on a scale of 1:200,000. This is divided into 15 sheets covering the regions of Italy: Umbria is covered on the sheet (No. D40) entitled 'Umbria, Marche'. These are also published in a handier form as an atlas (with a comprehensive index) called the 'Atlante Stradale d'Italia' in three volumes (the one entitled 'Centro' covers Umbria). These maps can be purchased from the Italian Touring Club offices and at many booksellers; in London they are obtainable at Stanfords, 12–14 Long Acre, WC2 9LP, and Robertson McCarta Ltd, 15 Highbury Place, N5 1QP.

The 'Istituto Geografico Militare' of Italy has for long been famous for its map production (much of it done by aerial photography). Their headquarters are in Florence (10 Via Cesare Battisti). Their maps are now available at numerous bookshops in the main towns of Italy. They publish a map of Italy on a scale of 1:100,000 in 277 sheets, and a field survey partly 1:50,000, partly 1:25,000, which are invaluable for the detailed exploration of the country, especially its more mountainous regions; the coverage is however, still far from complete at the larger scales, and some of the maps are out-of-date.

Public Transport

Railways. The Italian State Railways ('FS'—'Ferrovie dello Stato') now run five categories of trains. (1) 'EC' ('Eurocity'), international express trains (with a special supplement, approximately 30 per cent of the normal single fare) running between the main Italian and European cities (seat reservation is sometimes obligatory). (2) 'IC' ('Intercity'), express trains running between the main Italian towns, with a special supplement (on some of these seat reservation is obligatory, and some carry first-class only). (3) 'Espressi', long-distance trains (both classes) not as fast as the 'Intercity' trains. (4) 'Diretti', although not stopping at every station, a good deal slower than the 'Espressi'. (5) 'Regionali', local trains stopping at all stations.

In the last few years the Italian railways have been greatly improved, and the service reorganised. With the construction of the new 'Direttissima' line between Rome and Florence the time of the journey between these two cities has been reduced to c 2 hours (on 'Intercity' trains). In 1989 an extra fast service was introduced (ETR 450) which has daily connections between Milan, Bologna, Florence (Rifredi station), and Rome. These trains, which carry first-class only, cost considerably more, and advance booking is obligatory (the price of the ticket includes restaurant service). One of these, the 'Pendolino', operates non-stop, reaching a maximum speed of 250km an hour, between Milan and Rome in just under 4 hours.

Trains in Italy are usually crowded, especially on holidays and in summer; seats can be booked in advance from the main cities at the station booking office. The timetable of the train services changes on about 26 September and 31 May every year. Excellent timetables are published twice a year by the Italian State Railways ('Il Treno'; one volume for the whole of Italy) and by Pozzorario in several volumes ('Nord e Centro' covers Umbria). These can be purchased at newsstands and railway stations.

Fares and Reductions. In Italy fares are still much lower than in England. Tickets must be bought at the station (or at Agencies for Italian State Railways) before starting a journey, otherwise a fairly large supplement has to be paid to the ticket-collector on the train. Time should be allowed for this as there are often long queues at the station ticket offices. Some trains carry first-class only; some charge a special supplement; and on some seats must be booked in advance. It is therefore always necessary to specify which train you are intending to take as well as the destination when buying tickets. If you purchase a return ticket, you must write the date of the return by hand on the back of the ticket. In the main stations the better known credit cards are now generally accepted (but there is a special ticket window which must be used when buying a ticket with a credit card). There are limitations on travelling short distances on some first-class 'Intercity' trains.

Children under the age of four travel free, and between the ages of four and 12 travel half price, and there are certain reductions for families. For travellers over the age of 60 (with Senior Citizen Railcards), the 'Rail Europ Senior' card offers a 30 per cent reduction on Italian rail fares. The 'Inter-rail' card (valid one month) which can be purchased in Britain by young people up to the age of 26, is valid in Italy. In Italy the 'Carta d'Argento' and the 'Carta Verde' (both valid one year) allow a 20 per cent reduction on rail fares for those over 60, and between the ages of 12 and 26. The 'Biglietto Turistico di libera circolazione' ('Travel at Will ticket'), available to those resident outside Italy, gives freedom of the Italian railways for 8, 15, 21, or 30 days (and another scheme of this type is offered by the 'Italy Flexy Railcard'). These tickets can be purchased in Britain or at main stations in Italy. A 'Chilometrico' ticket is valid for two months for 3000 kilometres (and can be used by up to five people at the same time). There is a 15 per cent discount on Day Return tickets (maximum distance, 50km) and on 3-Day Return tickets (maximum distance 250km). A 'Carta Blu' is available for the disabled, and certain trains have special facilities for them (information from the main railway stations in Italy).

Left Luggage offices are usually open 24 hours at the main stations; at smaller stations they often close at night. **Porters** are entitled to a fixed amount (shown on notice boards at all stations) for each piece of baggage.

Restaurant Cars (sometimes self-service) are attached to most international and internal long-distance trains. A lunch tray brought to the compartment (including three courses and wine, and costing slightly less than the restaurant) is a convenient way of having a meal. Also, on most express trains, snacks, hot coffee and drinks are sold throughout the journey from a trolley wheeled down the train. At every large station good snacks are on sale from trolleys on the platform and you can buy them from the train window. These include carrier-bags with sandwiches, drink, and fruit ('cestini da viaggio') or individual sandwiches ('panini').

Sleeping Cars with couchettes or first- and second-class cabins are also carried on certain trains, as well as 'Sleeperette' compartments with reclining seats (first-class only).

Train services in Umbria are generally good, although most of the lines are secondary. Details of the services have been give in the text. Information about the State railways ('Ferrovie dello Stato') from the main railway station in Perugia (Piazza Vittorio Veneto), Tel. 075/5001091; or the railway station in Terni (Piazza Dante Alighieri), Tel. 0744/401283. A line between Città di Castello, Umbertide, Perugia, Todi, and Terni is run by the 'Ferrovia Centrale Umbra'. Information from the station of Sant'Anna in Perugia (Tel. 075/29121) or the station in Terni (Tel. 0744/415297).

Country Buses. Local country buses abound between the main towns in Italy, and offer an excellent alternative to the railways. It is difficult to obtain accurate information about these local bus services outside Italy. Details have been given in the text. The main bus companies operating in Umbria are: 'Auto Servizi Perugia' ('ASP'), località Pian di Massiano, Perugia (Tel. 075/751145); 'Società Spoletina di Imprese e Trasporti', Via Flaminia, Spoleto (Tel. 0743/221991); 'Azienda Trasporti Consortili' ('ATC'), 19 Piazza Europa, Terni (Tel. 0744/59541); and 'ACAP-SULGA', località Pian di Massiano, Perugia (Tel. 075/74641).

Town Buses. Now that most towns have been partially closed to private traffic, town bus services are usually fast and efficient. It is almost always necessary to purchase tickets before boarding (at tobacconists, bars, newspaper kiosks, information offices, etc.) and stamp them on board at automatic machines. **Taxis** (yellow or white in colour) are provided with taximeters; make sure these are operational before hiring a taxi. They are hired from ranks or by telephone; there are no cruising taxis. A tip of about 1000 lire is expected. A supplement for night service, and for luggage is charged. There is a heavy surcharge when the destination is outside the town limits (ask roughly how much the fare is likely to be).

Accommodation

Hotels in Italy are now classified by 'stars' as in the rest of Europe. Since 1985 the official category of 'Pensione' has been abolished. There are five official categories of hotels from the most expensive luxury 5-star hotels to the cheapest and simplest 1-star hotels. *Hotels in Umbria have been listed in the text, although only a small selection has been made. They have been given with their official star rating in order to give an indication of price. In making the selection for inclusion, smaller hotels have been favoured, and those in the centre of towns, or in particularly beautiful positions in the countryside.* Each local tourist board ('APT', see above) issues a free list of hotels giving category, price, and facilities. The Regione dell'Umbria also publishes annually a list of all the hotels, residences, youth hostels, and camping sites in Umbria in one booklet (free of charge). Local tourist offices help you to find accommodation on the spot; it is however advisable to book well in advance, especially at Easter and in summer. To confirm the booking a deposit should be sent. Hotels equipped to offer hospitality to the disabled are indicated in the 'APT' hotel lists.

Up-to-date information about hotels and restaurants can be found in numerous specialised guides to hotels and restaurants in Italy. These include the red guide to Italy published by 'Michelin' ('Italia', revised annually). In Italian, the Touring Club Italiano publish useful information about hotels in 'Alberghi in Italia' (published about every year) and in the 'Guida Rapida d'Italia' (four volumes, one of which covers Umbria, Tuscany and the Marches). The guides published in Italian by 'L'Espresso' to hotels and restaurants in Italy are now issued (in a reduced single volume) in English every year. Other specialised guides include the 'Charming Small Hotel Guide: Italy' (Duncan Petersen).

Charges vary according to class, season, services available, and locality. In all hotels the service charges are included in the rates. VAT is added in all hotels at a rate of 9 per cent (14 per cent in 5-star hotels). However, the total charge is exhibited on the back of the door of the hotel room. Breakfast (usually disappointing and costly) is by law an optional extra charge, although a lot of hotels try to include it in the price of the room. When booking a room, always specify if you want breakfast or not. It is usually well worthwhile going round the corner to the nearest bar for breakfast. Hotels are now obliged by law (for tax purposes) to issue an official receipt to customers: you should not leave the premises without this document.

A new type of hotel has been introduced into Italy, called a 'Residence'. They are normally in a building, or group of houses, of historic interest, often a castle or monastery. They tend to have only a few rooms, and can be delightful places to stay. Residences are listed separately in the 'APT' hotel lists, with their prices. At present there are only four of these in Umbria.

Agriturism has recently been developed throughout Italy, which provides accommodation in farmhouses in the countryside. Terms vary greatly from bed-and-breakfast, to self-contained flats. These are highly recommended for travellers with their own transport, and for families, as an excellent (and usually cheap) way of visiting Umbria. Some farms require a stay of a minimum number of days. Cultural or recreational activities are sometimes also provided, such as horse-back riding. Information about such holidays from 'Agriturist Umbria', 38 Via Savonarola, Perugia (Tel. 075/32028), who also publish an annual list of 'Agriturismo' accommodation in Umbria, and from local 'APT' offices.

Religious organisations sometimes run hostels or provide accommodation. Information from local 'APT' offices. In Assisi, numerous convents offer hospitality; an information and booking service is provided there by the 'Centro Prenotazione per le Case Religiose' (Tel. 075/8001515).

Renting accommodation for short periods in Italy has recently become easier and better organised. Villas, farmhouses, etc., can be rented for holidays through specialised agencies. Information from ENIT in London, and 'APT' offices in Italy.

Camping is now well organised throughout Italy. An international camping carnet is useful. In Umbria an annual list of camping sites is published by the Regione dell'Umbria (together with their hotel list), giving details of all services provided, size of the site, etc. In some sites caravans are allowed. The sites are divided into official categories by stars, from the most expensive 4-star sites, to the simplest and cheapest 1-star sites. Their classification and rates charged must be displayed at the camp site office. Some sites have been indicated in the text, with their star ratings. Full details of the sites in Italy are published annually by the Touring Club Italiano and Federcampeggio in 'Campeggi e Villaggi turistici in Italia'. The Federazione Italiana del Campeggio have an information office and booking service at No. 11 Via Vittorio Emanuele, Calenzano, 50041 Florence (Tel. 055/882391).

Youth Hostels. The Italian Youth Hostels Association (Associazione Italiana Alberghi per la Gioventù, 44 Via Cavour, 00184 Rome (Tel. 06/4871152) has 52 hostels situated all over the country. They publish a free guide to them. A membership card of the AIG or the International Youth Hostel Federation is required for access to Italian Youth Hostels. Details from the Youth Hostels Association, Trevelyan House, 8 St Stephen's Hill, St Albans, Herts AL1 2DY, and the American Youth Hostels Inc, National Offices, PO Box 37613, Washington DC 20013-7613. The regional office in Umbria is at the Ostello della Pace, Via Valecchi, 06081 Assisi (Tel. 075/816767). In Umbria there are youth hostels at: Assisi ('Fontemaggio', Strada per l'Eremo delle Carceri); Foligno ('Fulginium', Piazza San Giacomo); Gubbio ('Aquilone', località Ghigiano); San Venanzo ('Casa per Ferie Centro Turistico Giovanile', località Monte Peglia); Sigillo ('Ostello Centro di volo libero', località Villa Scirca); and at Trevi ('Casa San Martino', 4 Viale Ciuffelli).

Eating in Italy

Restaurants in Italy are called 'Ristoranti' or 'Trattorie'; there is now no difference between the two. Italian food is usually good and not too expensive. The least pretentious restaurant almost invariably provides the best value. Almost every locality has a simple restaurant (often family run) which caters for the local residents; the decor is usually very simple and the food excellent value. This type of restaurant does not always offer a menu and the choice is usually limited to three or four first courses, and three or four second courses, with only fruit as a sweet. The more sophisticated restaurants are more attractive and comfortable and often larger, and you can sometimes eat at tables outside. They display a menu outside, and are also usually considerably more expensive.

In the text below a small selection of restaurants open in Umbria in 1992 has been given, which is by no means exhaustive. The restaurants have been divided into three categories to reflect price ranges in 1992: 'LUXURY-CLASS RESTAURANTS' where the prices are likely to be over Lire 60,000 a head (and sometimes well over Lire 100,000 a head). These are the most famous restaurants in Umbria and they usually offer international cuisine. 'IST-CLASS RESTAURANTS' where the prices range from Lire 35,000 and above. These are generally comfortable, with good service, but are not cheap. The third category, called 'SIMPLE TRATTORIE AND PIZZERIE' indicates places where you can eat for around Lire 25,000 a head, or even less. Although simple, the food in this category is usually the best value.

Specialised guides to restaurants (in the 'Luxury-class' and 'Ist-class' categories, as described above) in Italy (revised annually) include the red guide published by Michelin ('Italia'), 'La Guida d'Italia' published by L'Espresso (also now in a reduced English version), and 'I Ristoranti di Veronelli'.

Prices on the menu do not include a cover charge ('coperto', shown separately on the menu) which is added to the bill. The service charge is now almost always automatically added at the end of the bill: tipping is therefore not strictly necessary, but a few thousand lire are appreciated. Restaurants are now obliged by law (for tax purposes) to issue an official receipt to customers; you should not leave the premises without this document ('ricevuta fiscale'). Fish is always the most expensive item on the menu in any restaurant.

Pizze (a popular and cheap food throughout Italy) and other excellent snacks are served in a 'Pizzeria', 'Rosticceria' and 'Tavola Calda'. Some of these have no seating accommodation and sell food to take away or eat on the spot. For **picnics** sandwiches ('panini') are made up on request (with ham, salami, cheese, anchovies, tuna fish, etc.) at 'Pizzicherie' and 'Alimentari' (grocery shops), and 'Fornai' (bakeries) often sell delicious individual pizzas, bread with oil and salt ('focaccia' or 'schiacciata'), cakes, etc. Some of the pleasantest places to picnic in towns or their environs have been indicated in the text below.

Bars ('cafés'), which are open all day, serve numerous varieties of excellent refreshments which are usually eaten standing up. The cashier should be paid first and the receipt given to the barman in order to get served. If you sit at a table the charge is considerably higher (at least double) and you will be given waiter service (and should not pay first). However, some simple bars have a few tables which can be used with no extra charge (it is always best to ask before sitting down). Black coffee ('caffè' or 'espresso') can be ordered diluted ('alto', 'lungo' or 'americano') or with hot milk ('cappuccino') or with a liquor ('corretto'). In summer, cold coffee ('caffè freddo') or cold coffee and milk ('caffè-latte freddo') are served. Ice-creams are always best in a 'Gelateria' where they are made on the spot: bars usually sell packaged ice-cream only.

Umbrian Food and Wine. The standard of cuisine in Umbria is still fairly high, and generally better than that to be found in many other regions of Italy. The region is famous for its pork. Good ham, sausages, and salami are produced (especially around Norcia and the Valnerina), as well as the famous 'porchetta', roast suckling pig with fennel, herbs, etc. Black and white truffles are a delicacy, often served with pasta. Excellent fish (including eels, and a fish soup called 'tegamaccio') is still served in the restaurants around Lake Trasimene. Trout are found in the rivers of the Valnerina and Clitunno. Mushrooms are a delicacy in season. Lentils are cultivated on the plain of Castelluccio. The quality of the meat in Umbria is usually good, and is best grilled. In and around Perugia bread is made with cheese in the form of a cake. Excellent cakes and biscuits are made all over Umbria, with almonds, candied fruits, pine nuts, chestnuts, walnuts, etc. The 'torciglione' or 'serpentone' is a delicious cake in the form of a snake made with almond paste.

The **wines** of Umbria are usually of good quality. The most famous white wine is produced around Orvieto, but is not now usually the best wine available. Among the best red wines are Torgiano, Rubesco, and Montefalco. Other 'DOC' wines in Umbria are: 'Colli Altotiberini' (red, white, and rosé) from the upper Tiber valley (particularly Umbertide); 'Colli Amerini' (red, white and rosé) from the area around Amelia; 'Colli del Trasimeno' (red and white) from the area around Lake Trasimene, notably Castiglione del Lago, Città della Pieve, and Corciano; 'Colli Martani' (red and white) from near Montefalco; 'Colli Perugini' (red, white and rosé) from near Perugia; 'Montefalco' (red) from near Montefalco. The deep red

'Sagrantino' also produced around Montefalco and Bevagna is one of the most exceptional wines in Umbria. All those interested in wine should not miss the Wine Museum in Torgiano.

Opening Times of Museums, Sites, and Churches

The opening times of **museums and monuments** have been given in the text but they vary and often change without warning; when possible it is always advisable to consult the local tourist office ('APT') on arrival about the up-to-date times. The opening times of State-owned museums and monuments are in the process of change: they are usually open 9–14, fest. 9–13, but in some cases they are now also open in the afternoon. On Monday, for long the standard closing day, many museums are now staying open (so that they remain open seven days a week). However, there is not, as yet, a standard timetable and you should take great care to allow enough time for variations in the hours shown in the text when planning a visit to a museum or monument. Some museums, etc., are closed on the main public holidays: 1 January, Easter, 1 May, 15 August, and Christmas Day (although there is now a policy to keep at least a few of them open on these days in the larger cities; information has to be obtained about this on the spot). Admission charges vary, but are usually between Lire 2000 and Lire 8000. British citizens under the age of 18 and over the age of 60 are entitled to free admission to State-owned museums and monuments in Italy (because of reciprocal arrangements in Britain). The 'Settimana per i Beni Culturali e Ambientali' is usually held early in December when for a week there is free entrance to all State-owned museums and others are specially opened, etc.

Churches, although they usually open very early in the morning (at 7 or 8), are normally closed for a considerable period during the middle of the day. Almost all churches close at 12.00 and do not reopen again until 15, 16, or even 17.00. Cathedrals and some of the larger churches (indicated in the text) may be open without a break during daylight hours. Smaller churches and oratories are often open only in the early morning, but it is sometimes possible to find the key by asking locally. The sacristan will also show closed chapels, crypts, etc. and sometimes expects a tip. Some churches now ask that sightseers do not enter during a service, but normally visitors not in a tour group may do so, provided you are silent and do not approach the altar in use. An entrance fee is becoming customary for admission to treasuries, cloisters, bell-towers, etc. Lights (operated by lire coins) have now been installed in many churches to illuminate frescoes and altarpieces, but a torch and binoculars are always useful. Sometimes you are not allowed to enter important churches wearing shorts or with bare shoulders.

Annual Festivals and Local Fairs in Umbria

There are a number of traditional festivals in Umbrian towns which are of the greatest interest. At these times, the towns become extremely lively, and, apart from the central race or competition, numerous celebrations take place on the side. All the local festivals have been mentioned in the text, and the most important ones described in detail, but a summary is given below, in case you are able to choose a period in which to visit Umbria when some of them are taking place. They are particularly exciting events for children. Information from local 'APT' offices and from 'AUDAC' ('Associazione Umbra Decentramento Artistico Culturale'), 20 Via del Verzaro, Perugia, Tel. 075-63645.

Castiglione del Lago: 'Coloriamo i cieli' (even years only) late April–beginning of May
Narni: 'Corsa all'Anello' second Sunday in May
Assisi: 'Calendimaggio' three days in early May
Gubbio: 'Festa dei Ceri' 15 May
Gubbio: 'Palio della Balestra' last Sunday in May
Spello: 'Infiorate' Corpus Domini
Bevagna: 'Le Gaite' second half of June
Montefalco: 'Corso del Bove' second half of June
Orvieto: 'Corpus Domini' Sunday in June after Corpus Domini
Spoleto: 'Festival dei Due Mondi' end of June–beginning of July
Città della Pieve: 'Palio dei Terzieri' second Sunday in August
Foligno:'La Giostra della Quintana' second and third Sunday in September
Sangemini: 'Giostra dell'Arme' end of September–beginning of October
Trevi: 'Palio dei Terzieri' early October

Another special feature of Umbria are the fairs held periodically, especially in Foligno (in September and around 26 January), Bevagna (in Spring), and Perugia (around 2 November). At Bastia Umbra the 'Mercatino Quattro Stagioni' is held on the first Sunday of each new season. A fair of artisans' products is held in August in Montefalco.

Among local products which can sometimes still be found are pottery (Deruta, Gubbio, Gualdo Tadino, Orvieto, Città di Castello); wrought-iron work (Gubbio, Assisi, Città della Pieve, and Norcia); objects in copper (Magione); and textiles, embroidery, and lace (Perugia, Città di Castello, Montefalco, Marsciano, Assisi, Panicale, Castiglione del Lago and Isola Maggiore on Lake Trasimene, and Orvieto).

Walking in Umbria

Hiking and walking has become more popular in Italy in recent years and more information is now available locally. There are numerous areas in Umbria ideal for walkers, and there are marked trails above Lake Trasimene, Monte Cucco, Castelluccio, and in the Valnerina. The local offices of the Club Alpino Italiano ('CAI') and the World Wildlife Fund provide all the information necessary. 'CAI' offices in Umbria: Foligno, Via Piermarini; Perugia, 9 Via della Gabbiaia; Spoleto, 4 Via Pianciani (Tel. 0743-28233); and Terni, 96 Via Roma. The 'Delegazione Umbria' of the World Wildlife

Fund is at 15 Via della Tartaruga, Perugia (Tel. 075-65816). Guides include 'Il Cammina Umbria' published in collaboration with the World Wildlife Fund, and '20 Sentieri ragionati in Valnerina' (published by the 'APT' for Valnerina). Maps are published by the Istituto Geografico Militare (see above), and by 'CAI' (including paths in the 'Comprensorio Spoletino' at a scale of 1:50,000).

Visiting Umbria with Children

A holiday can often be marred for parents as well as children if too much serious sight-seeing is attempted in too short a time. Umbria has a variety of sights which may be of special interest to children and may help to alleviate a day of undiluted 'Madonnas' and museums. A golden rule when allowing a 'break' for an ice-cream is to search for a 'Gelateria' (rather than a bar) where the locally produced ice-creams are generally excellent.

A few suggestions are given below of places that might have particular appeal to children, listed in the order of the routes by which the book is divided. These include some important monuments which are likely to give a clear impression of a particular period of art or architecture, a few museums, places of naturalistic interest, and the most exciting annual festivals. Detailed descriptions of all the places mentioned below are given in the main text (and can easily be found by reference to the index at the back of the book).

Rte 1. In Perugia: Rocca Paolina; Corso Vannucci; Sala di Udienza del Collegio del Cambio; San Severo; Oratorio di San Bernardino; Arco d'Augusto; Sant'Angelo; Convent of Beata Colomba or Sant'Agnese; the Roman mosaic; Archaeological Museum. In the environs of Perugia: the Ipogeo dei Volumni; Torgiano wine museum; and 'Città della Domenica'.

Rte 2. In Assisi: Basilica of San Francesco (particularly the Upper Church); Oratorio dei Pellegrini; Rocca Maggiore; Santa Chiara; Eremo delle Carceri; and Monte Subasio. 'Calendimaggio' medieval pageant, and 'Palio di San Rufino' (bow and arrow contest).

Rte 3. Lake Trasimene: boat trips to the Isola Maggiore and Isola Polvese; Hannibal's Battle route at Tuoro; bathing in the lake (at Tuoro); Museo della Pesca, San Feliciano; walking and horse riding; the castle of Castiglione del Lago; and the nature reserve on Monte Pausillo. 'Coloriamo i cieli' festival of kites at Castiglione del Lago, and 'Palio dei Terzieri' at Città della Pieve.

Rte 4. 'Alcatraz' holiday centre; Ethnographical museum, at Garavelle near Città di Castello.

Rte 5. Gubbio: cable car to Sant'Ubaldo on Monte Ingino; Fontana 'dei Pazzi'. The 'Festa dei Ceri' and 'Palio della Balestra'. In the environs of Gubbio: Gorge of Bottaccione and Monte Cucco. At Gualdo Tadino: Rocca Flea (when restored).

Rte 6. Foligno: 'Giostra della Quintana'. Colfiorito; Monte Pennino; 'Palio dei Terzieri' at Trevi; Fonti del Clitunno.

Rte 7. Bevagna: Roman mosaic and other Roman remains; rope-making in the streets; Good Friday and Easter Day processions. Montefalco: the tower of Palazzo Comunale; San Francesco; 'Corsa del Bove'.

Rte 8. Todi: Santa Maria della Consolazione.

Rte 9. Orvieto: funicular; Pozzo di San Patrizio; Duomo; Archaeological Museum. 'Corpus Domini' procession. Monte Peglia.

Rte 10 Marmore waterfalls; Lago di Piediluco; Roman remains of Carsulae. Narni: the Rocca (when restored), and the 'Corsa all'Anello'. Sangemini: 'Giostra dell'Arme'. Roman remains of Ocriculum. Amelia: the walls. Castle of Alviano (with its ethnographical museum). Oasis of Alviano (bird sanctuary). Fossil forest of Dunarobba (with related exhibition at Avigliano Umbro).

Rte 11. Spoleto: Ponte delle Torri; Rocca Albornoz (when restored); Roman theatre and archaeological museum; Roman house. 'Festival dei Due Mondi'.

Rte 12. Piano Grande di Castelluccio.

General Information

Public Holidays. The Italian National Holidays when offices, shops and schools are closed are as follows: 1 January, 25 April (Liberation Day), Easter Monday, 1 May (Labour Day), 15 August (Assumption), 1 November (All Saints' Day), 8 December (Immaculate Conception), Christmas Day and 26 December (St Stephen). Each town keeps its patron Saint's day as a holiday.

Italy for the disabled. Italy is at last catching up slowly with the rest of Europe in the provision of facilities for the disabled. All new public buildings are now obliged by law to provide access for the disabled, and specially designed facilities. In the annual list of hotels published by the local 'APT' offices, hotels which are able to give hospitality to the disabled are indicated. Airports and railway stations provide assistance, and certain trains are equipped to transport wheelchairs. Access is allowed to the centre of towns (normally closed to traffic) for cars with disabled people, where parking places are reserved for them. For all other information, contact local 'APT' offices.

Telephones and Postal Information. Stamps are sold at tobacconists (displaying a blue 'T' sign) and post offices (open 8.10–13.25, Monday–Saturday). Central offices in main towns are open 8.10–19.25. Correspondence can be addressed c/o the Post Office by adding 'Fermo Posta' to the name of the locality. It is always advisable to post letters at post offices or railway stations; collection from letterboxes may be erratic. There are numerous public telephones all over Italy in bars, restaurants, kiosks, etc. These are now usually operated by coins, telephone cards, or metal disks (200 lire) known as 'gettone'. These and telephone cards can be bought from tobacconists, bars, some newspaper stands, and post offices.

Working Hours. Government offices usually work from 8–13.30 or 14.00 six days a week. Shops (clothes, hardware, hairdressers, etc.) are generally open from 9–13, 16–19.30, including Saturday, and for most of the year are closed on Monday morning. Food shops usually open from 8–13, 17–19.30 or 20, and for most of the year are closed on Wednesday afternoon. From mid-June to mid-September all shops are closed instead on Saturday afternoon. Banks are usually open Monday–Friday 8.20–13.30, 14.30–15.45. They are closed on Saturday and holidays, and close early (about 11.00) on days preceding national holidays.

Public Toilets. There is a notable shortage of public toilets in Italy. All bars (cafés) should have toilets available to the public (generally speaking the larger the bar, the better the facilities). Nearly all museums now have toilets.

Help is given to British and American travellers who are in difficulty by the British and American consulates in Italy, and the British and American Embassies in Rome. They will replace lost or stolen passports, and will give advice in emergencies. The nearest consulates to Umbria are in Florence: British Consulate, 2 Lungarno Corsini (Tel. 055-284133); US Consulate, 38 Lungarno Vespucci (Tel. 055-2398276).

Health Service. British citizens, as members of the EC, have the right to claim health services in Italy if they have the E111 form (issued by the Department of Health and Social Security). There are also a number of private holiday health insurance policies. First Aid services ('Pronto Soccorso') are available at all hospitals, railway stations, and airports. **Chemist Shops** ('farmacie') are usually open Monday–Friday 9–13, 16–19.30 or 20. On Saturdays and Sundays (and holidays) a few are open (listed on the door of every chemist). In all towns there is also at least one chemist shop open at night (also shown on the door of every chemist). For emergencies, dial 113.

Crime. Pick-pocketing is a widespread problem in towns all over Italy: it is always advisable not to carry valuables in handbags, and be particularly careful on public transport. Crime should be reported at once to the police, or the local 'carabinieri' office (found in every town and small village). A detailed statement has to be given in order to get an official document confirming loss or damage (essential for insurance claims). Interpreters are provided. For all emergencies, dial 113.

Glossary

AEDICULE, small opening framed by two columns and a pediment, originally used in classical architecture.

AMPHORA, antique vase, usually of large dimensions, for oil and other liquids.

ANCONA, retable or large altarpiece (painted or sculpted) in an architectural frame.

ANTEFIX, ornament placed at the lower corners of the tiled roof of a temple to conceal the space between the tiles and the cornice.

ANTIPHONAL, choir-book containing a collection of *antiphonae*—verses sung in response by two choirs.

ARCA, wooden chest with a lid, for sacred or secular use. Also, monumental sarcophagus in stone, used by Christians and pagans.

ARCHITRAVE, lowest part of an entablature, horizontal frame above a door.

ARCHIVOLT, moulded architrave carried round an arch.

ATLANTES (or *Telamones*), male figures used as supporting columns.

ATRIUM, forecourt, usually of a Byzantine church or a classical Roman house.

ATTIC, topmost storey of a Classical building, hiding the spring of the roof.

BADIA, *Abbazia*, abbey.

BALDACCHINO, canopy supported by columns, usually over an altar.

BASILICA, originally a Roman building used for public administration; in Christian architecture, an aisled church with a clerestory and apse, and no transepts.

BORGO, a suburb; street leading away from the centre of a town.

BOTTEGA, the studio of an artist: the pupils who worked under his direction.

BOZZETTO, sketch, often used to describe a small model for a piece of sculpture.

BROCCATELLO, a clouded veined marble from Siena.

BUCCHERO, Etruscan black terracotta ware.

BUCRANIA, a form of classical decoration—heads of oxen garlanded with flowers.

CAMPANILE, bell-tower, often detached from the building to which it belongs.

CAMPOSANTO, cemetery.

CANEPHORA, figure bearing a basket, often used as a caryatid.

CANOPIC VASE, Egyptian or Etruscan vase enclosing the entrails of the dead.

CANTORIA, singing-gallery in a church.

CAPPELLA, chapel.

CARTOON, from *cartone*, meaning large sheet of paper. A full-size preparatory drawing for a painting or fresco.

CARYATID, female figure used as a supporting column.

CASSONE, a decorated chest, usually a dower chest.

CAVEA, the part of a theatre or amphitheatre occupied by the row of seats.

CELLA, sanctuary of a temple, usually in the centre of the building.

CENACOLO, scene of the Last Supper (often in the refectory of a convent).

CHALICE, wine cup used in the celebration of Mass.

CHIAROSCURO, distribution of light and shade, apart from colour in a painting.

CIBORIUM, casket or tabernacle containing the Host.

CIPOLLINO, onion-marble; a greyish marble with streaks of white or green.

CIPPUS, sepulchral monument in the form of an altar.

CISTA, casket, usually of bronze and cylindrical in shape, to hold jewels, toilet articles, etc., and decorated with mythological subjects.

CLOISONNÉ, type of enamel decoration.

COLUMBARIUM, a building (usually subterranean) with niches to hold urns containing the ashes of the dead.

COMMUNE, a town or city which adopted a form of independent self-government in the Middle Ages.

CONDOTTIERE, professional military commander.

CONFESSIO, crypt beneath the high altar and raised choir of a church, usually containing the relics of a saint.

CORBEL, a projecting block, usually of stone.

CORSO, main street of a town.

CRENELLATIONS, battlements.

CUPOLA, dome.

CYCLOPEAN, the term applied to walls of unmortared masonry, older than the Etruscan civilisation, and attributed by the ancients to the giant Cyclopes.

DIPTYCH, painting or ivory panel in two sections.

DOSSAL, altarpiece.

DOSSERET, a second block above the capital of a column.

DUOMO, cathedral.

EDICOLA, *see* aedicule.

EXEDRA, semicircular recess.

EX-VOTO, tablet or small painting expressing gratitude to a saint.

FRESCO (in Italian, *affresco*), painting executed on wet plaster. On the wall beneath is sketched the *sinopia*, and the *cartoon* (see above) is transferred onto the fresh plaster (*intonaco*) before the fresco is begun either by pricking the outline with small holes over which a powder is dusted, or by means of a stylus which leaves an incised line on the wet plaster. In recent years many frescoes have been detached from the walls on which they were executed.

GIALLO ANTICO, red-veined yellow marble from Numidia.

GONFALON, banner of a medieval guild or commune.

GRAFFITI, design on a wall made with an iron tool on a prepared surface, the design showing in white. Also used loosely to describe scratched designs or words on walls.

GREEK-CROSS, cross with the arms of equal length.

GRISAILLE, painting in various tones of grey.

GROTESQUE, painted or stucco decoration in the style of the ancient Romans (found during the Renaissance in Nero's Golden House in Rome, then underground, hence the name, from 'grotto'). The delicate ornamental decoration usually includes patterns of flowers, sphynxes, birds, human figures, etc., against a light ground.

HERM (pl. *Hermae*), quadrangular pillar decreasing in girth towards the ground surmounted by a bust.

HYPOGEUM, subterranean excavation for the interment of the dead (usually Etruscan).

ICONOSTASIS, high balustrade with figures of saints, guarding the sanctuary of a Byzantine church.

IMPASTO, early Etruscan ware made of inferior clay.

INTARSIA (or *Tarsia*), inlay of wood, marble, or metal.

INTONACO, plaster.

INTRADOS, underside or soffit of an arch.

KRATER, Antique mixing-bowl, conical in shape with rounded base.

KYLIX, wide shallow vase with two handles and short stem.

LATIN-CROSS, cross with a long vertical arm.

LAVABO, hand-basin usually outside a refectory or sacristy.

LOGGIA, covered gallery or balcony, usually preceding a larger building.

LUNETTE, semicircular space in a vault or ceiling, or above a door or window, often decorated with a painting or relief.

MAESTÀ, Madonna and Child enthroned in majesty.

MATRONEUM, gallery reserved for women in early Christian churches.

MEDALLION, large medal; loosely, a circular ornament.

META, turning-post at either end of a Roman circus.

MONOCHROME, painting or drawing in one colour only.

MONOLITH, single stone (usually a column).

NARTHEX, vestibule of a Christian basilica.

NIELLO, black substance used in an engraved design.

NIMBUS, luminous ring surrounding the heads of saints in paintings; a square nimbus denoted that the person was living at that time.

OCULUS, round window.

OPERA (DEL DUOMO), the office in charge of the fabric of a building (i.e. the Cathedral).

OPUS RETICULATUM, masonry arranged in squares or diamonds so that the mortar joints make a network pattern.

OPUS TESSELLATUM, mosaic formed entirely of square tesserae.

PALA, large altarpiece.

PALAZZO, any dignified and important building.

PALOMBINO, fine-grained white marble.

PAVONAZZETTO, yellow marble blotched with blue.

PAX, sacred object used by a priest for the blessing of peace, and offered for the kiss of the faithful. Usually circular, engraved enamelled or painted in a rich gold or silver frame.

PENDENTIVE, concave spandrel beneath a dome.

PERISTYLE, court or garden surrounded by a columned portico.

PIETÀ, group of the Virgin mourning the dead Christ.

PIETRE DURE, hard or semi-precious stones, often used in the form of mosaics to decorate cabinets, table-tops, etc.

PIEVE, parish church.

PISCINA, Roman tank; a basin for an officiating priest to wash his hands before Mass.

PLAQUETTE, small metal tablet with relief decoration.

PLUTEUS (pl. *plutei*), marble panel, usually decorated; a series of them used to form a parapet to precede the altar of a church.

POLYPTYCH, painting or panel in more than three sections.

PORTA, gate (or door).

PORTA DEL MORTO, in certain old mansions of Umbria and Tuscany, a narrow raised doorway, said to be for the passage of biers of the dead, but more probably for use in troubled times when the main gate would be barred.

PREDELLA, small painting or panel, usually in sections, attached below a large altarpiece, illustrating the story of a saint, the life of the Virgin, etc.

PRESEPIO, literally, crib or manger. A group of statuary of which the central subject is the Infant Jesus in the manger.

PRONAOS, porch in front of the cella of a temple.

PUTTO (pl. *putti*), figure of a boy sculpted or painted, usually nude.

QUADRATURA, painted architectural perspectives.

QUATREFOIL, four-lobed design.

REREDOS, decorated screen rising behind an altar.

RHYTON, drinking-horn usually ending in an animal's head.

ROOD-SCREEN, a screen below the Rood or Crucifix dividing the nave from the chancel of a church.

SCAGLIOLA, a material made from selenite and used to imitate marble or 'pietre dure', often used for altar frontals and columns.

SCENA, the stage of a Roman theatre.

SCHIACCIATO, term used to describe very low relief in sculpture, where there is an emphasis on the delicate line rather than the depth of the panel.

SCHOLA CANTORUM, enclosure for the choristers in the nave of an early Christian church, adjoining the sanctuary.

SINOPIA, large sketch for a fresco made on the rough wall in a red earth pigment called sinopia (because it originally came from Sinope on the Black Sea). By detaching a fresco it is now possible to see the sinopia beneath and detach it also.

SITULA, water-bucket.

SOFFIT, underside or intrados of an arch.

SPANDREL, surface between two arches in an arcade or the triangular space on either side of an arch.

STAMNOS, big-bellied vase with two small handles at the sides, closed by a lid.

STELE, upright stone bearing a monumental inscription.

STEMMA, coat of arms or heraldic device.

STEREOBATE, basement of a temple or other building.

STOUP, vessel for Holy Water, usually near the W door of a church.

STYLOBATE, basement of a columned temple or other building.

TABLINUM, room in a Roman house with one side opening onto the central courtyard.

TELAMONES, see *Atlantes*.

TESSERA, a small cube of marble, glass, etc., used in mosaic work.

THERMAE, Roman baths.

THOLOS, a circular building.

TONDO, round painting or bas-relief.

TRANSENNA, open grille or screen, usually of marble, in an early Christian church.

TRAVERTINE, tufa quarried near Tivoli.

TRICLINIUM, dining room and reception room of a Roman house.

TRIPTYCH, painting or panel in three sections.

TROMPE L'OEIL, literally, a deception of the eye. Used to describe illusionist decoration, painted architectural perspectives, etc.

VILLA, country house with its garden.

WESTWORK, W end of a Carolingian or Romanesque church with a massive central tower and, inside, a double storey, with the upper room open to the nave.

The terms QUATTROCENTO, CINQUECENTO (abbreviated in Italy '400, '500), etc., refer not to the 14C and 15C, but to the 'fourteen-hundreds' and 'fifteen-hundreds', i.e. the 15C and 16C, etc.

Piazza del Comune, Assisi

1

Perugia

PERUGIA (129,000 inhab.), capital of the province of the same name (6357 sq km), which comprises nearly the whole of Umbria, has a booming economy. Disorderly suburbs with ugly tower blocks (especially prominent on the approach from Florence and Siena) have sprawled onto the lower hills below the old town in the last ten years or so. The historical centre, however, preserves its character and numerous tortuous streets climb up and down the oddly-shaped hilly spurs of land (494m above sea level and some 300m above the Tiber) on which the town is built. It is perhaps the most difficult town in Italy in which to find one's bearings. It has numerous interesting monuments, including the Palazzo dei Priori on the delightful Corso, where the Pinacoteca has a magnificent display of Umbrian art. Lovely churches are situated on the edges of the hills. The famous painter, Pietro Vannucci was called 'Perugino' due to his long association with the town, and many works by him survive here, notably in the Collegio del Cambio. Students from all over the world come to Perugia to attend the famous 'Università per Stranieri' ('University for foreigners'). Perugia was the first hill town in Italy to resolve its traffic problems in the 1980s: this was achieved by constructing car parks connected to the historical centre by a series of escalators.

Information Offices. 'APT', Sala San Severo, Piazza 4 Novembre (Pl. II;1), Tel. 075/23327; headquarters at No. 21 Via Mazzini. 'Assessorato al Turismo della Regione dell'Umbria', 30 Corso Vannucci.

Railway Stations. The main station is in a modern part of the town at Fontivegge (Pl. I;13), below the historical centre to the SW. Frequent services to Foligno (with connections to Rome) and to Terontola (with connections to Florence). Bus Nos 26, 27, and 29 for Piazza Italia (Pl. II;8), and No. 36 for Piazza Matteotti (Pl. II;4). A private railway company (Ferrovia Centrale Umbra) operates two services from the Stazione Sant'Anna (Pl. I;11) and the Stazione Ponte San Giovanni (6km ESE) to Città di Castello and San Sepolcro, and to Terni via Deruta, Marsciano, and Todi.

Buses. For city buses from the railway station, see above. There is a wide network of buses from Piazza Partigiani (Pl. I;11) to the main towns of interest in Umbria, with frequent daily services: to Assisi in c 1hr (slower services via Santa Maria degli Angeli); to Spello (50min) and Foligno (1hr 15min); to Gubbio (1hr 10min); to Deruta (30min) and Todi (1hr 30min); to Lake Trasimene (Passignano 1hr, Tuoro 1hr 15min, and Castiglione del Lago 1hr 15min); to Città della Pieve (1hr 30min) and Chiusi (1hr 40min); to Gualdo Tadino (1hr 30min); to Torgiano (20min) and Bettona (30min); to Corciano (30min). Services once a day to Norcia (2hrs 50min); to Orvieto (2hrs 30min); and Spoleto (1hr 30min; better reached by train). Cortona is reached by train to Terontola and bus connection from there. Long distance *coach services* via the motorway to Florence (2hrs) and Rome (2hrs 30min).

There is a small **airport** at *Sant'Egidio*, 12km E of Perugia, with daily flights to Milan.

Car Parking. The historic centre (on the highest hills) is closed to traffic (7–13, 15–18), but visitors can obtain permission to reach hotels within this area. Car parks are clearly indicated on the approaches: the most convenient one for visitors is in *Piazza Partigiani* (Pl. I;11), signposted from Via Cacciatori degli Alpi or Via Baldassare Orsini. This huge two-storey underground car park has an hourly tariff (special reduced tariff for overnight periods). From here escalators (described below) mount through the Rocca Paolina to Piazza Italia (Pl. II;8), in the centre of the city. Another convenient car park (signposted from the railway station), also provided with escalators, is in *Viale Pellini*

(Pl. I;6) with an hourly tariff. On the approach to this car park, off Via Arturo Cecchi, there is free car parking in *Piazzale della Cupa*. From here an escalator ascends to Viale Pellini, from where more escalators continue up to emerge in Via dei Priori (Pl. I;6), which leads up right to Corso Vannucci. There is also a car park below the *Covered Market* (Pl. II;4) with a lift up to Piazza Matteotti (Pl. II;4).

Hotels. 5-star: 'Brufani', 12 Piazza Italia. 4-star: 'La Rosetta', 2 Via del Sette. 3-star: 'Palace Hotel Bellavista', 12 Piazza Italia. 2-star: 'Signa', 9 Via del Grillo; 'Priori', 3 Via Vermiglioli.

In the environs: *Corciano*: 'Colle della Trinità' (4-star). *Torgiano*: 'Le Tre Vaselle' (with luxury-class restaurant) (5-star). *Deruta*: 'Melody' (with 1st class restaurant) (3-star), 'Nel Castello' (with 1st class restaurant, 5km SE of Deruta) (3-star).

Camping Sites on Colle della Trinità: 'Paradise d'Etè' (3-star, open all year), 'Il Rocolo' (2-star, open in summer). **Youth Hostel**, 13 Via Bontempi (Pl. I;7).

Restaurants. Luxury-class: 'Osteria del Bartolo', 30 Via Bartolo. 1st class: 'Il Falchetto', 20 Via Bartolo; 'La Taverna', 8 Via Streghe; 'La Rosetta', 2 Via del Sette; 'La Piazzetta', 3 Via Deliziosa; 'La Bocca Mia', 36 Via Ulisse Rocchi; 'Del Sole', 28 Via Oberdan; 'Il Canto delle Sirene', 4G Via Campo di Marte (specilizing in fish; with a good 'tavola calda' adjoining). Trattorie: 'Dal Mi' Cocco', 12 Corso Garibaldi; 'Ubu' re', 17 Via Baldeschi; 'Aladino', 16 Via Sant'Elisabetta.

In the environs at *Corciano*: 'Ottavi', 10 Anita Garibaldi, Località San Mariano (Luxury-class). The 'Enoteca Provinciale', 18 Via Ulisse Rocchi, has a wide selection of Umbrian wines.

Good places to **picnic** can be found near the churches of Sant'Angelo and San Pietro. **Cafés** with good snacks on Corso Vannucci.

Theatre and Annual Festivals. 'Teatro Morlacchi', Piazza Morlacchi (Pl. I;6) for prose and concerts. A Festival of Jazz is held at the beginning of July. A large fair is held from 2 November for one week at Pian di Marsiano. A small antiques fair is held in Perugia on the last Sunday of each month.

History. *Perusia* was one of the 12 cities of the Etruscan Confederation and it submitted to the Romans under Q. Fabius in 310 BC. Its ancient walls of irregular blocks of travertine with seven gates were built probably at the end of the 2C BC. In the civil war between Octavian (Augustus) and Mark Antony, L. Antonius, brother of the triumvir, was besieged in Perusia in 41–40 BC. Famine compelled the city's surrender; but one of its citizens, Gaius Cestius, in panic set fire to his own house, and the flames spread, razing all Perusia to the ground. Augustus rebuilt the city and called it *Augusta Perusia*. It is said to have been besieged by Totila in 547, and saved by the wisdom of its bishop, St Herculanus. In 592 it became part of the Lombard duchy of Spoleto, and after the restoration of the Western Empire its history is one of obscure and intricate wars with neighbouring towns in which it generally took the Guelf side. The first despot was one of the Raspanti ('scratchers'; the nickname of the burghers), named Biordo Michelotti (1393), who murdered two of the noble family of the Baglioni, became leader of the Florentine army, and allied himself with Gian Galeazzo Visconti. The city passed to the latter family, and afterwards to Braccio Fortebraccio (1416–24), the famous 'condottiere' and a wise governor. Perugia subsequently suffered from the rivalry between the Oddi and Baglioni families. When the Baglioni got the upper hand, they in turn quarrelled, until the day (14 August 1500) when all their leaders were massacred as the result of a conspiracy, with the exception of Gian Paolo, who revenged himself upon the murderers. Pope Paul III seized the town in 1535 and built the Rocca Paolina (see below). From then onwards Perugia was ruled by a papal governor. In 1809 it was annexed to the French Empire, and it was called *Perouse* by the French; in 1815 it was restored to the Church. In 1859 the papal Swiss Guards occupied the city after an indiscriminate massacre, but a year later they were expelled, and a popular insurrection all but destroyed the Rocca Paolina.

The British 8th Army entered Perugia on 20 June 1944.

Art. Perugia was the chief centre of the splendid Umbrian school of painting, which was formed in the 12C. By the 15C it had became independent of Siena and Florence, and produced such masters as Gentile da Fabriano, Ottaviano Nelli, Nicolò da Foligno (L'Alunno), Matteo da Gualdo, Bartolomeo Caporali, and Benedetto Bonfigli (c 1420–

96), the first great Perugian painter. His immediate follower was Fiorenzo di Lorenzo (1445–1522), but the greatest Perugian painter was Pietro Vannucci (1446–1523), born at Città della Pieve, but called *Perugino*. Among his numerous disciples of the Umbrian school alone were Pinturicchio (Bernardino di Betto; 1454–1513), Andrea d'Assisi (L'Ingegno), Tiberio d'Assisi, Francesco Melanzio of Montefalco, Lo Spagna, Bernardino di Mariotto, Eusebio da San Giorgio, Domenico and Orazio Alfani, and Giannicola di Paolo. His most famous pupil was Raphael. The city also produced especially skilled woodworkers who carved numerous beautiful choir stalls which still survive in many churches of the city, and whose work culminated in the exquisitely panelled Sala della Mercanzia.

The approach to Perugia from the W or from the main station is by Via Venti Settembre (Pl. I;9,14), which winds uphill towards the old city. Off Largo Cacciatori degli Alpi (Pl. I;11), with its monument to Garibaldi by Cesare Zocchi (1887), is PIAZZA PARTIGIANI (Pl. I;11), where there is a two-storey underground car park (signposted). From the car park the stadium is conspicuous beside the 13–14C church of *Santa Giuliana* (Pl. I;14), with a graceful 14C campanile, and two cloisters (13C and 14C; now incorporated in a military hospital). A series of escalators (and some steps), opened in 1983, lead up from the car park to the centre of the city; beyond Via del Circo they traverse the huge vaulted foundations of part of the **Rocca Paolina** (Pl. II;8), a fortress built by Antonio Sangallo the Younger at the command of Paul III to dominate the Perugians who had rebelled against his salt tax. A whole medieval district, including the ruins of the old Baglioni mansions, was vaulted over for this 'bellissima e inutilissima opera'. Much of it, including the upper part on the site of the present Piazza Italia (see below), was destroyed by the Perugians in 1860 in anger against the papal rulers. The escalators emerge at a crossing where the subterranean *VIA BAGLIONA, an ancient road, descends past remains of medieval and Renaissance dwellings (some built on Etruscan foundations), and the huge brick vaults built by Sangallo to sustain the fortress above. Only some of the buildings, including the 13C towers and houses of the Baglioni family, are identified, but the succession of tall scenographic vaults and huge shadowy rooms produces a remarkable atmosphere. The area to the right of the road formed part of the defence works of the fortress, with embrasures in the bastions for the cannon, and here also were huge cisterns for its water supply. Via Bagliona emerges on Via Marzia beneath the splendid Etruscan *PORTA MARZIA (Pl. II;8; 3–2C BC), carefully re-erected in its present position by Sangallo. It is decorated on the outside face by a few worn sculptures in dark stone.

The subterranean road continues from the escalators up to the left past several plans of the Rocca, and the last flight of escalators ends beneath the portico of Palazzo della Provincia (1870; now the Prefettura, whose front bears the Perugian griffin in bronze), on PIAZZA ITALIA (Pl. II;8), flanked by imposing buildings. Behind the Prefettura is the charming little terraced *Giardino Carducci* with a *view extending from Monte Amiata to the summits of the central Apennines, with Montefalco, Assisi, Spello, Foligno, and Spoleto in the distance. Corso Vannucci begins at Piazza Italia.

Fontana Maggiore, Perugia

45

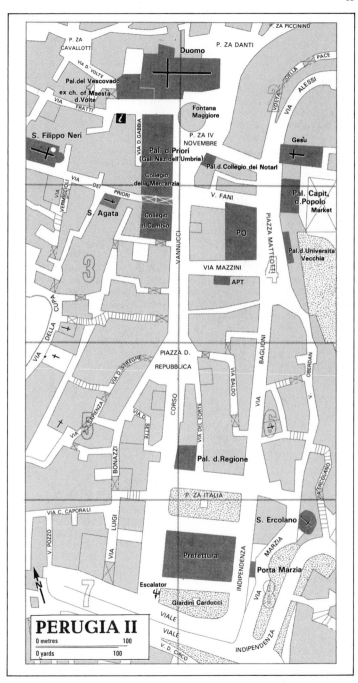

A.   Corso Vannucci: Palazzo dei Priori with the Collegio del Cambio and the Galleria Nazionale, and the Cathedral

The exceptionally wide and undulating *Corso Vannucci (Pl. II;3,5; totally closed to motor traffic), is at the centre of the old city, and it provides a magnificent setting for the 'passeggiata' at dusk when it is even more crowded than at other times. It is named in honour of Perugia's greatest painter. Towards the far end is the long curving façade of *Palazzo dei Priori (Pl. II;1), one of the largest and most splendid town halls in Italy. It stretches as far as Piazza IV Novembre, which has the oldest façade (described below). It was built by the local architects Giacomo di Servadio and Giovannello di Benvenuto (1293–97), and enlarged and completed by 1443 (restored in the 19C and again in 1990). It houses the Collegio del Cambio, the Collegio della Mercanzia, municipal offices, and the Galleria Nazionale dell'Umbria, and beneath it runs Via dei Priori. The front, on the Corso, has castellations above two rows of Gothic three-light windows placed unusually close together. On the ground floor are a series of arches on either side of the high archway over Via dei Priori, and the elaborately decorated main portal. The façade on the left of Via dei Priori (and the bell tower) incorporates a medieval tower and was added in the same style in the 15C. Here (at No. 25) is the entrance to the hall and chapel of the *COLLEGIO DEL CAMBIO (Pl. II;3), which has a main portal (covered for restoration) with bas reliefs and polychrome terracotta tiles in the arch, flanked by two smaller doorways. The wood doors are fine works by Antonio Bencivenni da Mercatello. The guild of money-changers played an important part in the public administration of the city, and passed judgement in law suits concerning financial disputes. It was founded before 1259 and still functions as a charitable institution. Since 1457 it has been housed in these rooms in Palazzo dei Priori, adapted by Bartolomeo Mattioli and Lodovico d'Antonibi.

The entrance (open 9–12.30, 14.30–17.30; winter 9–14; fest. 9–12.30; closed Monday) is through the *Sala dei Legisti* which became property of the Collegio dei Legisti in 1613. The fine walnut benches were carved by Giampietro Zuccari in 1615–21. The beautifully decorated **Sala di Udienza del Collegio del Cambio** is one of the best preserved rooms of the Renaissance in Italy, famous for its frescoes by Perugino, perhaps his masterpiece. The work was carried out, with the help of pupils, including Andrea d'Assisi, and possibly also Raphael, in 1498–1500 (although a final payment was made to Perugino in 1507). They illustrate the ideal combination of Christian virtues with Classical culture in a scheme drawn up by the Perugian Humanist Francesco Maturanzio. The ceiling has beautiful grotesques and medallions with pagan divinities. On the right of the portal is the figure of Cato, symbol of Wisdom. On the left wall is a lunette with Prudence and Justice seated above six standing figures of Classical heroes (all named). On the pilaster is a splendid self-portrait by Perugino. The second lunette has the figures of Fortitude and Temperance seated above Classical heroes; the figure of Fortitude has been attributed to Raphael, then only 17 years old. On the end wall, Transfiguration and Nativity, and on the right wall, the Eternal Father in glory above 12 figures of Prophets and Sibyls, perhaps the most successful composition in the room. The remarkable figure studies here include Daniel, thought to be a portrait of

Raphael. The frescoes are being restored, so that half of the room will be inaccessible for some years. The splendid carved and inlaid furniture is by Domenico del Tasso (1492) and Antonio Bencivenni da Mercatello (1508). In the niche is a gilded statue of Justice attributed to Benedetto da Maiano.

The *Cappella di San Giovanni Battista* is entirely frescoed with stories from the life of St John the Baptist by Perugino's pupil, Giannicola di Paolo (1515–18). The altarpiece is also by him. The woodwork is by Antonio Bencivenni da Mercatello.

The same ticket gives access (at the same times) to the *Sala di Udienza del Collegio della Mercanzia, entered at No. 15 in the Corso (on the right of the main portal, see below). The merchants' guild (still a charitable institution) has been housed here since 1390. Founded before the 13C, it was the most important guild in Perugia in the 14C. The vault and walls are entirely panelled with splendid carving and intarsia work, carried out during the early 15C by unknown craftsmen, showing Northern European influence.

The main portal of Palazzo dei Priori was erected in the 14C and is beautifully carved, but has recently been harshly restored. The outer pilasters, borne by lions, display the Perugian griffin, and in the lunette there are usually statues of Perugia's patron saints (removed). The doors are original. The entrance hall has fine vaulting and a large 15C safe. Stairs (or a lift) lead up to the THIRD FLOOR with the **Galleria Nazionale dell'Umbria (Pl. II;1), the most important collection extant of Umbrian paintings. It is undergoing a radical restoration, and at present the main works are temporarily exhibited in Room XXVI. When the other rooms are reopened the arrangement may be changed. Admission every day, 8.45– 13.45, 15–19; fest. 9–13. The collection was founded in 1863, and moved here in 1879.

The SALA MAGGIORE was the hall of the the Consiglio Generale del Comune. It contains interesting 13–15C frescoes of the Central Italian schools. Rooms I and II contain works of the late 13C. **RI.** 29. Duccio di Buoninsegna, Madonna and angels; 26. Maestro di San Francesco, Cruci- fix, with St Francis in adoration (dated 1272); 32. Vigoroso da Siena, Madonna and saints (dated 1269). **RII.** 894–6. Arnolfo di Cambio, Statuettes. **RIII.** Meo di Guido da Siena, 1. Polyptych, 13. Madonna and Child with four saints, 8. Madonna and Child. **RIV** contains 14C Perugian and Sienese works, and a stained glass window (168.) by Giovanni di Bonino. **RV.** Sienese 14C and early 15C. Taddeo di Bartolo, 72. Annun- ciation, 64. St Peter, 62. Five saints, 66. Madonna and saints (signed and dated 1403), 63. St Paul; Bartolo di Fredi, 58. Triptych with the Marriage of St Catherine, saints, Annunciation, 88. Madonna with saints and the prophet Elijah; *56. Lippo Vanni, Madonna and Child; 116. Domenico di Bartolo, Polyptych; 67. Taddeo di Bartolo, Pentecost. **RVI.** 79. Bicci di Lorenzo, Marriage of St Catherine (with a fine predella); 84. Pietro di Domenico da Montepulciano, Madonna between Saints Francis and Anthony Abbot; 129. Gentile da Fabriano, Madonna and Child (early work). **RRVII and VIII.** Revivial of Umbrian art in the mid 15C. **RVII.** *91–108. Fra Angelico, Madonna with angels and saints, part of a triptych; in the predella, Miracles and death of St Nicholas; *111–14. Piero della Francesca, Madonna with angels and saints, with a beautiful Annunciation above; in the predella, Miracles of St Anthony, St Francis, and St Elizabeth; 746. Francesco di Giorgio Martini, Scourging of Christ (bronze relief); 124. Benozzo Gozzoli, Madonna of Humility and saints. **RVIII.** Giovanni Boccati, 437. Pietà, 149. Madonna della Misericordia, 150–1. Madonna del Pergo-

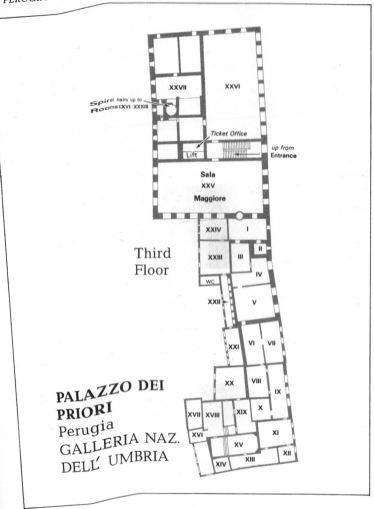

Spiral stairs up to
Rooms XXVI - XXXIII

XXVII   XXVI

Ticket Office

up from
Entrance

Lift

Sala
XXV
Maggiore

Third
Floor

XXIV   I

II

XXIII   III

IV

WC

XXII

V

XXI   VI   VII

XX   VIII

IX

XVII XVIII   XIX   X

XVI   XI

XV   XII

XIV   XIII

PALAZZO DEI
PRIORI
Perugia
GALLERIA NAZ.
DELL' UMBRIA

lato, 147. Madonna dell'Orchestra; 879. Francesco di Gentile da Fabriano, Madonna and Child and Annunciation, processional banner painted on both sides; 169, L'Alunno, Gonfalon of the Confraternità dell'Annunziata; 126–8. Giovanni Francesco da Rimini, Madonna and saints.

RIX. Benedetto Bonfigli, 138. Annunciation and St Luke, 140–1. Adoration of the Magi; in the predella, Baptism of Christ, Crucifixion, Miracle of St Nicholas. **RX.** Minor 15C works. Nicolò del Priore, 204. St Francis receiving the stigmata, 193–5. 197, 199. Dead Christ and saints, 339,40,

Crucifixion; 109. Antoniazzo Romano, Madonna; Perugian School, 152. Dead Christ, 174. Madonna and Child (fresco); Antoniazzo Romano, 109. Madonna and Child, 1054. Ecce Homo; Mariano di Antonio, 117–22. Miracles of Saints Anthony, John the Baptist, and Bernardine, 115. Scenes from the Passion; 236. Girolamo da Cremona, Madonna with angels. **RXI** Perugian 15C artists. Fiorenzo di Lorenzo, 235. Painted niche, signed and dated 1487; Bartolomeo Caporali, 160–3. Angels with the symbols of the Passion, 221. Pietà (fresco), 166–70. Assumption; above, Eternal Father; 153–4. Angel, St John the Evangelist, St Mary Magdalene, 125. Madonna with angels. **RXII.** Fiorenzo di Lorenzo, 231. St Sebastian, 208–19. Madonna and saints, 178–9, Adoration of the shepherds, 181–2. 206, Triptych of the Madonna and saints. **RXIII** Fiorenzo di Lorenzo, 177. Madonna with Sts Nicholas of Bari and Catherine (fresco), 435. St Sebastian (fresco); 856. School of Andrea della Robbia, St Francis; Perugino, 220. Pietà, 180. Adoration of the Magi (c 1475), 1056. St Jerome (fresco); 796. Benedetto Buglioni, Madonna in adoration (terracotta).

RXIV. *164, 237, 222-9. Benedetto Bonfigli, Pinturicchio, Perugino and others, Niche of St Bernardine of Siena (1465 and after); below, Gonfalon of St Bernardine (Bonfigli); on the side walls: *Miracles of the Saint (Pinturicchio and Perugino), with remarkable architectural details. **RXV.** Perugino, 238, 243, 245, 247, 249–61. Adoration of the Shepherds, Baptism of Christ, Saints Jerome and Mary Magdalene, Angel, Eternal Father; in the predella, adoration of the Magi; Presentation in the Temple, Marriage of Cana, Preaching of St John the Baptist, saints, 270. Madonna della Confraternità della Consolazione, *279. Madonna and Child with four saints (1500; predella in Berlin; in a beautiful frame), 278. Gonfalon of the Confraternità della Giustizia (much restored), 266–9. Transfiguration; in the predella, Annunciation, Nativity, Baptism of Christ; 280. Saints Francis, Jerome, John the Baptist, Sebastian, and Anthony of Padua, *248. Christ in the tomb (1494), 358. Lunette of the Adoration of the Shepherds (fresco); Pinturicchio, *274. Madonna, Saints Augustine and Jerome; in the predella, St Augustine and the Child and St Jerome in the desert; above, Annunciation, Christ in the tomb, the Holy Spirit; 276. Gonfalon of St Augustine.

RXVI. 983. Piero di Cosimo, Pietà. **RXVII.** Bernardino di Mariotto, 156. Madonna with St John and two saints, 155. Marriage of St Catherine, 175. Madonna and saints, 157. Coronation of the Virgin; 203. School of Luca Signorelli, Madonna with angels and saints; in the predella, St Bernardine, Dream of Innocent III, etc. **RXVIII.** Followers of Perugino. Giannicola di Paolo, 323. All Saints' Day, 324. Madonna and St John, 325. Crucifixion (fresco); 273. Lo Spagna, Blessed Colomba da Rieti; 271. Giovanni Battista Caporali, Madonna and Child enthroned with saints; Perugino *263, 200. Coronation of the Virgin, Crucifixion, painted on both sides. **RXIX.** Pupils of Perugino. Eusebio da San Giorgio, 287. Adoration of the Magi, 282. Madonna and saints, 343. Madonna with Saints John the Baptist and Benedict; 347. Three saints; Sinibaldo Ibi, 357. Madonna with four saints, 1005. Standard of St Anthony Abbot; 356. Sinibaldo Ibi and Berto di Giovanni, Madonna with Saints Augustine and Sebastian; Berto di Giovanni, 294. Birth of the Virgin, 295. Presentation of the Virgin, 303. Marriage of the Virgin, 304. Assumption (these four from the predella of Pinturicchio's Coronation of the Virgin, now in the Vatican), 309. Coronation of the Virgin, 307–26. St John the Evangelist.

RXX has ceiling frescoes by Tommaso Bernabei. The paintings are by 16C followers of Perugino and Raphael. 363. Pompeo di Anselmo and Domencio Alfani, Holy Family (after Raphael); Domenico Alfani, 364.

Madonna with Saints Gregory and Nicholas of Bari, 288. Eternal Father (after a drawing by Raphael; originally placed over Raphael's Descent from the Cross, which is now in the Galleria Borghese in Rome), *354. Madonna with angels and saints; 275. Pompeo Cocchi, Crucifixion; 414. Dono Doni, Birth of the Virgin. **RXXI.** Late Renaissance. 415. Giovanni Battista Naldini, Presentation in the Temple; 816. Vincenzo Danti. Bas-relief of Christ expelling the merchants from the Temple. **RXXII.** 733, 763. 14C croziers; *744. Cataluccio di Pietre da Todi, Silver-gilt chalice and paten from the church of San Domenico; *742. Reliquary of gilt metal; 762. Gold reliquary of St Juliana; 868, 317–8. Silver voting chest, used for the election of magistrates; 859. 17C ivory Crucifix. **RXXIII**, formerly the Prior's Chapel, with a majolica pavement. Bonfigli, Frescoes of the lives of St Ercolano and St Louis of Toulouse, patrons of Perugia (1454–96); stalls by Gaspare di Jacopo da Foligno and Paolino da Ascoli (1452; removed); 720-1. Voting chests. **RXXIV.** 855. Agostino di Duccio, Madonna and Child and other sculptural fragments.

From the Sala Maggiore the stair landing is reached and the entrance to Rooms XXVI–XXXVII, which display 16–18C works. **RXXVI**, in a fine large hall of the palace, contains works by late 16C painters including Lattanzio Pagni, Cristoforo Gherardi, Arrigo Fiammingo, and Francesco Baldelli; (on easels): 1084. Federico Barocci, Madonna and Child with the young St John; 1083. Orazio Gentileschi, Female saint at the piano; 1073, 1074. Valentin, Noli me tangere, Christ with the Samaritan woman. **RXXVII.** 535. Pietro da Cortona, Birth of the Virgin; Sassoferrato, 381. Virgin in prayer, 380. Head of the Madonna. A spiral staircase leads up to **RXXVIII.** 614. Francesco Trevisani, Martyrdom of St Andrew; 606. Benedetto Luti, Christ in the house of the Pharisee; 379. Corrado Giaquinto, Trinity. **RXXIX.** Giuseppe Maria Crespi and the local painters of the 18C. **RXXX.** Ludovico Mazzanti, St Bernard Tolomei curing the pestilence in Siena in 1348; works by Sebastiano Conca and Francesco Appiani. From RXXVIII, **RXXXI** is entered. Here is a historical topographical display with 16C views of Perugia. **RXXXII** contains wood carvings and Perugian textiles. **RXXXIII.** 18C topographical drawings by Giovanni Battista Wicar. From here a staircase leads down to the exit.

On the FIRST FLOOR (reached by two flights of stairs) is the **Sala del Consiglio Comunale** (sometimes unlocked on request; glass window in the door). Here have been placed the original bronze *Lion and *Griffin from the exterior of the palace (see below). On the inside, in a lunette above the carved portal, is a fresco of the Madonna and Child with angels by Fiorenzo di Lorenzo or Pinturicchio. For a long time this room was known as the 'Sala del Malconsiglio', named after the ill-advised consent of the Perugians to spare the lives of the English soldiers of Sir John Hawkwood (the famous condottiere known in Italy as Giovanni Acuto (died 1394), by whom they were afterwards defeated in 1366.

The Corso rises to end at the delightful PIAZZA QUATTRO NOVEMBRE (Pl. II;2), on a slope, which contains the *Fontana Maggiore. This has two polygonal marble basins, the lower one with 25 double reliefs, 12 illustrating the Labours of the Months, four with figures representing the Liberal Arts, and the others depicting fables, the story of Romulus and Remus, heraldic beasts, and scenes from the Old Testament. Decorating the upper basin are 24 statuettes including personifications of cities, personages from the Old Testament, saints, and contemporary figures. The simple bronze basin above supports three female figures. The fountain bears an inscription with the date of completion (1278), and the names of the artists who worked on it, including Fra Bevignate, Boninsegna, Nicola and Giovanni Pisano. The exquisite carving is by Nicola and Giovanni Pisano: one of the Labours of the Months (with two eagles) is signed by Giovanni, who also carved the figures of the Liberal Arts. The panels representing June and July and the statuette personifying Perugia are attributed to Nicola.

In the piazza is the main façade of **Palazzo dei Priori** (see above), with copies of the bronze Perugian griffin and the Guelf lion, bearing chains, carried off from the gates of Siena by the Perugians after a victory at Torrita in 1358. The latest suggestion about the sculptures is that the wings of the griffin were added before 1281 to an Etruscan body and the new lion made at that time. To the right is a portico of three arches with fine medieval capitals, probably from the church of San Severo, destroyed to make room for the palace. Here is the *Tourist Information Office*. A charming flight of steps leads up to a Gothic portal, the entrance to the huge *****Sala dei Notari** (open 9–13, 16–20; winter 9–13, 15–19; fest. 9–12, 15–19; closed Monday), one of the most impressive rooms in Italy, with remarkable vaulting. It was originally used for popular assemblies, and later as an audience hall by notaries of the city. It is now used for concerts and lectures. After 1860 Matteo Tassi covered the walls with the painted coats-of-arms of the podestà of the city from 1297–1424, but the most interesting decoration (difficult to see) is high up on the spandrels of the arches which bear frescoes of Old Testament scenes and fables by a close follower of Pietro Cavallini (1297).

On the opposite corner of the Corso is the mutilated *Palazzo del Collegio dei Notari* (15C), with good windows.

Along the upper side of the piazza is the flank of the **Cathedral** (Pl. II;2); San Lorenzo; closed 12–16), a Gothic building of the 15C, orientated towards the W with an unfinished façade on Piazza Danti. The S side, overlooking the fountain, has Gothic windows and 14C marble geometrical decoration. Here is an exterior pulpit built for St Bernardine in 1425, a doorway by Galeazzo Alessi (1568), and a bronze statue of Pope Julius II, by Vincenzo Danti (1555, the year of the Pope's death). The elegant Loggia di Braccio Fortebraccio, of four arches on octagonal travertine columns, was built in 1423.

The dark INTERIOR, imposing rather than harmonious, with aisles equal in height to the nave, has columns painted in imitation of impossible marble. Surrounded by a little altar on a pillar of the nave, is the handsome Madonna delle Grazie, attributed to Giannicola di Paolo. Above the W door, in an elaborate frame, Madonna and Child with the patron saints of Perugia, by Giovanni Antonio Scaramuccia (1616). In the right aisle, beside the tomb of Bishop Baglioni (died 1451), attributed to Urbano da Cortona, is the CAPPELLA DI SAN BERNARDINO, closed by a fine wrought-iron screen (15C). It contains a magnificent *Descent from the Cross, one of the best works of Barocci (1569), and a stained glass window (removed for restoration) by Costantino di Rosato and Arrigo Fiammingo. The carved bench dates from the same time (1565). The BAPTISTERY has carved marble decoration of 1477, a fresco of the Baptism of Christ by Domenico Bruschi (1876) and, above stained glass with the Eternal Father, also by Bruschi. The large wood Crucifix is a 17C work by Christophe Fournier. The CHAPEL OF THE SACRAMENT is attributed to Galeazzo Alessi (the painting of the Pentecost by Cesare Nebbia has been removed from the altar). Beyond, on the nave wall, Martyrdom of St Sebastian by Orazio Alfani. RIGHT TRANSEPT. On the altar, Giovanni Baglione, Martyrdom of St Stephen. In the chapel right of the choir, altarpiece by Francesco Appiani (1784). In the CHOIR are a bishop's throne (1520) and stalls (covered for restoration since they caught fire in 1985) of intarsia work by Giuliano da Maiano and Domenico del Tasso (1486–91). In the chapel left of the choir, Ippolito Borghese, Assumption (1624). In the left transept, 16C wood Crucifix. In the LEFT AISLE are bas-reliefs (*Pietà and Eternal Father) by Agostino di Duccio, and a gonfalon painted by Berto di Giovanni (with a lunette above by Giannicola di Paolo). In the CAPPELLA DEL SANTO ANELLO, at the W end of the aisle, is preserved the supposed marriage ring of the Virgin Mary, stolen by the Perugians from Chiusi. It is kept in a chased and gilded reliquary (1498–1511) by Bino di Pietro and Federico di Francesco Roscetto, under 15 locks and is exhibited only on 29 and 30 July. The altarpiece of the Marriage of the Virgin is by Jean Baptiste Wicar (1825). The fine intarsia bench is by Giovanni Battista Bastone (1520–29).

In the SACRISTY (closed for restoration), on the right side of the choir, are frescoes of the Life of St Laurence by Giovanni Antonio Pandolfi da Pesaro (1578) and inlaid cupboards by Mariotto da Gubbio (1494–97). A door here leads into the *Cloister* which has antique and medieval sculptural fragments beneath the portico. Beyond is another cloister with four pretty loggias. The *Museo dell'Opera* has been closed for a number of years. It was founded in 1923 and contains works of art from the cathedral. The paintings include a Madonna, with saints and a donor, by Luca Signorelli (1484), the Redeemer and saints, by Lodovico di Angelo and works by Meo di Guido, Bartolomeo Caporali, Andrea Vanni, and others. There is also a valuable collection of illuminated manuscripts, breviaries, missals, graduals, and antiphonals, as well as gold and silver reliquaries and other vessels.

At the end of Piazza IV Novembre is the 13C *Palazzo del Vescovado*, several times rebuilt. Nearby is the bell tower of the Cathedral (1606–12), which replaced an octagonal Gothic campanile pulled down in 1462. The picturesque medieval *Via delle Volte* descends to the former church of the *Maestà delle Volte* (1567–90), now used as an office (admission on request). The handsome late 16C façade is by Bino Sozi. Inside is a beautiful fresco fo the Maestà by an unknown 14C artist who is named after this work, the 'Maestro della Maestà delle Volte'. The cupola has fine decorations by Nicolò Pomarancio (1568). Outside is a Gothic arch and a 13C tower-house on the corner of the pretty Via Antonio Fratti. Via delle Volte continues downhill under a remarkably high flying arch to *Piazza Cavallotti*. Excavations beneath the piazza have revealed foundations of Roman houses and a Roman road (usually open in summer). In the adjoining Piazza is the *Teatro Morlacchi* built in 1780 by Alessio Lorenzini.

Below Corso Vannucci, and parallel to it, is the long PIAZZA MATTEOTTI (Pl. II;4), built in part on the foundations of Etruscan walls. Here is the impressive *Palazzo dell'Università Vecchia* built in 1453–1515 by Gasparino di Antonio and Bartolomeo Mattioli da Torgiano, seat of the University until 1811. Next to it is *Palazzo del Capitano del Popolo* (1472–81), another fine Renaissance palace, by Gasparino di Antonio and Leone di Matteo (1472–81). Both of these palaces are now occupied by the law courts. An archway leads out onto a terrace (used as a street market) above the large produce market (1932), reached by stairs or lift. From here can be seen medieval arches some 15m high against the walls. A 14C loggia above them is being restored. There is a fine view from the terrace with the large church of San Domenico prominent on the right. Also in Piazza Matteotti is the church of the *Gesù* (1571). The upper part of the façade was completed in 1934. It contains frescoes by Giovanni Andrea Carlone (1621) and a carved ceiling (covered for restoration). At the N end of the piazza is a characteristic narrow old street, the Volta della Pace, which rises beneath a 14C portico. Opposite the law courts is the Post Office, built in 1913 by Osvaldo Armanni.

From Piazza Danti on the upper side of the Duomo, Via del Sole leads up into an ancient part of the town, the Rione di Porta Sole. Via delle Prome diverges left to Piazza Rossi Scotti, from the terrace of which there is a fine view of an unspoilt valley. Below, near at hand, is Via Pinturicchio and a stretch of walls, and on the extreme right, the campanile of Santa Maria Nuova. To the left, the 18C façade of Palazzo Galenga Stuart is conspicuous, and, on the edge of the hill, Sant'Agostino with its small octagonal tower. In the distance, on the skyline, is the pyramidal cupola of Sant'Angelo, and, to the left, Porta Sant'Angelo. In the piazza is a fine large palazzo housing the *Biblioteca Comunale Augusta* which owns a good collection of manuscripts and incunabula. Beside the church to Sant'Angelo della Pace (closed; by Galeazzo Alessi) steps lead down to Via Bartoli.

Via del Sole continues up to *Piazza Michelotti* (Pl. I;7), the highest point of the city (494m), built on the site of the medieval castle, and now surrounded by 17C houses. From the piazza a passageway leads downhill; to the left, beyond a short undulating lane, steps continue down under another passageway to emerge in the secluded Piazzetta Raffaello, in a quiet corner of the old town. Here is the church of **San Severo** (Pl. I;7). According to tradition, in the 11C Camaldulensian monks built here, on the site of a temple of the Sun, a convent and church dedicated to Severus, Bishop of Ravenna. Both were rebuilt in the 15C, and in 1748–51 the church (usually closed) was given its present form. One chapel of the 15C church survives (entrance next door; open 10–13, 15–18 except Monday), with a celebrated *fresco by Raphael (c 1505; his earliest work of the kind; restored in 1976), representing the Holy Trinity with saints. Beneath, in 1512, Perugino, already in decline, painted six other saints. The seated statue of the Madonna and Child in terracotta dates from the 15C or early 16C.

Nearby, in Via Bontempi, is the Etruscan *Porta Sole* (or 'Arco dei Gigli'). There are numerous short narrow medieval streets worth exploring in this area. In Via Alessi is the church of *San Fiorenzo* (Pl. I;7), rebuilt in 1770, which contains a gonfalon by Benedetto Bonfigli. In Piazza Piccinino, which adjoins Piazza Danti (see above) is the church of the *Compagnia della Morte* by Bino Sozi (1575), and an *Etruscan Well* (entrance at No. 19 Piazza Danti, 9–12.30 except Monday). The well, 35m deep and some 5m in diameter, was probably constructed at the same time as the city walls to provide an emergency water supply.

B.   Via dei Priori and the Oratorio di San Bernardino

*Via dei Priori (Pl. I;6) is a splendid old medieval street which descends steeply from Corso Vannucci through Palazzo dei Priori. In Via della Gabbia (right) can be seen medieval houses incorporated in Palazzo dei Priori. On the left is the church of *Sant'Agata* (Pl. II;3), built in 1290–1314 which preserves interesting remains of frescoes, including a Crucifixion by the late 14C Umbrian school. Farther on, on the right, is the church of *San Filippo Neri*, with a grandiose Baroque façade by Paolo Marucelli (1647–

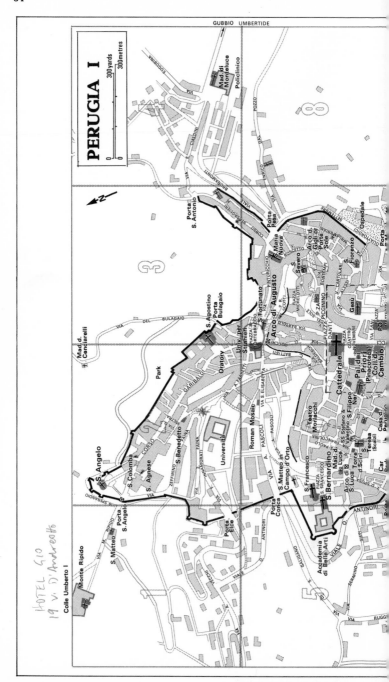

PERUGIA I

300 yards
300 metres

GUBBIO UMBERTIDE

HOTEL GIO
19 v. D'Andreotto
Colle Umberto I

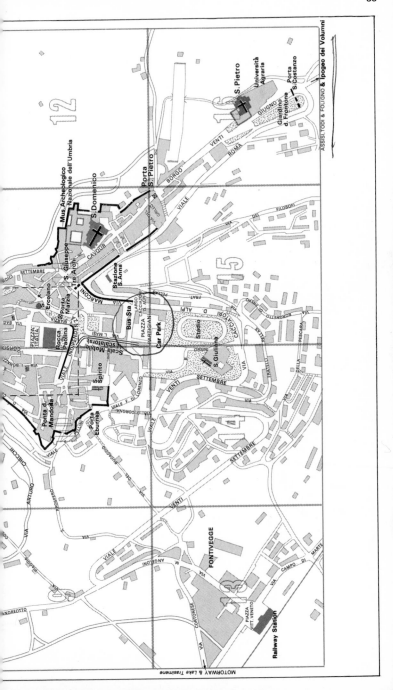

55

MOTORWAY & Lake Trasimene

ASSISI, TODI & FOLIGNO & Ipogeo dei Volumni

Railway Station

FONTIVEGGE

PIAZZA
VITT. VENETO

VIA CAMPO DI MARTE

VIA CORTONESE

VIA ANGELONI

VIA ARTURO

VIA CHECCHI

VIA SETTEMBRE

VENTI

VIALE

S. Giuliana

Stadio

VIA CACCIATORI

VIA D. CACCIATORI

VENTI SETTEMBRE

Car Park

Bus Sta.

PIAZZA PARTIGIANI

LARGO
CACCIANO

Stazione
S. Anna

VIA MARCONI

S. Domenico

Mus. Archeologico
Nazionale dell'Umbria

Porta
S. Pietro

S. Pietro

Università
Agraria

Porta
S. Costanzo

Giardino
d. Frontone

VIA ROMA

BORGO

VENTI GIUGNO

VIALE

CAVOUR

Tre Archi

S. Giuseppe

Ercolano

Porta
Marzia

PIAZZA
ITALIA

Rocca
Paolina

Scala Mobile
(Escalators)

CORSO

VIALE INDIPENDENZA

S. Spirito

Porta
Eburnea

Porta d.
Mandorla

VIA DELLA SPIGA

VIA DEI FILOSOFI

12

15

4

3

63). The high altarpiece is by Pietro da Cortona. The frescoes in the nave
(1762) are by Francesco Appiani, and those in the cupola (1730) by
Francesco Mancini (where the four Evangelists are by Giovanni Andrea
Carlone, 1668).

Via della Cupa diverges left. It leads down under several arches past (right) Via
Deliziosa (where at No. 17 Perugino is supposed to have lived; plaque) to the Etruscan
walls. Steps lead down to a little public park here.

Via dei Priori continues down to another small piazza on which is the
delightful miniature apse, surmounted by a bell-cote, of the church of *Santi
Stefano e Valentino*. A chapel was founded here in the 10C, and the church
now has two aisles, one of the 12C and one of the 14C. It contains 12–13C
fresco fragments, a painting of the Madonna and saints by Domenico
Alfani, and a copy made in 1911 of a triptych by Alunno. On Via dei Priori,
beside the entrance to the escalators which descend to the car parks in
Viale Pellini and off Via Arturo Cecchi, is the church of the *Scalzi* (1718, by
Alessandro Baglioni), usually closed. Next to it rises the *Torre degli Sciri*,
the only tall medieval tower (46m) left in Perugia (which once had some
500 towers). At No. 6 Via dei Sciri is the *Oratorio della Confraternità dei
Disciplinati di San Francesco*, with fine 16C decorations, and paintings by
Giovanni Antonio Scaramuccia (1611). Beyond an archway is a delightful
little piazzetta surrounded by a medley of medieval buildings and the
church of the *Madonna della Luce*, with an elegant façade of 1512–18. In
the small interior is a circular fresco of the Holy Father by Giovanni Battista
Caporali and, on the gilded wood high altar, a fresco of the Madonna and
saints by Tiberio d'Assisi. The *Arco di San Luca* or *Porta Trasimena* is a fine
tall Gothic archway, a gate opened in Etruscan times. On the right of the
Madonna della Luce is another church (closed) dedicated to *San Luca* by
Bino Sozi (1586), owned by the Knights of Malta, whose headquarters is
next door in a 15C palace with handsome square windows.

Beyond is PIAZZA SAN FRANCESCO, surrounded by green lawns. The
*Oratorio di San Bernardino (Pl. I;6) has a beautiful façade decorated in
1457–61 with bas-reliefs by Agostino di Duccio, and rich in polychrome
marbles. It is the most important sculptural work in the town. In the bare
interior is the tombstone of Fra Angelo who ordered the construction of the
oratory. A fine 4C palaeo-Christian sarcophagus serves as high altar.
Behind the E end is the Oratory of Sant'Andrea with a good ceiling (1558).
The adjoining convent is now the seat of the *Accademia delle Belle Arti*, a
16C foundation, which has a gipsoteca with a fine collection of plaster casts,
and a gallery of 19C paintings. Also here is the Cappella della Concezione,
restored in 1928, with a gonfalon by Bonfigli, painted after the plague of
1464. The large 13C church of **San Francesco al Prato** has a façade of
unusual design (rebuilt in 1927). The church has suffered from landslides
since the 18C, and is now in a ruined state; inhabited by birds, it presents
a strange sight. Beyond is the charming little 14C church of *San Matteo in
Campo d'Orto* (closed) with a very tall façade on top of which is a bell-cote.
From here Via Pascoli winds downhill (with the new building of the
University prominent across the hillside) to Via Sant'Elisabetta (see Rte 1D).

C. San Domenico, the Museo Archeologico Nazionale dell'Umbria, and San Pietro

From Piazza Matteotti (see Rte 1A) Via Oberdan descends and (left) the stepped Via Ercolano continues to curve under the Etruscan *Porta Cornea*, later the Gothic *Arco di Sant'Ercolano*. The polygonal church of **Sant' Ercolano** (Pl. I;11) is a very unusual building dating from 1297–1326 with tall blind arcading, preceded by a double staircase (1607). The good Baroque interior (in very poor condition) follows the lines of the octagonal Gothic structure. It contains frescoes by Giovanni Andrea Carlone (1680) and in the apse is a good copy of an altarpiece by Perugino, and paintings by Mattiuccio Salvucci. A well-preserved Roman sarcophagus serves as the high altar. Above, Via Marzia skirts the Rocca Paolina and Porta Marzia, both described before (Rte 1A), with the escalators that connect Piazza Partigiani with Piazza Italia.

From Viale Indipendenza, Corso Cavour descends past the flank of the old stone church of *San Giuseppe* (formerly *Santa Croce*) which contains a fresco of the Madonna and saints in a niche by the school of Bonfigli and a painting of the Madonna of the Misericordia with St Sebastian. The neo-classical *Tre Archi* (1842) were built beside a smaller arch in the Etruscan and Roman walls. Beyond, in a small piazza with a 15C well-head is **San Domenico** (Pl. I;11), the largest church in Perugia (122m in length). It was founded in 1305 and rebuilt after the collapse of the vaulting, by Carlo Maderno in 1632. The façade is unfinished. Part of the Gothic structure can be seen on the exterior. The Gothic campanile by Gasparino di Antonio (1464–1500) was lowered in the 16C.

The INTERIOR is dominated by the huge stained glass window at the E end. SOUTH AISLE. In the fourth chapel, a relic of the earlier church, is a beautiful marble and terracotta dossal by Agostino di Duccio (1459) and his pupils, recomposed and finished later. It includes four statues in carved niches, and a seated statue of the Madonna and Child flanked by two kneeling angels in the lunette above. The frescoed decoration was carried out by Bernardo di Girolamo Rosselli da Firenze (1532). The painting around the statue of the Madonna of the Rosary is by Domenico Bruschi (1869). By the side door is a funerary monument with the terracotta effigy of Guglielmo Pontano (1555). CHAPELS AT THE E END. In the second chapel right of the Choir, 14C votive frescoes and an altarpiece of the Martyrdom of St Peter Martyr by Bonaventura Borghesi (1705). In the first chapel right of the Choir, vault frescoes by a follower of Taddeo di Bartolo, and Gothic *Monument to the Blessed Benedict XI (died 1304) by the early 14C Umbrian school. On the right pilaster of the CHOIR, monument to Elisabetta Cantucci with a bust by Alessandro Algardi (1648). The high altar dates from 1720. The huge stained glass *window (23m x 9m) bears the signatures of Fra Bartolomeo di Pietro da Perugia and Mariotto di Nardo, and the date 1411, but it is thought that the upper part is a later work. It is the largest stained glass window in Italy, except for those in the Duomo of Milan. The carved and inlaid choir stalls date from 1476. On the left pilaster of the Choir is the funerary monument of the Danti family, with a bust of the sculptor Vincenzo by Valerio Cioli. In the first chapel left of the choir, the vault has very ruined frescoes attributed to Allegretto Nuzi. The altarpiece of the Circumcision is by Giuseppe Berrettini. The tomb (1429)

Detail of the 14C monument to the Blessed Benedict XI,
San Domenico, Perugia

with the effigy of Bishop Benedetto Guidalotti, and two reliefs of female
virtues, is attributed to Urbano da Cortona. The second chapel left of the
Choir has votive frescoes. In the N transept is an elaborate organ, begun
in 1660. NORTH AISLE. The fifth chapel has important fresco fragments (very
damaged) attributed to the late 14C Umbrian school; in the fourth chapel,
the altarpiece of the Madonna and Child with two saints is by Giovanni
Lanfranco. The third chapel has a gonfalon painted by Giannicola di Paolo
(1494), and the first chapel, a 17C wood Pietà showing the influence of
Michelangelo, and a detached 14C fresco in a tabernacle. The marble font
dates from the 14C. Benedict's robes are preserved in the sacristy.

The convent of San Domenico now houses the *Archivio di Stato* and the
*Museo Archeologico Nazionale dell'Umbria (Pl. I;11; open every day,
9–13.30, 15–18 or 19; fest. 9–13). The museum has been undergoing
restoration for years, and at present the arrangement is still rather hap-
hazard and the exhibits poorly labelled. The rooms are not numbered. The
museum consists of two collections: the Etruscan-Roman section was
founded in 1790 and housed in the University from 1812–1936; in 1946 the
contents were installed here. The Prehistoric collection, one of the most

important of its kind, was founded on the collection of Giuseppe Bellucci, and was first exhibited in 1937. Since 1952 it has been combined with the Etruscan-Roman collection and displayed in San Domenico. When more rooms are opened the arrangement may well change. Special exhibitions sometimes remain on display for some years.

The fine LARGE CLOISTER has recently been restored. It was begun in 1455 by Leonardo Mansueti and completed in 1579. Here, at the moment, are displayed an inscription of the Augustan era found in 1970 near Perugia, and four cippi with inscriptions set up in honour of Augustus when he authorized the rebuilding of Perugia. In a room off the cloister: sarcophagus with the myth of Meleagar dating from the early 2C AD, possibly by the 'Master of the column of Marcus Aurelius', found at Farfa Sabina, and a puteal of the 2C AD with reliefs of Sabines, also from Farfa. Also here is a display of material found in the Cutu family tomb discovered in 1983 at Monteluce di Perugia. The tomb, in use from the Etruscan to Roman period (3C–1C BC) contained a sarcophagus and 50 cinerary urns, some with polychrome decoration. A room off the cloister is to be opened to display all the Cutu material.

The entrance to the Museum is at the upper level of the large cloister. A corridor (where temporary exhibitions are held) leads to the SMALL CLOISTER. Here are displayed four Roman portrait heads, including one of a man, dating from the 1C BC. The following description follows the chronological order of the display. Beyond a glass door, and to the left, is the ***Prehistoric Collection**. Of particular interest are the discoveries made in 1928–29 at the site of Belverde, near the foot of Monte Cetona (see *Blue Guide Tuscany*). Off a corridor (with a view at the end of Assisi and Monte Subasio beyond orchards and fields) are eight small rooms (at present the four on the left, topographically arranged, are closed). The collection includes objects of flint and pottery illustrating the development in Central Italy of civilisation from the Paleolithic to the Neolithic Age. At the other end of the corridor, steps lead up to the *SALONE, with a splendid display (starting with the right-hand cases) relating to the Bronze Age. It includes axes, daggers, and other implements, objects in copper and bronze; material from the caves of Belverde; vases, some with geometrical decoration, bone implements, agricultural tools, bronze shields and discs, armlets, articles of household use and adornment, and a fine bronze sword. From the windows are good views of Perugia.

At the foot of the steps and to the right is another corridor where the **Etruscan-Roman Collection** begins. In the first case in the corridor are Villanovian finds (8C BC) from recent excavations at Monteluce. The chronological order of the display continues in the rooms off the corridor to the left: R1 contains a stele with the representation of two warriors (from Monte Gualandro) and an archaic sphinx from Cetona. R2. A large sarcophagus from Sperandio showing a victorious return from battle has been removed for restoration. The circular cippus has fine bas-reliefs. Rooms 3 and 4 contain *bronzes from Castel San Mariano, found in 1812 and dating from the 6C BC. These include beautiful plaques in relief which formerly decorated chariots. R5 contains bronzes from the necropolis of Monteluce (6–4C BC), also found in the 19C, and red- and black-figure vases. In R6 (the last room), there are 5–4C BC bronzes from the necropolis of Frontone.

In the corridor are two more cases of material found near Perugia (Palazzone necropolis, and Ponte San Giovanni) including a ceramic fragment with letters of the alphabet (6C BC?). On the other side of the corridor are the last five rooms (7–11) overlooking the Small Cloister. At the end of the corridor is a cippus in travertine, with the celebrated 'Inscription of Perugia' of 151 words, one of the most important monuments of Etruscan epigraphy. R7 contains two red-figure vases of the 5C BC found near Perugia, and finds from the necropolis of Santa Giuliana. R8 has Hellenistic material from tombs near Perugia and bronzes from the necropolis of Santa Giuliana. In R9 are finds from the tomb of Bettona, dating from the 2C BC up to the time of Tiberius; jewellery, and bronzes, including a large bronze shield probably from Pila. R10 displays bronzes from the Crocifisso del Tufo necropolis in Orvieto, and R11 contains a votive hoard from Colle Arsiccio, dating from the Archaic period up to the time of Constantine. The bronzes include an elongated stylised figurine of the 3–2C BC. In the corridor is a terracotta statuette of a seated divinity, signed by the artist.

Other material not at present on view includes: inscriptions, Etruscan urns, fragments of Roman bas-reliefs, and a colossal head of Claudius from Carsulae.

Corso Cavour leads on to (300m) *Porta San Pietro*, with a lovely outer façade by Agostino di Duccio and Polidoro di Stefano (1473). Beyond the gate, Borgo XX Giugno continues along a narrow ridge for another 400m to the Benedictine church of *San Pietro* (Pl. I;16), with a graceful polygonal Gothic tower (rebuilt in 1463) crowned with a spire, a characteristic feature of the city and visible for many miles around. The church belonged to a convent (the buldings are now used by the Faculty of Agriculture of the University) founded at the end of the 10C by the monk Pietro Vincioli, who became the first Abbot. At the end of a short avenue is the portal which leads into the COURTYARD, both built by Valentino Martelli in 1614. Under the portico on the left is the entrance to the church. The carved doorway dates from the late 15C and has a lunette of the Madonna with two angels by Giannicola di Paolo. Two Romanesque arches with 14–15C frescoes have been uncovered from the old façade of the basilica.

The dark basilican INTERIOR (closed 12–15), with ancient marble and granite columns, was transformed in the early 16C. It is entirely decorated with paintings of particularly high quality (but many of them are in very poor condition). The red and white tiled floor dates from 1614, and the fine carved and gilded ceiling from c 1554. In the NAVE are 11 large canvases by l'Aliense (1592–94). On the W wall are frescoes transferred to canvas by Orazio Alfani and Leonardo Cungi. SOUTH AISLE. Eusebio da San Giorgio (attributed), Madonna and two saints (removed for restoration); Orazio Alfani, Assumption. Between the first and second altars, Giacinto Gemingnani, Miracle of the Column; second altar, Cesare Sermei, Miracle of St Mauro (1648). Between the second and third altars, Ventura Salimbeni, David and angels; third altar, Eusebio da San Giorgio (attributed), St Benedict; Ventura Salimbeni, Procession of St Gregory the Great. The fine CHAPEL OF ST JOSEPH (light to the left) was decorated in 1857 by Domenico Bruschi. The altarpiece is a copy from Raphael by Carlo Fantacchiotti. Above the door is an early 16C fresco, and on the right wall, Holy Family by the 16C Florentine school. On the wall of the aisle is an amusing painting by François Perrier of Samson. On the wall opposite, Pietà by the school of Sebastiano del Piombo. Above a door are three small paintings: the Madonna and the young St John with a female saint, attributed to Bonifacio Veronese, and two saints, copies from Perugino by Sassoferrato. Opposite, Virgin by Giovanni Domenico Cerrini. On the aisle wall, Orazio Alfani, Resurrection. Above the sacristy door, three small paintings by Sassoferrato, and, opposite, Cerrini, St John the Baptist.

The SACRISTY (opened on request) has numerous interesting small paint-ings, including four *saints by Perugino (1496; the fifth one of St Scolastica is a copy of one stolen in 1916), St Francesca Romana and the angel attributed to Spadarino, and a Head of Christ by Dosso Dossi. A fragment survives of the Deruta majolica pavement (1563). The bronze Crucifix is by Alessandro Algardi. The intarsia work is by Giusto da Fiesole and Giovanni da Incisa (1472). Illuminated choir-books are displayed in a room off the N aisle. In the *CHOIR are stone pulpits with reliefs by Francesco di Guido (1521) and thrones by Benedetto da Montepulciano (1556). The 16C high altar bears a ciborium of the early 17C. The *stalls, among the finest in Italy, are richly inlaid and carved by Bernardino Antonibi and Stefano Zambelli, with numerous assistants (1526). A *door (usually locked), at the end of the choir, inlaid by Fra Damiano (1536), a brother of Stefano, leads out onto a balcony from which there is a splendid view of Assisi, Spello, etc. The autograph of the poet Carducci (1871) is indicated.

At the end of the NORTH AISLE, Pietà with two saints by Fiorenzo di Lorenzo (1469). The VIBI CHAPEL was built in 1507 by Francesco di Guido. It contains a marble tabernacle attributed to Mino da Fiesole and, above, a lunette of the Annunciation frescoed by Giovanni Battista Caporali. In the nave, copy by Sassoferrato of Raphael's Deposition. The RANIERI CHAPEL is also by Francesco di Guido. On the left wall, *Christ on the Mount by Guido Reni. On the nave wall, Sassoferrato, Judith, opposite St Peter and St Paul by the school of Guercino. In the 18C CAPPELLA DEL SACRAMENTO are three paintings by Vasari. In the nave, Eusebio da San Giorgio, Adoration of the Magi; third altar, Assumption by Orazio Alfani; second altar, wood Crucifix of 1478. Between the second and first altars, Pietà, a late work by Perugino.

The ex-convent buildings include a large cloister and staircase by Fran-cesco di Guido and a small cloister by Galeazzo Alessi (1571). Outside the refectory is a lavabo by Benedetto Buglioni (1488).

From the *Giardino del Frontone*, on the other side of the road, there is another fine view in the direction of Foligno. Outside the *Porta San Costanzo*, dating from 1587 when the Roman road was diverted and the old medieval gateway was included in the hanging garden of the monastery, is the church of *San Costanzo* (1143–1205), partly rebuilt and decorated by Leo XIII, who was Bishop of Perugia before his election to the Holy See in 1878.

D.   From the Arco d'Augusto to the church of Sant'Angelo

From Piazza Danti (see Rte 1A) the narrow old Via Ulisse Rocchi, formerly Via Vecchia, so called to distinguish it from the parallel Via Nuova, now Via Bartolo, descends steeply N to the so-called *Arco d'Augusto (Pl. I;7), a noble gateway in which three periods of civilization are represented. The Etruscan lower part dates from the 3–2C BC; the upper part, with the inscription 'Augusta Perusia', was added after 40 BC. It is flanked by two trapezoidal towers, to one of which a graceful Renaissance loggia was added in the 16C. Outside the arch is the busy **Piazza Fortebraccio** where numerous roads meet. It is dominated by **Palazzo Gallenga Stuart** with a colourful façade (recently restored) built in 1740–58 by Pietro Carattoli on

Arco d'Augusto, Perugia

a design by Francesco Bianchi. It was given a new wing in harmony with the 18C palace in 1935–37, and is now the seat of the *Università Italiana per Stranieri.*

This institution was founded in 1926 for the diffusion abroad of Italian language, literature, and culture. In 1931 it received a gift of $100,000 from the American F. Thorne Rider, for its enlargement. It owns a library (30,000 volumes) of Italian, English, French, and German books. The University is open to students of all nationalities, and it is one of the best known places in Italy at which to study the Italian language. On the left of the Arco d'Augusto is the church of *San Fortunato* (closed), rebuilt in the 17C.

From Piazza Fortebraccio the long narrow **Corso Garibaldi** (Pl. I;2), an old medieval street, leads up out of the town along a spur towards Porta Sant'Angelo. It is lined with fine old houses and a number of convents. The park of Porta Sant'Angelo is just beyond the houses off the right side of the Corso. A short way along on the right is the church of **Sant'Agostino** (Pl. I;3). It has an attractive pink-and-white chequered façade, and an 18C interior by Stefano Canzacchi. In the INTERIOR the first S chapel is a good

16C architectural work by Francesco di Guido di Virio da Settignano with delicately carved details in pietra serena. On the altar is a fresco of the Madonna delle Grazie by Giannicola di Paolo. In the apse, the *Choir is finely carved and inlaid by Baccio d'Agnolo (1502). On the N side, beyond a chapel showing the influence of Sanmichele, the second altar has an early 16C fresco of the Madonna enthroned between two saints, and the first altar, a Crucifixion and Nativity by Pellino di Vannuccio (1387). The *Oratory of the Confraternity of Sant'Agostino* is entered from the piazza (it is sometimes shown on request by the sacristan of Sant'Agostino). It was beautifully decorated in the 17C, and has paintings by Mattia Battini, Giulio Cesare de Angelis, and Bernardino Gagliardi.

The Corso continues uphill past some interesting houses (including No. 126 with an outside stair), and after c 300m Via della Pietra leads left to the ex-monastery of *San Benedetto* (being restored; sometimes open in the morning) which has a 16C majolica pavement, probably of Deruta manufacture. On the right of the Corso at No. 191 is the *Monastery of Beata Colomba* (ring for access). The Dominican nuns show the cell of the Blessed Colomba of Rieti (1467–1501) in which is a remarkable painting of *Christ carrying the Cross, delicately painted in tempera on a very thin cloth, attributed to Lo Spagna. Also here are a charming 15C painting of the Saint, and mementoes including her carefully preserved and labelled clothes, etc. In the church of the convent (to the left of the entrance), above a colourful scagliola altar is an interesting painting of Christ and St Thomas.

Beyond the arch the church of *Sant'Angelo* (Pl. I;2) can be seen on the right, at the end of Via del Tempio. It is preceded by a delightful lawn with cypresses, in a peaceful corner of the town. The church is a remarkable circular building derived from Roman models, erected in the 5C as a temple dedicated to St Michael Archangel. In the beautiful INTERIOR the rotunda has a drum supported by a ring of 16 splendid Roman *columns of different heights and varying materials. There were formerly four chapels forming a Greek-cross plan: only the semicircular Cappella del Crocifisso and one rectangular chapel survive. The drum was reduced in height in the 14C and the building restored in 1948. The altar is made up from Roman fragments. A few frescoes survive from the 14C and 15C, and above a Roman pedestal is the 'Madonna del Verde' (transferred to canvas), a 14C work.

Steps lead down from the garden to *Porta Sant'Angelo* (restored in 1989) rebuilt in 1326 by Lorenzo Maitani, with a tower of a castle built by Fortebraccio. Outside the gate beautiful countryside reaches up to the well-preserved medieval walls providing a remarkably unspoilt approach to the town. Nearby is the 13C church of *San Matteo* (closed). Beyond, on a little hill, can be seen the *Convent of Monte Ripido* (Pl. I;1), founded in the 13C, with an 18C library. In Corso Garibaldi a lane opposite Via del Tempio (see above) leads up to the convent of *Sant'Agnese* (Pl. I;1; ring for access, 9–11, 15–18). One of the sisters will show visitors a chapel with a fresco by Perugino of the Madonna and Saints Anthony Abbot and Anthony of Padua. Another delightful fresco by Eusebio da San Giorgio may not be viewed since it is in part of the convent which is occupied by a closed order.

From Piazza di Fortebraccio (see above), Via Pinturicchio, named after the artist who lived here, leads to the 14C church of **Santa Maria Nuova** (Pl. I;7). In the INTERIOR the organ dates from 1584. On the second S altar is a gonfalon (in very poor condition) by Benedetto Bonfigli with a view of Perugia with its towers in the background. In the chapel to the right of the apse, wood sarcophagus of Braccio I Baglioni (1479). In the apse are fine carved stalls (1456). In the chapel to the left of the apse are frescoes by Vasari's ancestor, Lazzaro Vasari. On the second N altar, copy of a Madonna and saints by Perugino made by Giuseppe Carattoli in 1822. In a chapel at the W end, 16C fresco of the Madonna enthroned. Near the church is the *Porta Pesa*, so called from the time when produce brought in from the country was weighed here. About 500m farther on is the *Madonna di Monteluce* (Pl. I;4), with a rose window and a double portal (13C) in its façade, and containing a marble tabernacle by Francesco Ferrucci (1487). Adjoining is the *Policlinico*, the hospital of Perugia, whose buildings are spread over the E part of the Colle di Monteluce.

From Piazza di Fortebraccio (see above) steps lead down beside the University for Foreigners to Via Goldoni which leads into Via Sant'Elisabetta. Here, beyond the span of a narrow footbridge (once a 13C aqueduct), a modern building of the University (on the right) covers a monochrome **Roman Mosaic** (Pl. I;6) (2C), with the story of Orpheus charming the wild beasts (closed Sunday). The main buildings of the UNIVERSITY, founded in 1307, are in Via Fabretti (Pl. I;2) in what was once a monastery of Olivetan monks, who were suppressed by Napoleon. From Via Sant'Elisabetta Via Pascoli (left) winds up to the SW past fields to Piazza San Francesco (see Rte 1B).

E. Environs of Perugia

The Ipogeo dei Volumni

About 5km from Porta San Costanzo (beyond the church of San Pietro, see Rte 1C) begins the old road to Foligno. Just before the suburb of *Ponte San Giovanni* (also reached by an exit from the Perugia by-pass) is the *Ipogeo dei Volumni (admission 9.30–12.30, 16.30–18.30; winter 9.30–12.30, 15–17; fest. 9.30–12.30). It can also be reached by bus from Piazza Italia (infrequent service: three times daily). This is one of the finest Etruscan tombs known, and it was discovered in 1840. Probably dating from the second half of the 2C BC, it has the form of a Roman house with atrium, tablinum, and two wings. The walls are decorated with stucco and reliefs. The coffered ceiling has heads hewn out of the rock. In the central chamber nine travertine urns containing ashes of the Volumnii family (particularly the urn of Aruns Volumnius) show Roman influence; a tenth, in marble, belongs to the 1C AD. Above the hypogeum, in a modern building, are several urns which were found in the adjacent cemetery.

Torgiano, Bettona, and Deruta

Beyond the church of San Pietro (see Rte 1C) Via San Costanzo leads to a road junction where the old road for Todi begins (N317). At 6km the road diverges left via the Madonna del Piano for Torgiano. 9km. On the Marsciano road (right; 1km) is *San Martino in Campo* where a chapel called 'La Madonnuccia' contains frescoes by the school of Perugino.

A by-road continues to (14km) **Torgiano**, situated between the Tiber and Chiascio rivers, famous for its wine. A private *WINE MUSEUM was opened here in 1974. The exhibits are excellently displayed and labelled in the cool cellars of Palazzo Baglioni, also used for exhibitions (open every day 9–12, 15–20; in winter: 9–12, 15–18; ring for access). This particularly interesting collection illustrates the history of wine, with archaeological material (Roman amphorae, an Attic kylix from Vulci, etc.); a section illustrating wine making, including agricultural tools, wine presses, etc; and Italian majolica (including Deruta, Gubbio, and Faenza ware).

The road from Torgiano continues through thick olive groves to (20km) **Bettona**, the ancient *Vettona*, which has a fine view from its little hill (355m). On the approach the road passes the remarkable golden-coloured Etruscan walls. In the simple little piazza with a fountain is *Palazzo del Podestà* (enquire at the police station for access) with a small collection of Umbrian paintings, which includes two works by Perugino and a predella by Dono Doni. These were rediscovered in 1990 in Jamaica after their theft in 1987 and are being restored. A Madonna with six saints, and a Nativity (from the church of San Crispolto), both by Doni, are also kept here. Below the fountain is the church of *San Crispolto* (the first bishop of Bettona) with a pyramidal campanile. To the right of the church is the restored cloister, and (beyond glass doors) a pretty covered passageway (restored) leads out on to the hillside with a view of the town and its walls. The contents of the other church in the piazza, Santa Maria Maggiore, have been removed for safe-keeping.

At *Passaggio*, 3km beyond Bettona, is the former abbey of San Crispolto, with a fine crypt perhaps dating from the 11C, and the 18C Villa del Boccaglione.

Deruta, on a low hill (218m) 5km S of Torgiano (see above) is famed for its majolica, which is still made in great quantity in modern factories in the new town below. In the old town the Palazzo Comunale houses a PINA-COTECA and collection of majolica (open 10–12.30; Friday, Saturday, and Sunday 15–18; closed Monday). In the first room are works by Baciccia, L'Alunno (Madonna and Child, 1453), and a detached *fresco (c 1478; in very poor condition) from the church of San Francesco by Fiorenzo di Lorenzo. It includes a view of Deruta with Saints Roch and Romano (the head is attributed to Perugino). A gonfalon by L'Alunno is being restored. The second room has portraits by Antonio Amorosi (1660–1736) and two small works by Francesco Trevisani. Beyond is a room with a display of Deruta majolica from the 14C and 15C onwards, and three more rooms on the upper floor contain 19C and 20C majolica.

Opposite the Museum is the church of *San Francesco* with 14C and 15C frescoes. The church of the *Madonna di Bagno*, 3km outside the town, on the Todi road, has a remarkable collection of 17C and 18C ex-votos in majolica.

Corciano

The old road to Magione and Lake Trasimene (N75bis) leaves Perugia near the railway station. The 'superstrada' for Lake Trasimene follows close to this route, with an exit for Corciano. In the suburb known as Ferro di Cavallo, on the right of the road by (6km) the little church of San Manno (remains of 13C frescoes), is the *Ipogeo di San Manno* (owned by the Knights of Malta; admission only with special permission), with a spacious vault faced with travertine slabs and an arched ceiling. The Etruscan inscription states that this tomb belonged to the Precu family.

A large children's amusement park known as *'Città della Domenica'* lies c 2km N. N75bis continues to (10km) the picturesque medieval village of **Corciano**, with well-preserved walls and a 13C castle. The church of *San Cristoforo* has a little museum and *Santa Maria* has a gonfalon by Benedetto

Bonfigli, and a late work by Perugino (Assumption; 1513). At *Pieve del Vescovo*, 2km N, is a 14C castle restored in the 16C by Galeazzo Alessi. The road from Pieve continues for another 4km to *Colle Umberto I* with the *Villa del Cardinale* built in 1580 on a design by Galeazzo Alessi for Cardinal Fulvio della Corgna, surrounded by a fine garden. From Colle a road leads directly back to Perugia via the suburb of San Marco, and enters the town at Porta Sant'Angelo (see Rte 1D). Outside the gate Via Sperandio leads to the *Ipogeo di Villa Sperandio* (privately owned; admission only with special permission), another vaulted Etruscan tomb discovered in 1900.

2

Assisi

ASSISI, on a commanding spur of Monte Subasio (360–505m), is a little medieval town (3000 inhab.) which has retained its beautiful rural setting with olive trees and cultivated fields reaching right up to its walls. St Francis of Assisi, one of the most fascinating characters in history, here founded his Order. In the great Basilica begun two years after his death, the story of his life provided inspiration to some of the greatest painters of his time including Cimabue, Giotto, Simone Martini, and Pietro Lorenzetti. The impressive and moving frescoes here are among the most important works of art in Italy. In this century Assisi has become one of the most famous religious shrines in the world; it is uncomfortably crowded in spring and summer when it is given over to the reception of thousands of Italian and foreign visitors. In the winter months the town, which is slowly becoming depopulated, retains its quiet medieval character: at this time its famous Basilica, as well as its Roman remains, beautiful churches and picturesque streets can be appreciated to the full.

Information Office. 'APT', 12 Piazza del Comune (Tel. 075/812534).

Railway Station. At Santa Maria degli Angeli, 5km SW of the town on the Terontola–Perugia–Foligno branch line (slow trains only). To Perugia (25 mins); to Terontola (c 1hr). Bus c every half hour from the station to Piazza Matteotti via Piazza Unità d'Italia and Largo Properzio.

Buses. Town mini-buses ('A' and 'B', see below. Bus services run by 'ASP' from Piazza Matteotti to Santa Maria degli Angeli, via the railway station, every half hour (c 20 mins). To Perugia, and Foligno via Spello (c 1hr). From mid June–mid September *Coach Excursions* once a week to Gubbio, Urbino, Lake Trasimene, Siena, La Verna, Cascia, Norcia, Spoleto, Todi, and Orvieto. Long distance coaches (run by 'Sulga') from Piazza San Pietro once a day to Florence (2hrs 40 mins) and to Rome (3hrs).

Car Parking. The movement and parking of vehicles within the walls are limited to certain times of the day. Visitors are strongly advised to leave their cars outside the walls, preferably in the free car parks (limited space) off Viale Vittorio Emanuele (near Porta del Sementone) and below Viale Marconi. Apart from these, there are car parks (with an hourly tariff) at Porta San Pietro (the nearest park to San Francesco), Porta Moiano, and Porta Nuova (with an escalator up to Via Borgo Aretino). A mini-bus service ('A' and 'B') runs c every 20 minutes along Viale Vittorio Emanuele past the above car parks and through the centre of the town. A new car park is under construction in Piazza Matteotti.

Many **Hotels** are closed in winter. 4-star: 'Subasio', 2 Via Frate Elia; 'Fontebella', 25 Via Fontebella. 3-star: 'Umbra', 6 Via degli Archi (off Piazza del Comune); 'San Francesco', 48 Via San Francesco; 'Dei Priori', 15 Corso Mazzini. 2-star: 'Country House', 178 Via San Pietro Campagna (in the country below the town, c 15 minutes walk from San Pietro); 'Pallotta', 6 Via San Rufino; 'La Fortezza', 19 Vicolo della Fortezza (above Piazza del Comune). Numerous convents and monasteries of every nationality also provide hospitality (information and booking service at 'Centro Prenotazione per le Case Religiose' Tel. 075/8001515).

In the environs: *Armenzano* (12km E) 'Le Silve' (4-star); *San Gregorio* (12km NW) 'Castel San Gregorio' (3-star); *Bastia Umbra* (10km W) 'Progetto La Villa' (4-star); 'Lo Spedalicchio' (at Ospedalicchio), and 'Turim' (both 3-star); *Petrignano d'Assisi* (9km W) 'Poppy Inn' (3-star), with the 1st class restaurant 'Locanda del Papavero'.

   Youth Hostels 'Fontemaggio' (Via Eremo delle Carceri), and 'Victor', 102 Via Sacro Tugurio. **Camping Sites**: 'Internazionale Assisi', 110 Via San Giovanni Campiglione (3-star); 'Fontemaggio', 8 Via Eremo delle Carceri (2-star).

Restaurants. Luxury-class: 'Da Alberto', 4 Via Arco dei Priori; 'San Francesco', 50 Via San Francesco. 1st class: 'La Fortezza', 26 Vicolo della Fortezza. Trattorie: 'La Rocca', 27 Via Porta Perlici; 'Pallotta', 4 Via San Rufino. On the way up to the hermitage of the Carceri on Monte Subasio 'La Stalla' (2km from the centre) has tables outside in summer.

   Beautiful **picnic places** can be found in the vicinity of Assisi. On Monte Subasio, above the Hermitage of the Carceri on the road across the summit towards Collepino, or on the road along the side of the hill (signposted 'San Benedetto'); or on the hillside around the Rocca Maggiore.

Annual Festivals connected with St Francis, with processions and liturgical ceremonies are held in Easter Week, Ascension Day, Corpus Domini, 22 June ('Festa del Voto'), 1–2 August ('Festa del Perdono'), 11 August ('Festa di San Rufino'), 12 August ('Festa di Santa Chiara'), 3–4 October ('Festa di San Francesco'), and at Christmas. A medieval pageant (when the town divides into two parts) known as the 'Calendimaggio' is held for three days around 1 May to celebrate the arrival of spring. An Antiques Market is also held in May.

History. An Umbro-Etruscan settlement here became the important Roman town of 'Asisium'. Sextus Propertius (c 46 BC–c AD 14), the elegiac poet, was probably a native of Assisi, and his house is supposed to have been that discovered beneath the church of Santa Maria Maggiore. The town was evangelised by St Rufino, who was martyred here in 238. Later under the dominion of the Dukes of Spoleto, it became a republic in 1184. It was famous in the 12C as the birthplace of St Francis. It flourished from the 13C, but at the end of the 14C was captured by Perugia, and from then until the 16C it was involved in numerous wars with neighbouring towns in the struggle between Guelfs and Ghibellines. It passed to the church in the 16C. After the Council of Trent it lost much of its religious significance as the shrine of St Francis. In 1786 Goethe described his walk up to Assisi from Santa Maria degli Angeli when he 'turned away in distaste from the enormous substructure of the two churches on my left, which are built one on top of the other like a Babylonian tower, and are the resting place of St Francis' in order to proceed directly to the temple of Minerva, the 'first complete classical monument' he had ever seen. In 1818 the coffin of St Francis was rediscovered and a new interest in the saint developed. Assisi has become increasingly famous as a centre of pilgrimage in this century: in 1982, the anniversary of the saint's birth, some 5 million pilgrims visited Assisi. In 1986 it was chosen as the place to celebrate a 'Day of World Peace' by representatives of races and religions from all over the world.

St Francis of Assisi (1181–1226) was the son of a rich merchant, Pietro Bernardone, the husband of Pica (perhaps de Bourlemont, a Provençal), He was baptised Giovanni, but his father, who at the time was trading in France, called him Francesco. At the age of 24, after a year's imprisonment at Perugia, followed by an illness, he changed his way of life. He gave all he had to the poor, looked after the sick, and led a humble, exemplary life. He extended his devotion to animals and birds. As he was praying in San Damiano he heard a voice telling him to 'Rebuild my Church', and in the Chapel of the Porziuncola he heard the command 'Freely you have received, freely give'. He retreated with some followers to a stable in Rivotorto, and then settled in a hut around the Porziuncola. He and his companions also stayed on Monte Subasio in prayer and meditation. In May 1209 he obtained from Pope Innocent III the verbal approval of his Order founded on a rule of poverty, chastity, and obedience. He preached his gospel in Italy, in Spain, in Morocco, in Egypt (1219), where the Sultan Melek-el-Kamel received him kindly, and in the Holy Land. In 1221 the Franciscan Rule was sanctioned by Pope Honorius III, and three years later Francis himself retired to La Verna. On 14 September 1224 he had a vision of a seraph with six wings and found on his own body the stigmata or wounds of the Passion. He returned to Assisi and died at the Porziuncola on 3 October 1226. St Francis was canonised on 16 July 1228 and became a patron saint of Italy in 1939. The Franciscan Order has various divisions: the first, a religious order divided into four families (Friars Minor, Conventuals, Capuchins, and Tertiary Religious Order); the second, the Poor Clares, and the third, a secular Order of Tertiary lay brothers.

St Clare (Chiara), the daughter of a rich family, disciple of St Francis, and foundress of the Poor Clares, was born at Assisi in 1194, and died in her own convent in 1253.

Among famous **painters** who came to work here in the basilica of San Francesco in the 13–14C were Cimabue, Giotto, Pietro Lorenzetti, and Simone Martini. In the 15C Andrea d'Assisi (L'Ingegno) and Tiberio d'Assisi, both pupils of Perugino, were born here. Other native artists include Dono Doni (died 1575) and the painter and architect Giacomo Giorgetti (1603–79). Cesare Sermei (1581–1668) worked here most of his life.

The prettiest **approach to Assisi** off the Perugia–Foligno 'superstrada' (N75) is via N147 which passes **Bastia Umbra.** This was important for its castle in the Middle Ages, remains of which can still be seen. In the church of Santa Croce are works by Tiberio d'Assisi, Nicolò Alunno, and Cesare Sermei.

A by-road leads N via *Petrignano*, with a detached fresco by the school of Perugino in its church, to **Rocca Sant'Angelo** (6km), a castle in a splendid position above the Chiascio valley. At the top of the hill, outside the castle walls, is the convent of Santa Maria della Rocchicciola, founded in the 13C. In the church are 14C frescoes in the apse, a Crucifix painted by Matteo da Gualdo, and frescoes by Bartolomeo Caporali and Lo Spagna. From Rocco San Angelo a minor road leads all the way into Assisi.

The straight road (N147) from Perugia via Bastia Umbria provides splendid views of the pale pink-and-grey stone buildings of Assisi beneath its ruined castle, as it traverses the fields at its foot. It climbs up round the N spur of the hill on which the massive tiered vaulting and buttresses built by Sixtus IV in the 15C support the huge convent around the church of San Francesco. At a junction beneath the walls Viale Marconi continues left for the car park nearest to San Francesco outside Porta San Pietro, while Viale Vittorio Emanuele skirts the walls in the opposite direction past several other car parks. *Porta San Pietro* leads into the town near the church of San Pietro (described in Rte 2D) and the picturesque Piaggia San Pietro leads up left to cross Via Fontebella (see Rte 2D) near the 13C Porta San Francesco. Via Frate Elia continues steeply up past the Hotel Subasio, opened here in 1868, to the colonnaded *Piazza Inferiore di San Francesco*, laid out in the 15C.

A. The Basilica of San Francesco

The two-storeyed * *Basilica of San Francesco**, the principal monument to the memory of St Francis, contains a magnificent series of frescoes.

On his death St Francis was interred in the church of San Giorgio, now included as a chapel in the basilica of Santa Chiara. A fund for a memorial church was started in April 1228, and its foundation stone was laid by Pope Gregory IX the day following the canonisation ceremony. Frate Elia, close friend and follower of St Francis and

Vicar-General of the Franciscans, took an active part in the construction of the church and it is thought may himself have been the architect; the work has also been attributed to Filippo da Campello, Giovanni della Penna, and Lapo Lombardo. The lower church was soon ready and on 25 May 1230 the tomb of St Francis was translated to it. The completed church was consecrated by Innocent IV in 1253. The beautiful tall CAMPANILE dates from 1239.

Admission times. The church is open all day in summer but is closed 12–14 in November–March. The E end of the lower church is illuminated from 9–17; otherwise the lighting is poor and it is difficult to study the frescoes in the other chapels in detail (binoculars are useful). The light upper church should, if possible, be visited at different times of day.

At the end of the piazza is the entrance to the lower church which, because of the sloping terrain, has no façade. A double flight of steps (rebuilt in 1731) leads up to the lawn in front of the upper church (also approacₗₑd directly from the lower church, as described below). The ex-oratorio di San Bernardino, with a Renaissance double door, a graceful Lombard work of 1459–72, is beside the entrance to the huge CONVENT (now a missionary college; no admission) with a fine library. A Renaissance PORCH by Francesco di Bartolomeo da Pietrasanta (1486–7) protects the Gothic *POR-TAL (1; 1271) which leads into the **Lower Church**. Beneath the rose window is a tiny fresco of St Francis. The wood doors were carved in the late 16C. The porch and portal have recently been heavily restored. On the wall to the left is a 16C frescoed lunette and a 14C tomb.

The dark INTERIOR, lit by stained glass *windows, resembles a huge crypt with Gothic vaulting and low arches. Its form is that of a Tau cross; the narthex and side chapels were added at the end of the 13C. In the ENTRANCE TRANSEPT or Narthex are frescoes by Cesare Sermei and Girolamo Martelli (1646); the latter also decorated the little chapel of San Sebastiano (2). On the wall beyond (3) is a Madonna enthroned with saints by Ottaviano Nelli (1422). On the opposite wall (4) is a 13C funerary monument of a member of the Cerchi family with a huge porphyry vase. Beneath it to the left is the tomb of Andrea Gabrielli (died 1638) with his portrait by Cesare Sermei. Beyond a 15C Cantoria (5), with 17C decoration, is the *Tomb (6) of John of Brienne, King of Jerusalem and Emperor of Constantinople, friend of St Francis and a Franciscan Tertiary, who was present at the canonisation ceremony of the saint. The two carved angels are particularly fine. The frescoes in the last part of this transept are by Cesare Sermei. In the CAPPELLA DI SANT'ANTONIO ABATE (7), now the Chapel of the Holy Sacrament, are two 14C tombs. The picturesque cloistered cemetery (8; 1492) is usually closed. The CAPPELLA DI SANTA CATERINA (9; poorly lit) was decorated in 1367 for Cardinal Albornoz who found a temporary resting place here before his body was transferred to Toledo. The chapel was designed by Matteo di Gattapone and the frescoes of the story of the life of St Catherine are by Andrea de' Bartoli. The fine stained glass window dates from c 1320. From the transept there is access to the CAPPELLA DI SANTO STEFANO (10), with stories from the life of St Stephen by Dono Doni (1574), and 14C stained glass. In the little CAPPELLA DI SAN LORENZO (11), beyond, are frescoes by Andrea de' Bartoli.

NAVE. The floor slopes down towards the altar. Here are the oldest *frescoes (1253) in the basilica, damaged when the side chapels were opened. The Passion scenes (right wall), the Life of St Francis (left wall) and the geometric decoration of the rib vaulting are all attributed to an anonymous artist, known as the 'Maestro di San Francesco'. On either side of the nave a staircase (12) descends to the CRYPT, opened in 1818 when

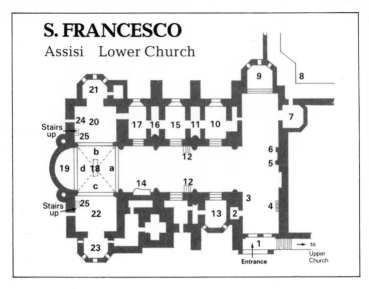

the stone coffin of St Francis was rediscovered (it had been rendered inaccessible in the 15C as a precaution against Perugian raids). The neo-classical form of the crypt was altered in 1932. Round the tomb are grouped the sarcophagi of the saint's four faithful companions: Fra Leone, Fra Angelo, Fra Masseo, and Fra Rufino.

NORTH SIDE. The CAPPELLA DI SAN MARTINO (13) contains a splendid cycle of *frescoes illustrating the story of St Martin by Simone Martini (c 1312–15). The chronological order of the scenes starts on the lower register (left side): St Martin divides his cloak; Christ appears to the saint in a dream; (right side) investiture by the Emperor; the saint renounces the sword. Upper register: (left) the saint resuscitates a child; meditation of the saint; (right) Mass at Albenga; the saint is honoured by the Emperor. In the vault: two scenes of the Death of the saint. Above the entrance arch, Cardinal Gentile da Montefiore, who commissioned the frescoes, is shown kneeling before the saint. On the intrados are paired saints in niches. Simone Martini may also have designed the beautiful stained glass in this chapel. Beneath the third N bay (14) is a Cosmatesque tribune with a fresco of the Coronation of the Virgin by Puccio Capanna (c 1337).

SOUTH SIDE. The CAPPELLA DI SANT'ANTONIO DA PADOVA (15) has stories of the Life of St Anthony by Cesare Sermei (1610). The stained glass windows date from c 1317. Beyond the CAPPELLA DI SAN VALENTINO (16) with the pavement tomb (often covered by benches) of Friar Ugo of Hartlepool (died 1302) is the CAPPELLA DELLA MADDALENA (17) with worn Cosmatesque panels and frescoes (c 1309) of the *Life of St Mary Magdalene, thought to be by Giotto, with the help of assistants including Palmerino di Guido. Left wall: Supper in the house of the Pharisee, Raising of Lazarus. Right wall: Noli me Tangere, Journey of St Mary Magdalene to

Marseilles and the miracle of the Princess and her newborn child found alive on a rock in the middle of the sea. In the lunettes: the saint with angels, receiving the clothes of the hermit Zosimus, and kneeling before a priest, and her soul ascending to Heaven. In the vault, with stars on a blue ground, are tondoes with figures of the Redeemer, St Mary Magdalene, Lazarus, and St Martha. The rest of the decoration consists of figures of saints. The stained glass, with scenes of the life of the saint, predates the frescoes.

The pretty HIGH ALTAR (18), consecrated in 1253, is directly above the tomb of St Francis, which can be seen through a grille. The EAST END OF THE CHURCH (well illuminated) has beautiful and well-preserved frescoes executed in a carefully worked out scheme relating to St Francis: above the altar are the Franciscan Virtues and the Glory of the Saint, and in the transepts the Childhood and Passion of Christ. The decoration, which replaces earlier frescoes here by the 'Master of San Francesco' and Cimabue, was begun in the S transept and Cappella di San Nicola c 1306, continued in the central cross vault (c 1315) and terminated in the N transept (c 1320). The CROSS-VAULT above the altar, known as the 'Quattro Vele', contains four celebrated *frescoes representing allegories of the three Virtues of St Francis: Poverty (a), Chastity (b), and Obedience (c); and his Triumph (d), richly decorated in gold. Traditionally attributed to Giotto, they are now ascribed to an Umbrian pupil known as the 'Maestro delle Vele' from these frescoes, and to a Tuscan follower of Giotto, possibly Stefano Fiorentino. In the APSE (19) a Last Judgement by Cesare Sermei (1623) replaces a Glory of Angels by Stefano Fiorentino. The beautifully carved stalls were completed by Apollonio da Ripatransone (1471). SOUTH TRANSEPT (20). In the vault and on the end wall are large scenes of the *Childhood of Christ, traditionally attributed to Giotto but now thought to be by assistants working under his direction, including an artist known as the 'Maestro di San Nicola'. On the right wall the *Crucifixion may be by the hand of Giotto himself. Next to it is a *Madonna enthroned with four angels and St Francis by Cimabue. This survives from the earlier fresco decoration of c 1280 in this part of the church, and the figure of St Francis is one of the most famous representations of the saint. The tomb of five companions of St Francis bears their portraits by Pietro Lorenzetti. To the left of the door, half-length figures of the Madonna and Child with two King-Saints, and (on the end wall), five saints including one traditionally thought to be St Clare, all by Simone Martini. The CAPPELLA DI SAN NICOLA (21) is decorated with *frescoes of the life of St Nicholas attributed by some scholars to Giotto and by others to his assistants, including one called from these frescoes the 'Maestro della Cappella di San Nicola', and Palmerino di Guido. Above the tomb of Giovanni Orsini (died 1292/4) is a frescoed tripytch of the Madonna and Child between St Nicola and Francis attributed to the hand of Giotto. The glass is contemporary with the frescoes. NORTH TRANSEPT (22). The vault and walls are covered with moving frescoes of the *Passion by Pietro Lorenzetti (c 1320), including a large Crucifixion (damaged in the 17C) and a Descent from the Cross. On the left wall is a charming *Madonna and Child with Saints Francis and John the Evangelist. In the CAPPELLA DI SAN GIOVANNI BATTISTA (23) there is a frescoed triptych of the Madonna and Child with Saints John the Baptist and Francis also by Pietro Lorenzetti. The central panel of stained glass is attributed to Jacopo Torriti.

Beyond a door (24) in the S transept steps lead down past the vaulted apse to the CHAPTER HOUSE (c 1240) with a fresco of the Crucifixion by Puccio Capanna (c 1340). Here are exhibited reliquaries of St Francis, including his chalice and paten, clothes, etc, and a horn and staff of office presented to him by Sultan Melek-el-Kamil. Also here is the Rule of the Franciscan Order sent to the saint by Pope Honorius III in 1223.

Stairs (25) lead up from both transepts to a terrace outside the apse of the upper church overlooking the Cloister of Sixtus IV. Here a door leads into the SALA GOTICA, where the *Treasury has been beautifully arranged (there are views of the countryside from the windows). It is open from Easter to October, 9.30–12, 14–18 except Sunday, but is closed from November to March. Though several times despoiled it still contains precious treasures. In the entrance is the magnificent Flemish *tapestry of St Francis, presented by Sixtus IV in 1479. Also here, *altar-frontal (1473–78) presented by Sixtus IV in 1478. The figures of the Pope kneeling before St Francis are by Antonio del Pollaiolo, and the frieze above attributed to Francesco Botticini. In the main hall, the first cases contain a 12C Processional Cross and a 13C painted Crucifix by a follower of Giunta Pisano; (on the wall) Umbrian Crucifix (c 1220–40). Cases 10–12: reliquary of St Andrew (c 1290), presented by Nicholas IV; panel painting of St Francis (1265–75); and a sinopia of the head of Christ from the Upper church. On a raised platform in the centre: silver gilt Reliquary presented by Queen Joanna of Burgundy in the 14C; Madonna and Child, a 13C ivory of French workmanship; and the illuminated Missal of St Louis of Toulouse (French, 1260–64). On the left wall: sinopia of St Martin by Simone Martini from the Lower Church; tabernacle designed by Galeazzo Alessi and made by Vincenzo Danti (1570), and medieval ceramics found in Assisi in 1968. Case 17: silver gilt *Chalice of Nicholas IV (c 1290) by Guccio di Mannaie, with a portrait of the Pope in enamel. Cases 18–25 contain 14–16C reliquaries and Crosses, including a 14C Venetian Cross in rock-crystal with enamels. On the platform are displayed more reliquaries and Crosses of the 16–17C. At the end of the hall, 18C and 19C church silver, and on the wall, paintings by Tiberio d'Assisi (Crucifix and Saints) and Lo Spagna (Madonna enthroned).

The room beyond was opened in 1986 to display the **Mason Perkins Collection** of paintings (some of them recently restored) left to the Convent by the art historian, collector and dealer, Frederick Mason Perkins (1874–1955), particularly interesting as an example of a private collection formed in Italy in the first half of this century. It includes works by Mariotto di Nardo, Lorenzo Monaco (Madonna of Humility), Pier Francesco Fiorentino, Lorenzo di Nicolò, Ortolano (St Sebastian), the 'Maestro di San Martino alle Palme' (portable triptych), Segna di Bonaventura, Taddeo di Bartolo (St Elizabeth of Hungary), Pietro Lorenzetti (Madonna and Child), and Bartolo di Fredi.

Two more staircases continue up from the terrace to the transepts of the **Upper Church**. The tall light interior provides a strong contrast to the Lower Church. The façade is described below. The architectural unity of this remarkable 13C Gothic building is enhanced by its contemporary frescoes and stained glass. It shows a close affinity to Northern Gothic churches, and may be the work of a French or even English architect. The *FRESCOES, carried out probably from 1277 to 1300, are by the greatest artists of the day, including Cimabue, Jacopo Torriti, and probably Giotto, together with anonymous masters. They follow a carefully worked out scheme which illustrates the importance of St Francis in his role as an intermediary between man and God.

In the TRANSEPT, CROSSING, and APSE are the earliest frescoes (c 1277) with scenes from the life of the Virgin, the Apostles, and the Apocalypse. They are very damaged and have lost their colour, taking on the appearance of negatives, for reasons still not fully explained. NORTH TRANSEPT. Scenes from the Apocalypse by Cimabue, and a dramatic Crucifixion. In the CROSSING the vault is decorated with the four Evangelists, also by Cimabue. In the APSE, scenes from the Life of the Virgin by an anonymous Northern painter (finished by Cimabue). The Papal throne also dates from the 13C and is probably the work of Roman sculptors. The stalls date from 1501. SOUTH TRANSEPT. The frescoes, with scenes from the life of Saints Peter and Paul, and another Crucifixion, were begun by an anonymous Northern painter, and continued by Jacopo Torriti and assistants of Cimabue.

NAVE. In the two UPPER REGISTERS, between the windows, are frescoes (difficult to see) of stories from the Old Testament (S wall) and New Testament (N wall), commissioned on the election of the first Franciscan pope, Nicholas IV, in 1288. Many of them are damaged. These were all ascribed by Vasari to Cimabue, but are now generally thought to be in part by pupils of Cimabue, and in part by painters of the Roman school, including Jacopo Torriti. Giotto is also now considered by some scholars to have been involved in some of the scenes; if this is so these would be his earliest works in the basilica. The chronological order of the scenes follows the upper register, starting on the SOUTH SIDE in the fourth bay with the Creation of the World and Creation of Adam, and continuing to the first bay, and then follows the middle register starting in the fourth bay with the creation of the Ark. The two remarkable scenes in the second bay of Isaac blessing Jacob and Esau before Isaac are attributed to the 'Maestro di Isacco', now usually identified with Giotto. The New Testament scenes on the NORTH SIDE of the church start on the upper register of the fourth bay with the Annunciation, and continue to the first bay with the Baptism of Christ. The story continues in the middle register at the fourth bay with the Marriage at Cana and ends in the first bay with the Maries at the Sepulchre. On the INNER FACADE are two scenes of the Pentecost and Ascension and Saints Peter and Paul. In the VAULT of the first bay of the nave are the four Doctors of the Church, now usually attributed to Giotto, and in the third bay, the Redeemer, the Virgin, St John the Baptist, and St Francis.

The LOWER REGISTER of frescoes in the NAVE are the famous scenes from the Life of St Francis, traditionally thought to be early works by Giotto and assistants (c 1290–95), but not attributed to Giotto by all scholars. Giotto received commissions for other Franciscan fresco cycles in Rimini and Padua, both now lost, and in the Bardi chapel of Santa Croce in Florence. A close study of the 28 scenes (recently well restored) reveals that several different hands were at work here. The story begins on the SOUTH WALL, in the fourth bay: 1. The young saint is honoured in the piazza of Assisi by a poor man who lays down his cloak before him; 2. St Francis gives his cloak to a poor man (with a panorama of Assisi in the background); 3. The saint dreams of a palace full of arms; 4. The saint in prayer in San Damiano hears a Voice exhorting him to 'Rebuild My Church'; 5. The saint renounces his worldly goods in front of his father and the Bishop of Assisi; 6. Innocent III dreams of the saint sustaining the Church; 7. Innocent III approves the saint's Order; 8. The saint appears to his companions in a Chariot of Fire; 9. Fra Leo dreams of the throne reserved for the saint in Paradise; 10. The expulsion of the Demons from Arezzo; 11. The saint before the Sultan offers to undergo the Ordeal by Fire; 12. The saint in Ecstasy; 13. The saint celebrates Christmas at Greccio. WEST WALL: 14. The saint causes a fountain to spring up to quench a man's thirst; 15. The saint preaches to the birds. NORTH WALL: 16. The Death of the Knight of Celano as foretold by

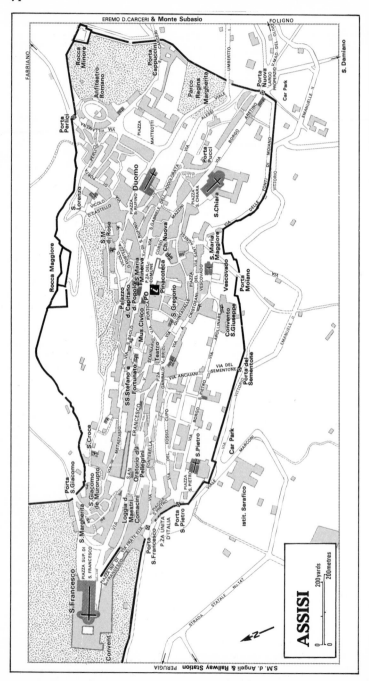

ASSISI

the saint; 17. The saint preaches before Honorius III; 18. The saint appears to the friars at Arles; 19. The saint receives the Stigmata; 20. The death of the saint and his funeral; 21. The apparition of the saint to the Bishop of Assisi and Fra Augustine; 22. Girolamo of Assisi accepts the truth of the Stigmata; 23. The Poor Clares mourn the dead saint at San Damiano; 24. Coronation of the saint; 25. The saint appears to Gregory IX in a dream; 26. The saint heals a man, mortally wounded, from Ilerda; 27. The saint revives a devout woman; 28. The saint releases Pietro d'Alife from prison.

The medieval *STAINED GLASS is the most important in Italy. The earliest windows are those in the apse (c 1253), probably by German artists. The glass in the S transept and nave is attributed to the 'Maestro di San Francesco' and French masters.

The *FAÇADE, with a beautiful rose window and fine Gothic portal, overlooks a green lawn.

B.   San Francesco to Piazza del Comune

From the lawn in front of the upper church of San Francesco, Via San Francesco leads towards the centre of the town. On the right is the 19C Oratorio dell'Immacolata Concezione. Next to it the Capuchin monks opened a museum in 1972 relating to the Indians of Amazonia. Beyond is Palazzo Bernabei, built by Giacomo Giorgetti after 1646. On the left (No. 14) is a 13C house known as the *Loggia dei Maestri Comacini*. From here a stepped alley (Vicolo di Sant'Andrea) leads up through a quiet medieval district of the town towards Porta San Giacomo (described at the end of this route). Beyond, on the left, is *Palazzo Giacobetti* with balconies over its two portals, now the seat of the Biblioteca Comunale. The rooms on the piano nobile have 17C painted decoration. On the right, beyond a palace built in 1883 with terracotta decoration round the windows and doorway, is the **·Oratorio dei Pellegrini**, the relic of a 15C hospital where pilgrims used to be lodged. The worn fresco on the façade is by Matteo da Gualdo, who also painted the delightful frescoes inside on the altar wall. The vault and side walls were decorated in 1477 by Pierantonio Mezzastris with stories from the life of St James including the Miracle of the two hens resuscitated in order to proclaim the innocence of a young pilgrim who had been unjustly accused, and the Miracle of a hanged man supported by the saint, and found alive by his parents. On the left wall are two stories from the life of St Anthony Abbot: the saint receiving some camels who have journeyed alone to bring provisions to the monks, and the saint distributing alms to the poor. The inner façade has figures of three saints, once thought to be early works by Perugino but now considered by some scholars to be by l'Ingegno.

On the left is the 16C Palazzo Bartocci-Fontana (being restored), and opposite, the *Portico del Monte Frumentario* with seven columns. The frescoes by followers of Giotto have all but disappeared. This was one of the first public hospitals in Italy (founded in 1267). Next to it is a public fountain attributed to Galeazzo Alessi. From the top of Vicolo Frondini there is a good view of the plain. The road now passes beneath an arch in the Roman circuit of walls, to Via del Arco del Seminario. The huge building of the former Missionary college on the left has a handsome loggia crowned by a balcony, built by Attilio Cangi in 1911. Opposite is the high red-and-white stone wall of the former monastery of Sant'Angelo di Panzo, with a fresco by Girolamo Marinelli. Farther on, on the right, is Palazzo Rossi, attributed to Galeazzo Alessi, with a balcony over its portal and, in a little piazza, the Teatro Comunale Metastasio (now a cinema) built in 1836 by Lorenzo Carpinelli. Via Fortini and Via Portica continue steeply up, with a view ahead of the Torre del Popolo and dome of San Rufino. On the right a pastry shop has a beautifully carved portal attributed to Franceschino Zampa (c 1470). Opposite is the entrance to the **Museo Civico** (admission daily 10–13, 14.30–17.30; cumulative ticket with the Pinacoteca and Rocca) arranged in 1933 in a crypt, all that remains of the church of San Niccolò founded in 1097. The collection, formed in 1793 by the Accademia Properziano del Subasio, consists of Umbrian and Roman material found in Assisi and environs. The works are numbered and a hand-list is lent to visitors. On the left, Roman sarcophagus and cinerary urn of the 2C AD. On the right is a fragment of an interesting funerary stele (1C AD). Beyond the entrance to the corridor (see below) are a number of urns (1C BC–1C AD) from a necropolis. Against the far wall are two statues dating from the 1C AD, and, on the left wall, a fragment of a seated female statue (1C AD). In the last part of the room are finds made in 1864 in a Roman house near the piazza, including interesting fresco fragments.

A corridor, with Roman paving stones and a drainage canal, lined with Roman inscriptions and funerary stelai, leads into an area first excavated in 1836. Once thought to be the Forum of the Roman city, this is now usually interpreted as a sacred area at the centre of the city in front and below the so-called Temple of Minerva (see below). This consisted of a paved piazza surrounded on three sides by a colonnade (now almost totally disappeared): the corridor runs along the upper side of the piazza past a rectangular platform thought to be an altar or a base for votive statues. Aligned with this, to the right, is another rectangular structure of the 1C AD, well preserved with an inscription relating to the statues of the Dioscuri which once stood here. The main corridor continues past stairs which led up to the temple and remains of a monumental fountain which once decorated the piazza. At the end of the corridor the bases of two columns from the portico survive and on the end wall are remains of Roman buildings thought to have been shops.

In Via Portico is a pretty public fountain, reconstructed in 1926 and a little pulpit carved by Niccolò da Bettona (1354). The beautifully-shaped **Piazza del Comune** is the centre of the town. It is on the site of a Roman piazza, once thought to be the Forum, but now usually identified as a sanctuary around the so-called Temple of Minerva: the position of the altar and statue base (visible in the Museo Civico, see above) in front of the temple have been outlined in white marble in the pavement. The so-called **˙Temple of Minerva** has a perfectly-preserved pronaos of six Corinthian columns on plinths which support a low tympanum. The flight of travertine steps continues between the columns. It dates from sometime between the 1C BC and the Augustine Age, and may have been dedicated to the Dioscuri. It was particularly admired by Goethe when he visited Assisi in 1786, as it was the first Classical building he had ever seen. It is in need of restoration. The cella was transformed in 1539 into the church of Santa Maria della Minerva and given a Baroque interior by Giacomo Giorgetti in 1634. The interior, with 18C statues and paintings by Martin Knoller, Antonio Maria Garbi, and Francesco Appiani, is closed for restoration.

The very tall **Torre del Popolo** was erected in the 13C. At its base is a relief of 1348 showing various measures. Next to it is the 13C *Palazzo del*

Podestà, reconstructed in the 16C. The neo-Gothic Post Office was built in 1927 by Silvio Gabrielli and Ruggero Antonelli (and decorated inside by Adalberto Migliorati). Next to it steps lead up to a tabernacle with a fresco of the Madonna del Popolo by a local follower of Simone Martini. Opposite the temple is the 16C Palazzo Bonacquisti (now a bank) and the rest of this side of the piazza is occupied by **Palazzo Comunale** and *Palazzo dei Priori*. An open archway has its vault decorated with pretty grotesques (1556). On the ground floor of Palazzo dei Priori is the **Pinacoteca Comunale** (admission daily 10–13, 14.30–17.30) inaugurated in 1912, which contains numerous detached frescoes from street tabernacles and oratories in the town (many of them in poor condition).

R1. On the right wall are interesting fragments of frescoes detached from Palazzo del Capitano del Popolo, including 13C Gothic scenes with knights on horseback and representations of the seasons. On the opposite wall, early 14C fragment of the Crucifixion with figures kneeling at the foot of the Cross. A painted Cross is attributed to the 'Maestro Espressionista di Santa Chiara' (perhaps Palmerino di Guido). The detached fresco fragment of the Prayer in the Garden is attributed to Pace di Bartolo. On a stand: Pace di Bartolo, Madonna and Child with angels (a fragment) and, behind, a charming fragment of the Child with St Francis by Puccio Capanna. Other 14C fresco fragments include the martyrdom of St Stephen and three armed men. The damaged fresco detached from Palazzo del Capitano del Popolo, of the Madonna enthroned in a painted niche is attributed to the bottega of Giotto. R2. Standard of the Madonna of the Misericordia (with St Biagio enthroned behind) by l'Alunno. Frescoes by Tiberio d'Assisi, and a lunette by l'Ingegno. Among the 15C votive frescoes is a scene of St Julian murdering his parents. R3. Good frescoes detached from the Castello di San Gregorio attributed to Tiberio d'Assisi or Francesco Tartaglia. R4 has paintings by Giacomo Giorgetti, Dono Doni, and Cesare Sermei.

The delightful fountain in the piazza was designed in 1762 by Giovanni Martinucci. Beneath the Arco dei Priori a road descends to the **Chiesa Nuova** built on the supposed site of the house which belonged to the parents of St Francis. In the piazza are two bronze statues of them (1984) and a Madonna and Child in majolica tiles (1927). The handsome centrally-planned church dates from 1615, and contains contemporary frescoes, and stuccoes of 1769. The two chapels on either side of the entrance have monochrome frescoes attributed to Cesare Sermei. In the chapel on the right are frescoes attributed to Vincenzo Giorgetti and an 18C altarpiece, and in the sanctuary, the high altarpiece and frescoes are by Cesare Sermei. In the chapel on the left, the altarpiece is by Andrea Polinori and the frescoes by Giacomo Giorgetti. In the pilaster is a tiny cell where St Francis is supposed to have been imprisoned by his father (the wood statue of the saint here dates from the 17C). A door leads out to an alley with an oratory of the 13C indicated as the birthplace of the saint.

From Piazza del Comune Via San Paolo leads past the church of *San Paolo* (closed), founded in 1071, next to the door of a Benedictine priory. Beyond the two-storeyed 14C Confraternity of Santo Stefano, the stepped Vicolo di Santo Stefano descends past a tabernacle with a worn fresco of 1363 by Pace di Bartolo to a little garden with a view of the valley. Here is the picturesque church of **Santo Stefano** with a bell-cote and pretty apse, in a peaceful corner of the town. The simple little church has interesting old vaulting above the presbytery and contains a very ruined fresco of the early 14C. Via San Paolo continues beyond an arch over the road down to the Renaissance Palazzo Locatelli, now the seat of the 'Opera Casa Papa Giovanni'. Beyond the huge Palazzo Spagnoli (1925; being restored) Via Metastasio continues past the entrance gate to the monastery of *San Giacomo de Murorupto* (closed 12–15.30). It has a picturesque cloister and Romanesque church. Via San Giacomo leads down past Casa Tini with architectural fragments in its façade to the old *Porta San Giacomo* in the 14C walls. On the left the stepped Vicolo Sant'Andrea descends beneath a wide arch to a picturesque and quiet part of the town around the little churches of Santa Margherita and Sant'Andrea. There is a splendid view of the upper church of San Francesco from here; the lawn is reached by another flight of steps.

C. San Rufino and the Rocca

From Piazza del Comune, Via San Rufino leads up to the charming, quiet *PIAZZA DI SAN RUFINO, with its wall fountain of 1532, on the site of a Roman terrace which may have been the Roman Forum. It provides a splendid setting for the **Cathedral (San Rufino)**. Tradition relates that a chapel was built here c 412 to house the relics of St Rufino, the first bishop of Assisi, martyred in 238. A church, which occupied the site of the present piazza, was built by Bishop Ugone c 1029. The *CAMPANILE, which stands over a Roman cistern, and the crypt (described below) survive from this building. The church was rebuilt in 1140 by Giovanni da Gubbio (who also heightened the campanile). The *FAÇADE has rectangular facing between its doors which are decorated with intricate carvings. Above a gallery are three lovely rose windows, the central one with good carved symbols of the Evangelists and telamones. It was heightened with a Gothic blind arch before the church was consecrated in 1253.

The INTERIOR (closed 12–14) was transformed by Galeazzo Alessi in 1571. At the beginning of the N aisle a little door gives access to a well-preserved Roman cistern with a barrel vault beneath the campanile. The statues on the W wall of Saints Francis and Clare are by Giovanni Duprè and his daughter Amalia (1881–88). At the beginning of the SOUTH AISLE is the font at which St Francis and St Clare were baptised. The Emperor Frederick II may also have been baptised here in 1187 (at the age of three). It is surrounded by a terracotta tabernacle of 1882. On the altar, Berto di Giovanni, Standard of St Joseph. The CAPPELLA DEL SANTISSIMO SACRAMENTO was built in 1663 on a design by Giacomo Giorgetti, with paintings in fine frames by Giovanni Andrea Carlone, and an oval in the vault by Giorgetti. On the last altar in this aisle, with stuccoes by Agostino Silva, is an altarpiece of Christ in glory with saints by Dono Doni. Beneath the high altar in the PRESBYTERY, St Rufino is buried. On the right and left altars are a Deposition and Crucifixion both by Dono Doni. The choir stalls were inlaid by Giovanni di Piergiacomo da Sanseverino. NORTH AISLE. The black stucco statues of Prophets, and the stucco decoration of the altars is by Agostino Silva (1672). On the fourth altar is a wood Crucifix (1561) and on the second altar, designed by Giacomo Giorgetti, is an altarpiece by Francesco Appiani.

From the S aisle a door leads into a corridor where the outside wall of the church can be seen. Here are displayed numerous lapidary fragments from the 11C church, and 17C paintings including works by Cesare Sermei. In the sacristy (1907, by Carlo Gino Venanzi) are paintings by Giacomo Giorgetti, Cesare Sermei and Martin Knoller. From the corridor there is access to the MUSEO CAPITOLARE (admission 9.30–12, 14–18; but closed November–Easter). It contains detached frescoes by Puccio Capanna from San Rufinaccio in Assisi, triptychs by l'Alunno and Matteo da Gualdo,

Detail of the 12C façade of the Cathedral of Assisi

works by Dono Doni and Cesare Sermei, and a standard of the martyrdom of St Catherine of Alexandria and Saint Giacomo and Anthony Abbot by Orazio Riminaldi (1627).

From a little door in the piazza (right of the façade) steps lead down through a Carolingian cloister (restored), with a well, to the entrance to the CRYPT of the 11C church (open at the same times and with the same ticket as the Museo Capitolare; see above), discovered in 1895. It has primitive vaulting and Ionic capitals, and in the apse are scant remains of the original frescoes. Nearby is a Roman wall and a channel which led to the reservoir (see above). The Roman *sarcophagus (3C AD), with reliefs relating to the myth of Diana and Endymion, was used as the tomb of St Rufino.

In front of the church Via Santa Maria delle Rose leads through a pretty district of the town past the ancient church of *Santa Maria delle Rose*, while Via Porta Perlici continues uphill. On the left the stepped Vicolo del Castello leads up past a gate in front of a little garden with cypresses and a tabernacle protecting a fresco by Cola Petruccioli (c 1394) which belonged to the *Confraternità di San Lorenzo*. The steps emerge on a road which continues up to the **Rocca Maggiore** (open daily, 10–16; Easter–November

The 'Rocchiciola' above Assisi

9–20) which dominates the town. There are splendid views to the N and E towards the wooded Monte di San Rufino and gorge of the Tescio, and the other citadel, known as the *Rocchiciola* (no admission), erected by Cardinal Albornoz in 1367, with the walls enclosing the picturesque little borgo of Perlici. In the other direction is the plain in front of Assisi. The hill was fortified in ancient times and the castle rebuilt in 1365 by Cardinal Albornoz. The entrance is beside a circular tower added by Paul III in 1538. The inner keep is surrounded by a high wall with slits for marksmen. From the courtyard is access to the kitchen, storerooms, and (on the floor above) the dormitory. A walkway leads to a polygonal tower (from which there is a remarkable view of the Basilica of San Francesco).

Via Porta Perlici (see above) continues uphill from San Rufino through two arches and then continues right with fine views of the wooded hills behind Assisi to end at the 14C Porta Perlici. To the right, Via dell'Anfiteatro Romano follows the form of the *Roman Amphitheatre* (1C AD) past the Fonte di Perlici (13C) and a public fountain erected in 1736. To the S is the large **Piazza Matteotti**, with a *bus station*, and a *car park* (under construction) and the *Parco Regina Margherita* laid out in 1882 by Alfonso Brizi planted with ilexes, elms, and cedar trees.

D. Santa Chiara to San Pietro

Corso Mazzini, the busiest street in the town, leads out of Piazza del Comune past several 16–17C palaces. Beyond the Portella di San Giorgio, a medieval gateway on the line of the Roman walls, is Piazza Santa Chiara with a beautiful view of the valley and hillside behind with the Rocca. The polygonal fountain was built in 1872 on a design by Attilio Cangi. Here is the splendid red and white Gothic basilica of ***Santa Chiara** (closed 12–14.30), built in 1257–65. The simple *FAÇADE has a portal flanked by high reliefs of two lions beneath a splendid rose window and a tympanum. The great flying buttresses that span one side of the piazza were added in 1351; beneath them are remains of a medieval public fountain. The CAMPANILE is the tallest in Assisi. On this site was the church of San Giorgio where St Francis was first buried, and his canonisation ceremony took place (his body was translated to San Francesco when that church was completed). The present church was begun in 1257 as the shrine of St Clare, who was also first buried in San Giorgio in 1253. The dark INTERIOR has stained glass windows in the apse by Francesco Moretti (1897–1925). Off the S side of the nave are two chapels on the site of the former church of San Giorgio. In the ORATORIO DEL CROCIFISSO is preserved the painted *Crucifix (late 12C) that spoke to St Francis at San Damiano (see Rte 2E). At the end, behind a grille, are a triptych by Rinaldo di Ranuccio (c 1270) and reliquaries of St Francis and St Clare, pointed out by a veiled nun from the closed order of Poor Clares. In the CAPPELLA DEL SACRAMENTO are charming frescoes (on the entrance wall) of the Annunciation, Nativity, Adoration of the Magi, and St George by Pace di Bartolo, and (on the left wall) a frescoed polyptych of the Madonna and saints by Puccio Capanna beneath scenes of the Passion. Outside the chapel, steps lead down to the CRYPT built in a neo-Gothic style in 1851–72 where St Clare is buried. In the SOUTH TRANSEPT are interesting frescoes (in poor condition; and very difficult to see as they are high up) with scenes of the Apocalypse and Life of Christ and, below, the Death and Funeral of St Clare, attributed to a close follower of Giotto known from these frescoes as the 'Maestro Espressionista di Santa Chiara', sometimes identified with Palmerino di Guido. Above the altar is a painting of St Clare with eight stories from her life, also attributed to the 'Maestro di Santa Chiara'. Above the HIGH ALTAR is a painted Cross dating from before 1260, and in the cross vault Madonna and Child with saints by a Giottesque master (c 1337). In the NORTH TRANSEPT, high up at the top of the walls, are 13C frescoes of scenes from Genesis in two registers. Below is a 14C fresco of the Nativity. On the altar is a Madonna and Child (c 1265) also attributed to the 'Maestro di Santa Chiara'. The huge CONVENT OF SANTA CHIARA (closed order) is built on the right side of the church. It was enlarged in the 14C and 16C.

Via Borgo Aretino leads out of the piazza away from the centre of the town beneath the 13C Arco di Santa Chiara. The Borgo, with fine views of the church and convent of Santa Chiara, ends at the 14C *Porta Nuova*.

From Piazza Santa Chiara, Via Sant'Agnese leads downhill. Beyond steps (left) which descend to *Porta Moiano* in the walls, near a medieval public fountain, the road ends in Piazza del Vescovado with a few trees and a 16C fountain. A delightful palace here with a tall façade bears the name of its first proprietor Ignatio Vannola (gonfalon of the town in 1625) and a lion sleeps above the ingenious door. The church of **Santa Maria Maggiore**

Santa Chiara, Assisi

(usually closed; key on request at No. 5) has a simple pink and white chequered façade with a good wheel window (1163). Above the doorway has been placed half a Roman marble fountain basin. The interior has 14–17C fresco fragments and a crypt dating from the 9C. Behind the pretty campanile there is a good view of Santa Chiara.

Below the church is a *Roman House* (admission only with special permission from the Soprintendenza Archeologica in Perugia), with interesting wall paintings, which may have belonged to Sextus Propertius. Next door is the courtyard of the Palazzo Vescovile.

From the upper end of the piazza the pretty medieval *Via Bernardo da Quintavalle* leads past the church of *San Gregorio* (closed) with a very damaged fresco on the exterior to Piazza Garibaldi. This piazza can also be reached by Via Antonio Cristofani which leads out of the centre of Piazza del Vescovado. From Piazza Garibaldi the picturesque *Via Fontebella* continues down to Porta San Francesco past the Fonte Marcello (1557) and the Hotel Giotto, opened in 1900.

Via Giovanni di Bonino leads out of Piazza del Vescovado downhill to Via Sant'Apollinare in which is the Benedictine monastery of *San Giuseppe* (closed for restoration; but admission usually granted on request at the gate). It incorporates the two façades of San Paolo and Sant'Apollinare which stand beside each other, and a campanile with a domed top. The wide Via Borgo San Pietro continues downhill with a view ahead of the campanile of San Pietro past the modern buildings of the 'Pro Civitate Christiana' founded in 1939, with a library and gallery of modern religious art. The road ends in the piazza with a view of the plain in front of the 12C abbey church of **San Pietro**. The fine *FAÇADE has a portal, guarded by two lions, and three large rose windows. The INTERIOR has interesting vaulting and a raised sanctuary beneath an unusual brick dome. There are several Gothic arcaded tomb recesses in red and white marble, and in the N transept frescoes by Pace di Bartolo.

E. Environs of Assisi

The Eremo delle Carceri and Monte Subasio

A road (well signposted) from Porta Cappuccini at first passes ugly new buildings before narrowing and climbing with hairpin bends up the lower slopes of Monte Subasio to (4km) the entrance gate to the *Eremo delle Carceri (open 6.30–17 or 19.30). A short walk (300m) leads to the forest hermitage in a remarkably secluded and peaceful spot (790m), nestled in a ravine covered with thick woods of ilexes and oaks. Here St Francis and his followers would come at times to live as hermits in caves, and in 1426 St Bernardine founded a convent here. Beyond the entrance to the monastery is a triangular terrace (inhabited by doves) with two wells, overlooked by the little buildings (no admission) of the convent with the refectory and dormitory. Ahead a door leads in to the CAPPELLA DI SAN BERNARDINO with a 15C Crucifixion with St Francis and a tiny 13C French stained glass window. The CAPPELLA DI SANTA MARIA DELLE CARCERI has a worn fresco of the Madonna and Child with St Francis by Tiberio d'Assisi and a 13C Crucifixion. A tiny and very steep flight of steps leads down to the Grotto of St Francis, a cave where the saint had his bed hollowed out of the rock. A miniature doorway leads out to another terrace; above the door is a worn fresco of St Francis preaching to the birds. In the ravine iron bars support an ancient ilex tree on which birds are supposed to have perched to receive his blessing. A bridge leads over the ravine past a little bronze statue of the saint by Vincenzo Rosignoli (1882) into the lovely woods where walks can be taken. From the bridge there is a good view back of the hermitage buildings. The exit is indicated up steps past the little Cappella della Maddalena; a path continues round the back of the monastery to the entrance gate.

From the hermitage a wide (unsurfaced) road, signposted 'Collepino' is open from 7–18 (7–20 in summer) for the summit of *Monte Subasio (7km; 1289m). The views are magnificent and include, on a good day, the chain of the Appenines. This is a pleasant cool spot to picnic in summer, although many of the fields are fenced to provide pasture for animals. In spring cowslips and wild hellebores grow here. From the summit the road continues down to Collepino (18km) which is 6km above Spello (see Rte 6). Another road above the Carceri (signposted 'San Benedetto' and 'Assisi') provides an alternative, but longer route (8km) back to Assisi. It leads along the side of the hill though woods past numerous picnic places, with views down to the plain. The road is surfaced but extremely narrow, and passes the abbey of *San Benedetto* founded c 1051, but abandoned by the monks in 1391. In 1945 it was returned to the Benedictines of San Pietro, who have restored it, and the 11C church survives. The road then descends steeply with fine views ahead of Assisi beneath its Rocca.

San Damiano and Rivotorto

A road (signposted) leads downhill from Viale Vittorio Emanuele near Porta Nuova to **San Damiano** (also reached on foot by a pretty lane from Porta Nuova). Here in 1205 St Francis renounced the world, and St Clare died. It was a Benedictine priory documented in 1030, and it was restored in 1212. St Francis stayed here on a number of occasions. Lord Lothian (Peter Kerr) left the convent to the Franciscans in 1983 and it can be visited (10–12.30, 14–16.45 or 18). In front of the church is an arcaded courtyard with votive frescoes. To the right is the entrance to the CAPPELLA DI SAN GIROLAMO with a fine Madonna and Saints by Tiberio d'Assisi (1517). The adjoining CAPPELLA DEL CROCIFISSO has a venerated wood Cross of 1637. The little CHURCH has a vaulted single nave with 14C frescoes showing St Agnes, St Francis in prayer before the Crucifix (a damaged scene), St Francis throwing down his money in front of the priest, and (on the W wall) the figure of the father of St Francis threatening the saint with a stick. The MONASTERY (at present closed for restoration) can also normally be visited, including the 15C cloister which has a vestibule frescoed by Eusebio da San Giorgio (1507).

A road continues downhill (keep right; just over 2km) to the plain, as far as the conspicuous church of RIVORTORTO with its campanile crowned by a short spire. It is named after a stream which runs down from Monte Subasio and passes in front of the church. The Franciscan convent here is being restored (ring at the door beside the campanile for admission to the church). The CHURCH was built in 1600–40 over a hovel where St Francis came to live in 1208. After the earthquake of 1853 the church was reconstructed in neo-Gothic style, but the 19C decorations have recently been eliminated. The restored hut survives in the middle of the church. Twelve paintings of the Life of St Francis by Cesare Sermei have been removed from the church during restoration work. Off the avenue which leads from the church towards Santa Maria degli Angeli can be seen a *British Military Cemetery*.

Santa Maria degli Angeli

A road (5km) leads from below the walls of Assisi down to the plain and the conspicuous domed basilica of **Santa Maria degli Angeli** (frequent bus service to the church from Assisi). It is open 5.45–12.30, 14–dusk. It is now surrounded by an unattractive small suburb. Visited by thousands of pilgrims because of its associations with St Francis, it has all the usual characteristics of a famous holy shrine. It has an ugly monumental approach, laid out in 1950, with flagstaffs and incongruous trees. The church was designed in 1569 by Galeazzo Alessi and built by Girolamo Martelli, Giacomo Giorgetti, and others, and finished in 1679. It was rebuilt after an earthquake in 1832 by Luigi Poletti except for the fine *cupola and apse which survive from the 16C church, and the side chapels, decorated in the late 16C–18C. The unattractive FAÇADE is by Cesare Bazzani (1928). The church was built on a place which belonged to the Benedictines, known as the 'Porziuncola', where St Francis and his companions first came to live in simple huts and where, in a little chapel, he founded his Order. The church was built to cover this little 11C oratory (Cappella della Porziuncola), and other chapels used by St Francis. This was the meeting place of Saints Francis and Dominic, and here St Francis died.

INTERIOR. The decorations in the side chapels, mostly commissioned between 1590–1630, are interesting works of this period. SOUTH SIDE. First chapel: altarpiece of St Anthony Abbot by Giacomo Giorgetti; Miracle of the Saint (left wall) by Anton Maria Garbi, and paintings in the vault by Francesco Appiani. The second chapel was decorated by Cesare Sermei in 1602 and the wrought-iron gate dates from 1700. The altarpiece of the Baptism of Christ is by Giacomo Giorgetti. Third chapel: altarpiece of the Birth of the Virgin by Cristoforo Roncalli, and frescoes of the Presentation in the Temple and Marriage of the Virgin by Antonio Circignani. The fourth chapel was decorated by Baldassarre Croce in 1602–03. Fifth chapel: altarpiece of the Nativity by Domenico Pace (1830). SOUTH TRANSEPT. In the right chapel, altarpiece by Francesco Appiani and a 15C statuette of the Madonna and Child (formerly in the tabernacle on the roof of the Chapel of the Porziuncola). The elaborate altar of San Pietro is decorated with stuccoes by Giovanni Reinhold (1675). Above the door into a corridor (see below) is an Annunciation by the bottega of Federico Barocci. In the CROSSING are four frescoes in the pendentives by Francesco Appiani. The little CAPPELLA DELLA PORZIUNCOLA stands beneath the cupola. It is a simple rustic hut built of stone. Over the wide entrance is a fresco of the Pardon of St Francis by Nazareno Friedrich Overbeck (1829) and a neo-Gothic tabernacle of 1832. In the simple interior the splendid altarpiece of the *Life of St Francis, the only known work by Ilario da Viterbo (1393), decorates the E wall. On the exterior are remains of 15C frescoes and an inscribed stone recording the burial place of Pietro Cattani, companion of St Francis (died 1221). On the pretty E end is a fine fresco of the Crucifixion attributed to Perugino (heavily restored in 1830). The tiny CAPPELLA DEL TRANSITO concealed behind the entrance to the chancel (right) was built over the cell where St Francis died. Through the fine wrought-iron gate can be seen frescoes of the first companions of St Francis by Lo Spagna and a statue of the Saint by Andrea della Robbia. The girdle of St Francis is preserved in a glass case. On the outside wall is a fresco of the Death and Funeral of St Francis by Domenico Bruschi (1886).

NORTH TRANSEPT. The Oratorio del Sacramento was opened in 1984 on the left side of the presbytery. It has a gilded wood altarpiece (1691). The 18C altar in the transept in polychrome marbles incorporates a wood Crucifix by a Northern artist of c 1530. NORTH AISLE. Fifth chapel: altarpiece of the Madonna of the Rosary by Domenico Maria Muratori and paintings by Baldassare Orsini and Carlo Morelli. The fourth chapel was decorated in 1603 by Simeone Ciburri. Third chapel (1602): altarpiece of the Deposition by Baldassarre Croce, and, in the vault, Resurrection by Ventura Salimbeni, and good stucco work. Second chapel: altarpiece of St Francis receiving the Stigmata by Giacomo Giorgetti and (left) Verification of the Stigmata, also by him. The vault was decorated by Cesare Sermei. First chapel: 18C works by Benedetto Cavallucci and Anton Maria Garbi.

From the S transept a door leads into a corridor. Ahead is the SACRISTY with fine carved cupboards of 1671. The CRYPT is also entered off the corridor (for admission, ask in the Sacristy). It was excavated in 1968 beneath the high altar to reveal remains of the first Franciscan convent, and contains a beautiful enamelled terracotta altarpiece by Andrea della Robbia. Also off the corridor is access to a portico which leads past a garden of the thornless roses of St Francis which bloom yearly in May. The bronze statue of the saint with a lamb is by Vincenzo Rosignoli (1916). The CAPPELLA DELLE ROSE, in two parts, has beautiful frescoes by Tiberio d'Assisi, the best of which are in the second larger barrel-vaulted chapel, built by St Bonaventura over the cave of St Francis. Beyond the grille are frescoes of the Redeemer (in the vault) and, around the altar, St Francis and his companions, also by Tiberio.

Another corridor leads past a garden with a fig tree, recalling another episode in the life of St Francis, to the CAPPELLA DEL PIANTO restored in 1926. A corridor leads back towards the church past a room with old pharmacy jars and the cloister of the convent. The MUSEO (open 9–12, 14–17.30; but closed November–Easter) has a small collection of paintings including a *Portrait of St Francis, by an unknown master, known as the 'Maestro di San Francesco', a *Crucifix by Giunta Pisano, another portrait of the saint by the school of Cimabue, and a detached fresco of the Madonna enthroned attributed to Pierantonio Mezzastris. There is also a display of church vestments and a delightful missionary museum. The pulpit from which St Bernardine preached, in a room near the entrance to the museum, is shown on request. A staircase leads up to the CONVENT OF ST BERN-ARDINE OF SIENA with cells, including that of St Bernardine.

3

Lake Trasimene

*LAKE TRASIMENE** has preserved its natural beauty to a large extent. It is surrounded by low fertile hills covered with olive groves and vineyards, and its shores are grown with reeds. It has picturesque lakeside villages, and three lovely islands. The colour of its waters changes constantly according to the weather, and it is subject to sudden storms in winter. From a distance it provides one of the most breathtaking views in Umbria (particularly from the hills around Cortona).

Lake Trasimene is the largest lake on the Italian peninsula, and the fourth largest lake in Italy, with a circumference of about 53km. It is 257m above sea level and has an average depth of 4.90m. It abounds in fish (eels, carp, tench, perch, shad, and pike) which are still caught in round nets attached to wooden piles in the water from flat-bottomed boats. Inhabited since the Paleolithic era, by 507 BC it was under the rule of Lars Porsena, king of Chiusi. It is famous as the site of the resounding victory of Hannibal over the Romans in 217 BC on its N shores (described at Tuoro, see below). Its central position on the borders of several warring communes meant that it was often used as a battlefield in the Middle Ages when numerous castles and fortified villages were built on its shores or on the neighbouring hills. In the 12C it came under the dominion of Perugia. Up until the 16C it was surrounded by thick woodlands, famous as hunting grounds. Attempts have been made to regulate the level of the lake since Roman times, when the first outlet was constructed. Leonardo da Vinci produced a study in 1503 in which he proposed linking the lake to the Chiana, the Arno and the Tiber. Up until the end of the 19C the lake was constantly subject to flooding, and the swamplands on its shores caused malaria epidemics. In the 18C and 19C there were various proposals to drain the lake, but in 1896 a new outlet was constructed, next to the Roman one, which finally solved the problem of flooding. In this century work has had to be carried out to try to ensure that the lake will not dry out in years of drought, as its level is constantly diminishing because of the formation of peat. The first public boat service on the lake was inaugurated in 1905. The lake was admired by Goethe in 1787 and by Stendhal in 1827.

Information Offices. 'APT del Trasimeno', 10 Piazza Mazzini, Castiglione del Lago (Tel. 075/9652484). *Passignano*: 'Pro Loco', 36 Via Roma; *Tuoro*: 'Pro Loco' by the ferry landing stage (open in summer); *Città della Pieve*: 'Associazione Turistica Pievese', Piazza Matteotti.

Transport. Bus services ('ASP') from Perugia to Castiglione del Lago, Tuoro, and Passignano, and from Perugia to Città della Pieve. Railway Station at Castiglione del Lago on the old Florence–Rome line (a few slow trains a day from Florence in 1hr 40mins–2hrs). Railway Station at Tuoro and Passignano on the branch line from Terontola to Perugia and Foligno (slow trains from Perugia to Passignano in c 30min).

    Passenger Boat Services run by 'SPNT' (information office in Passignano, Tel. 075/827157). There is a regular service throughout the year (c nine times daily) from Passignano via Tuoro to the Isola Maggiore (and vice versa) in c 30 minutes. From 1 May to the end of September there are more services from Tuoro to the Isola Maggiore (10 mins) on holidays. From 1 April–30 September services at least eight times a day also from Isola Maggiore to Castiglione del Lago (and vice versa) in 30 minutes. On holidays in April and daily from May to the end of September, services from San Feliciano 12 times a day to the Isola Polvese (and vice versa). From 1 July to the end of September service four times a day from Sant'Arcangelo to the Isola Polvese, and from the Isola Polvese to the Isola Maggiore.

Hotels. *Isola Maggiore*: 'Da Sauro' (2-star); *San Feliciano*: 'Da Settimio', Via Lungolago (1-star); *Monte del Lago*: 'Da Santino' (2-star); *Castiglione del Lago*: 'Miralago', 6 Piazza Mazzini (2-star); *Città della Pieve*: 'Vannucci', Viale Vanni (2-star). There are also 3-star and 2-star hotels in and around *Passignano*. *Castel Rigone*: 'La Fattoria' (3-star); *Panicale*: 'La Barca' and 'le Grotte di Boldrino', both 3-star; *Piegaro*: 'Da Elio' (2-star; with restaurant).

    There are also numerous self-catering flats and holiday houses to rent in the vicinity of the lake (detailed information from the 'APT' in Castiglione del Lago).

    Camping Sites near the lake are open from 1 April to 30 September. 3-star: 'Il Villaggio', Sant'Arcangelo, Magione; 'Kursaal', Viale Europa, Passignano; 'Punta Navaccia', Tuoro. 2-star: 'La Badiaccia', Castiglione del Lago; 'Cerquestra', Monte del Lago; 'Europa', Passignano. Numerous 1-star sites on the lakeside at San Feliciano, Castiglione, and Torricella.

Restaurants. Many restaurants serve fish from the lake. 1st class: *Isola Maggiore*, 'Da Sauro'; *Passignano*, 'Del Pescatore', 5 Via San Bernardino; *Città della Pieve*, 'Barzanti', 53 Via Santa Lucia. Trattorie: *San Feliciano*, 'Da Settimio', Via Lungolago; *Castiglione del Lago*, 'La Cantina', 89 Via Vittorio Emanuele; 'Il Lido Solitario', Via Lungolago (pizzeria). Luxury Class: *Panicarola*, 'Il Bisteccaro'.

    Beautiful places to **picnic** all round the lake and on Isola Polvese and Isola Maggiore.

Bathing in the lake is permitted in various localities including Tuoro, Passignano, and Castiglione del Lago. There are also facilities for wind surfing and sailing.

Hiking and horseback riding facilities have recently been introduced in the area surrounding the lake. These include marked tracks and paths (red-and-white C.A.I. signposts). Detailed information with illustrated guides and maps from the 'APT' in Castiglione del Lago.

A **Festival** of Kites 'Coloriamo i cieli' is held biennially (even years) at Castiglione del Lago for 3 days at the beginning of May.

There is a good **road** round the shore of the lake, described below: the prettiest stretch is between Monte del Lago and Castiglione del Lago, as the N shore is disturbed by the 'superstrada' (which connects Perugia to the AI motorway) which runs between the old road and the lake. However the 'superstrada' has relieved Passignano and Magione of much heavy traffic.

The Islands

*Isola Maggiore, with a circumference of c 2km and some 100 inhabitants, mostly fishermen, is the only island on the lake connected by regular boat services throughout the year with the shore (see above). It has no cars. It was visited in 1211 by St Francis of Assisi. Near the landing stage is the delightful brick-paved street, Venetian in character, with some 15C houses, and several simple restaurants. At its N end (left) a path leads to the 12C church of *San Salvatore* (restored in 1972). A path continues round the shore of the island with beautiful views across the lake. At the S end is the *Castello Guglielmi*, a Romantic mock-Gothic pile designed and built by the Roman senator Giacinto Guglielmi in 1885–91. It has been abandoned for many years and has now fallen into ruin. Paths lead up through olive groves to the church of *San Michele Arcangelo* at the highest point of the island. It was founded before 1200 and contains 14–15C frescoes, some attributed to Bartolomeo Caporali. The craft of lace-making was introduced to the island in 1904 by Elena Guglielmi and still survives here.

Isola Minore, once renowned for the skill of its fishermen, was abandoned by the end of the 16C. It was later invaded by snakes and is now privately owned.

*Isola Polvese (c 85 hectares; reached by boat in summer from San Feliciano; see above) is the largest island on the lake. It had five churches and 200 inhabitants in the 14C when the castle was built, but it was abandoned by the 17C because of malaria. Acquired in 1972 by the Province of Perugia, it has been a protected area since 1974, of the greatest interest for its birdlife. By the landing stage is a short avenue of huge lime trees. To the right there is access to a little beach (with a bar and restaurant open in summer), and to the left a path leads to the impressive remains of the 14C castle near poplars, tamarisk, and cypresses. Fruit trees grow inside its walls. A beautiful path leads round the shore of the island in c 1hr. The sound of the birds who nest in the reeds is remarkable: they include grebes, coots, cormorants, bitterns, kites, kingfishers, and ospreys. The vegetation ranges from ilexes, willows, oaks, and ash, with olives and cypresses in the centre of the island, across which another path runs, near the ruins of a 12C Olivetan monastery.

Castiglione del Lago (304m) is the most important place on Trasimene. It is situated on a small promontory planted with olive trees jutting into the W side of the lake, which is dominated by its magnificent castle. There was a 'castrum' here in Roman times, and in the Middle Ages its fortress was contended by Perugia and Cortona, the inhabitants always taking the side of Cortona. In 1247 Frederick II reconstructed the castle. The Baglioni family of Perugia ruled the town after 1490: Machiavelli was a guest here of Gianpaolo Baglioni, as was Leonardo da Vinci who drew the castle in 1503. In the 16C Ascanio Della Corgna married Giovanna Baglioni and, as nephew of Julius III, became Marquis of Castiglione. He was a famous condottiere, his military achievements culminating in the victory at the battle of Lepanto.

The little town has an interesting plan, with two parallel main streets terminating in the gardens in front of the castle at the edge of the promontory. It is best to park outside Porta del Rondò at the top of the hill, or below the walls (from which steps lead up through Palazzo Della Corgna). In Corso Matteotti on the left is the church of *Santa Maria Maddalena* built in 1836–60 on a plan by Giovanni Caproni. The pronaos dates from 1868, and the tall campanile from 1893. In the centrally-planned interior are

Castiglione del Lago: the passageway from Palazzo Della Corgna to the castle

frescoes by Mariano Piervittori (1850) and, on the left altar, Madonna and Child by Eusebio da San Giorgio. From Piazza Mazzini Via Vittorio Emanuele continues past a palace (No. 51) with good terracotta decoration, and the parallel Via del Forte leads past the church of *San Domenico*, with a 17C interior and 18C wood ceiling.

The two roads end in Piazza Gramsci with a view of the lake. Here is *Palazzo Della Corgna*, approached by a double ramp and with an L-shaped plan. A 13C tower house was incorporated into a hunting lodge by the Baglioni in the 16C, and in 1560 Ascanio Della Corgna rebuilt the palace, probably using Vignola as architect, and surrounded it by fine gardens (now diminished). The building was damaged by fire in 1824 and restored in 1934. The interior (used in part for municipal offices and in part for exhibitions) has numerous 16C frescoes (admission on request). In the entrance hall are frescoes attributed to Salvio Savini symbolising the marriage of Ascanio Della Corgna with Giovanna Baglioni. In the Main Hall the frescoes by Giovanni Antonio Pandolfi and Niccolò Circignani (Pomarancio), with geometric decorations by Cesare Nebbia, represent various episodes in the life of the great general. A chapel in the hospital in the piazza (formerly the Convent of Sant'Agostino) has a fresco of the Madonna attributed to Giovanni Battista Caporali or Giovanni Spagna.

A long narrow fortified passageway (entrance to the left of the gardens) with an old wood roof and stone floor, connects Palazzo Della Corgna with the *Castle (open daily), which can also be entered by a gate at the end of the gardens. Many times destroyed and reconstructed, it was largely rebuilt by Frederick II in 1247, probably on a design by Frate Elia of Cortona, when it became one of the most impregnable fortresses in Europe. Its interesting plan is an irregular pentagon with walls following the slope of the hillside and four angle towers. The triangular keep is 39m high. Its fortifications were strengthened by Ascanio Della Corgna who was also a military architect. Inside, the walkways are open, with splendid views down to the lake. An open-air theatre is set up within its walls in summer, where there are also ruins of an ancient chapel.

From Castiglione N454 leads away from the lake towards Montepulciano, passing close to several villages on the old Etruscan road which linked Chiusi to Cortona, including *Pozzuolo* (8km). Here Palazzo Moretti (1667) is now the property of the Comune and is to become the seat of a museum, and the church dates from 1783. At *Petrignano*, 5km N, the church of Sant'Ansano (rebuilt in the early 19C) contains an altarpiece attributed to Andrea della Robbia and a wooden Ecce Homo (early 18C). On the N454 beyond Pozzuolo a by-road leads right to *Laviano*, where St Margaret of Cortona was born in 1247. A little church in the vicinity dates from c 1000. The road continues across the A1 motorway to Montepulciano (28km; see *Blue Guide Tuscany*).

Another by-road from Castiglione leads inland to the Etruscan settlements of *Gioiella* and *Vaiano* (10km) at both of which tombs have been unearthed. At Vaiano the 17C parish church was renovated in 1740, and in the church of Santa Lucia is a fresco of the Madonna enthroned by the school of Perugino. Four km NW of Castiglione is *Piana* with a neo-classical church by Giovanni Caproni (1809).

A road (N71) runs N from Castiglione along the shore of the lake, and at 9km diverges right from the Arezzo road for *Borghetto*, a pretty little lakeside hamlet with a good view of Castiglione. Only one angle tower survives from its 15C castle. The road passes under the 'superstrada' and climbs up with a good view of the lake to continue towards Tuoro (keep right). It passes the old customs house, *La Dogana*, with a portico, which marked the boundary between the Grand-ducal lands of Tuscany and the Papal States. Plaques recall travellers who have passed this way including Michelangelo, Galileo, Goethe, Stendhal, Byron, and Hans Christian Anderson. To the N is *Monte Gualandro* (442m) in the castle of which, owned by the Montemelini, Frederick II is thought to have stayed in 1246. The road descends to a plain on the edge of the lake, enclosed by hills, which was the site of the battlefield where Hannibal routed the Romans in 217 BC. At that time the lake reached further inland. On a corner is a signpost (right) for the first halting place in an interesting *Itinerary of the Battlefield* ('Percorso Storico Archeologico della Battaglia') which can be followed by car. Maps and explanatory panels are provided (if somewhat erratically) as well as viewing platforms. A rough road leads past a farm and the abandoned *Pieve di Confini* dating from 1165, which was once one of the most beautiful Romanesque churches in the area. The portal with interesting carvings survives. Just beyond is the first platform ('Sosta No. 1') with a splendid view of the lake and its islands, but only just above the 'superstrada'.

In the early hours of the morning of 24 June 217 BC the Roman consul Flaminius (who built the road still named after him) with some 25,000 soldiers marched through the fog along the edge of the lake here and was ambushed by Hannibal and his 40,000 soldiers who had encamped on the surrounding hills. The massacre lasted only a few hours as the Romans were taken completely by surprise. Flaminius died in the encounter and about 15,000 of his men, trapped between the hills and the lake, died or were taken prisoner; the others fled and eventually returned to Rome. Hannibal is thought to have lost only about 1500 soldiers. He killed the Roman prisoners but let those from other Italic tribes go free to demonstrate his goodwill towards them. The dead were burned in 'ustrina', remains of which have been found in the area.

On the other side of the main road (left; inconspicuous sign) a good unsurfaced road leads inland up past several halting places (near a necropolis where soldiers' tombs and the base of a funerary monument have been found) to the hamlet of *Sanguineto* whose name ('a name of blood from that day's sanguine rain') commemorates Hannibal's victory. A road continues right (keep right) and descends to another halting place ('Sosta No. 6') with a platform which provides the best view of the battlefield in a natural amphitheatre. The by-road continues (keep right) and becomes paved as it enters (by a back road) **Tuoro sul Trasimeno** (17km by direct road from Castiglione) on a low hill, now set back from the lake. Palazzo del Nardo (or 'del Capra') is supposed to be built on Roman remains. A road descends towards the lake, and, on the modern Via Cartaginese (right; unsignposted) a column from   Roman Forum was set up in 1961 to mark the edge of the lake in Roman times. Some of Hannibal's troops are thought to have been stationed near here. The main road continues down to the lakeside district of Tuoro. Here is a landing stage for the ferries to the Isola Maggiore (see above), a bathing lido and several restaurants. An open-air sculpture park known as the 'Campo del Sole' has columns of pietra serena carved by various sculptors in 1985–88.

The old road for Passignano continues past a fortified house (above the road to the left) known as Mariottella (1541) and a by-road 1km outside Tuoro leads inland to *Vernazzano* whose medieval castle defended the N shore of the lake. One leaning tower survives. Just before Passignano an avenue leads up to the 18C Villa of *Pischiello* built by Uguccione Bourbon di Sorbello. 23km **Passignano sul Trasimeno** is an attractive little resort on the side of the lake, and the headquarters of the boat services for the islands. It also has moorings for private boats, as well as bathing beaches, hotels, and restaurants. Passignano was the Roman 'Passum Jani' and during the Middle Ages it was contested between warring communes. By the mid 13C it had come under the control of Perugia, and at that time the fortress was built. In the early 20C it had important seaplane construction works and it was bombed in the Second World War. From Piazza Garibaldi in front of the landing stage (built in 1967) several narrow lanes lead up to remains of the castle with a triangular 14C tower in an old fortified district.

The road for Magione continues along the side of the lake and at 27km a by-road diverges left, with fine retrospective views of the lake for **Castel Rigone** (6km) in a beautiful position on Monterone (653m) with splendid views. The Madonna dei Miracoli is a fine Renaissance church (1494). The portal, with a relief in the lunette, is by Domenico Bertini of Settignano (1512). Inside are frescoes by the Perugian school, a Madonna of the Rosary by Bernardo di Girolamo Rosselli (1558), an Assumption attributed to Giovanni Battista Caporali, and a fine Epiphany by Domenico Alfani (1528–34) in a frame by Bernardino di Lazzaro of Perugia. Remains of the castle and an old 15C hospice survive. The by-road continues to Umbertide (27km; see Rte 4).

The main road from Passignano continues alongside the 'superstrada' to a fork; on the left the road climbs up towards Magione. It passes a turning for *Montecolognola* (410m) where the inhabitants of Magione built a castle in 1293 (restored in the 15C), the walls of which are well preserved. In the parish church are 14–16C frescoes, an Annunciation in Deruta majolica (1460), and a fresco by the Futurist painter Gherardo Dottori. There is a magnificent view of the lake. 35km **Magione** (299m) was the birthplace of Fra' Giovanni da Pian di Carpine, one of the first followers of St Francis, who in 1246 travelled to Karakorum to convert the successor of Genghis Khan. He wrote a history of Mongolia used by later travellers to the East, including Marco Polo. A hospital of the Knights Templar existed in Magione in the 11–12C, parts of which survive in the four-square *Badia* or *Castello dei Cavalieri di Malta* with a fine courtyard by Fieravante Fieravanti (c 1420). The *Parish Church* was frescoed by Gherardo Dottori in 1947 when it was reconstructed after war damage. The church of the *Madonna delle Grazie* preserves a fresco of the Madonna enthroned, attributed to Andrea di Giovanni da Orvieto (1371). On the hillside to the N is the isolated 13C *Torre dei Lombardi*, which was damaged by earthquake in 1846 and has been propped up by scaffolding for many years. A by-road leads SE from Magione into the hills above the lake and the little fortified villages of *Montesperello* (a castle was built here before 997) and *Montemelino*.

The beautiful road which continues round the lake to the W of Magione passes *Torricella*, once an important posting stage, and now with a number of camping sites. 32km *Monte del Lago* with remains of its 14C castle (recently damaged by new buildings) juts into the E side of the lake. The road follows the lake past the picturesque *Castello di Zocco* (no admission) in a group of pine trees. On the site of a Franciscan convent, it was built c 1400 and was one of the most important fortresses on the E side of the lake. Abandoned some fifty years ago, it is now in a ruined state, but preserves its walls with five towers and an ancient chapel. 35km **San Feliciano**, named after St Feliziano of Foligno who came here in 220 AD, is now an attractive little village with a harbour for fishing boats. Some of the inhabitants work the reeds which abound in this part of the lake. The delightful *Museo della Pesca* (open daily except Wednesday in summer, 9.30–12.30, 16.30–19.30), in an old boat house on the side of the lake, illustrates the work of the fishermen on the lake, and the exhibits include boats and fishing equipment from the past. There is a regular boat service in summer from San Feliciano to the Isola Polvese (see above). 37km *San Savino*, stands on a little hill with remains of a walled castle, first built in 1006 with a tall triangular keep. In the vicinity is the subterranean emissary from the lake built by the Romans and several times reopened. Next to it is the outlet constructed in 1896.

The road now goes uphill and there are splendid views across fields and reedy marshes down to the lake with the Isola Polvese and the promontory of Castiglione del Lago beyond. This is a protected area where kingfishers and herons nest. 40km *Monte Buono* had another important 11C castle (now transformed); nearby is the abandoned church of Santa Rufina (10C). Beyond the little church of *Santa Maria delle Ancaelle* (closed), a late Romanesque building with traces of frescoes and a 14C painting of the Umbrian school, at 43km, above the road to the left, in a fine position, is the *Badia di Sant'Arcangelo* a former abbey which flourished in the 14C. The views of the lake are magnificent. 47km turning for the *Castello di Montalera* (487m) on a hill planted with ilexes. The castle, which had great strategic importance in the Middle Ages, was restored as a residence in 1534 by Braccio Baglioni.

A by-road from the Montalera turning leads up through Casalini and Lemura to the picturesque little medieval village of **Panicale** (8km) on a hill with one of the best views of the lake from its old walls (13–14C). It has Etruscan origins and was allied to Tuscany up until the 13C. It was the birthplace of the remarkable painter Tommaso Fini, known as Masolino da Panicale (1383–c 1440), master of Masaccio. The famous 14C condottiere Giacomo Paneri, called Boldrino di Panicale, was also born here. The attractive *Piazza Umberto I* was built on a slope in order that the rainwater would be collected in the well, replaced since 1473 by the present lovely fountain. Here is the massive fortified flank of the 17C *Collegiata* which contains a Nativity attributed to Giovanni Battista Caporali. A road leads on up to *Palazzo del Podestà* (partly 14C) at the top of the hill. From Piazza Umberto I another road leads to the *Teatro Cesare Caporali* (named after the famous poet born here in 1530 or 1531) built at the end of the 18C (restored in 1991), with a backcloth painted by Mariano Piervittori and stuccoes by Alceste Ricci. Outside the walls, in a less attractive part of the village, is the church of *San Sebastiano* (ring for the custodian at the bottom of the steps on the right, at No. 13) with two beautiful frescoes by Perugino: the Martyrdom of St Sebastian and a Madonna and Child (detached and damaged).

A winding road (5km) leads W to **Paciano**, another well-preserved little medieval village in a fine position, with a 14C castle. The church of *San Giuseppe* (reconstructed in the 18C) preserves the gonfalon of the Comune, a Madonna of the Misericordia dating from c 1460 and attributed to the school of Bonfigli or to Fiorenzo di Lorenzo. Next door is the little 17C church of *San Carlo Borromeo*. In the *Sala della Confraternità del Santissimo Sacramento* is an unusual fresco of the Crucifixion by Francesco di Città della Pieve (1452), by some considered to be the master of Perugino. Outside the village and below it are the churches of *San Sebastiano*, with a fresco of the Martyrdom of St Sebastian (1496) and the *Madonna della Stella* (1572) with frescoes by Silla Piccinino (1579). On the outskirts, at *Ceraseto* the church has a fresco of Christ enthroned between Saints John the Baptist and Peter, attributed to Giovanni Battista Caporali (c 1510). Above the village in woods is the *Torre d'Orlando*, part of the earliest castle of Paciano (restored and privately owned). On *Monte Pausillo* is a nature reserve (picnic places) with deer and wild boar and interesting bird life. A road leads down to join the fast road from Chiusi for Castiglione del Lago.

The lakeside road (N599) continues to a fork: 1km along the road to the left (for Chiusi) is *Panicarola* where an Iron Age necropolis has been found. The parish church is built on foundations of a pagan temple. The road continues along the lake (with fine views of Castiglione del Lago) and passes close to the *Santuario della Madonna della Carraia* built in 1661–63 (the cupola was rebuilt in 1856). On the left bank of the Pescia torrent is the 17C Torre di Pescia, with a 19C wing (reconstructed after war damage). 58km Castiglione del Lago (described above).

From Castiglione del Lago, N71 leads S passing close to Chiusi (see *Blue Guide Tuscany*) to **CITTÀ DELLA PIEVE** (26km), in a beautiful position (508m) above the Val di Chiana, with a distant view of Lake Trasimene. Etruscan in origin, it was then a Roman settlement. In the Middle Ages the town was controlled by Orvieto until 1198 when it was taken by Perugia, against whom the inhabitants rebelled for many centuries. In 1446 the great painter Pietro Vannucci, called Perugino, was born here. Since the 13C most of its buildings have been built in red brick, which give the town its characteristic appearance. Apart from its works by Perugino, it is particularly interesting for its 18C and early 19C architecture. The 'Palio dei Terzieri' is held here on the second Sunday in August.

The main brick-paved steet, named after Perugino, leads into the town from the N past a medieval well. Next to the *Palazzo Vescovile* (1772–80, by Clemente Moghini) is the church of *Santa Maria dei Bianchi*, also by Moghini. It contains 18C decorations by Giovanni Miselli and Stefano Cremoni. In the sacristy is a fresco of the Presentation in the Temple by Antonio Circignani (Pomarancio), who was a native of the town. It adjoins the *Oratorio di Santa Maria dei Bianchi* (open 10.30–12.30, 15.30–dusk; fest. 10–13, 15–19; if closed ring at No. 42 or ask locally for the custodian). This contains a fresco of the *Adoration of the Magi by Perugino (1504; restored in 1984) with Lake Trasimene in the background. It was painted in 29 days. Next door is the 14C *Casa Canestrelli* and, opposite, *Palazzo Giorgi-Taccini* with a neo-classical façade by Giovanni Santini. Via Vannucci ends in Piazza Plebiscito in front of the *Cathedral* begun at the end of the 15C above the ancient church of Santi Gervasio e Protasio. It was consecrated in 1584 and enlarged in the 17C. The façade incorporates 9–10C sculptural fragments. The campanile was designed by Andrea Angelelli in 1738. In the INTERIOR the works are labelled and provided with lights. SOUTH SIDE. First altar, 16C sculptured Crucifix attributed to Pietro Tacca; second altar, Madonna and Child with saints by Domenico di Paride Alfani (1521). In the APSE (covered for restoration) is a Madonna in glory with saints by Perugino, and paintings of the Madonna (right) by Giannicola di Paolo and (left) by Salvio Savini. The frescoes above are by Antonio Pomarancio. In the CHAPEL OF THE HOLY SACRAMENT are frescoes by Giacinto Boccanera (1714) and a painting of the Blessed Giacomo Villa by Giacinto Gemignani. In the CHAPEL OF THE ROSARY, Madonna by Salvio Savini and a wood sculpture of the Madonna attributed to Giovanni Tedesco. The font of 1548 is by 'Master Giovanni' of Montepulciano. NORTH SIDE. Second altar, Antonio Pomarancio, Marriage of the Virgin (repainted in the 18C), and first altar, Perugino, Baptism of Christ. There is a small MUSEUM attached to the cathedral (usually closed) and in the courtyard is archaeological material including Etruscan urns.

The splendid *Torre Civica*, next to the façade, was erected in the 12C, reusing travertine from an older building, and heightened in the 15C. Opposite the tower is the 14C *Palazzo dei Priori* (renovated in the 19C). On the corner of Via Vannucci is the large *Palazzo Della Corgna* (now the Biblioteca Comunale), built by Ascanio Della Corgna on his nomination as governor of the town in 1550, probably designed by Galeazzo Alessi. It contains frescoes by Salvio Savini (1580). At the foot of the stairs has been placed a curious sandstone obelisk, thought to be a sundial of ancient origin (formerly in the convent of San Francesco). In Piazza Plebiscito is the neo-classical *Palazzo Cartoni* (1845, by Giovanni Santini) and, opposite, a little house (with a coat-of-arms) on the site of the house which may have belonged to Perugino's family. Via Vittorio Veneto leads out of the piazza; in Via Roma (right) is the 16C *Palazzo Bandini*, perhaps by Galeazzo Alessi. Beyond the former church of *Sant'Anna* (1752) is the *Rocca* (with the local tourist office), erected in 1326 with four angle towers. It is connected to Porta Romana by a stretch of 13C walls. In Piazza Matteotti is the church of the *Gesù* with a façade by Clemente Moghini (1779). Beyond, across Largo della Vittoria, is the church of *San Francesco* with a 13C brick façade. In the interior (first altar on the S side), Madonna enthroned by Domenico Alfani, and (first altar on the N side), Descent of the Holy Spirit by Antonio Pomarancio. Next door is the entrance to the *Oratorio di San Bartolomeo* (open 10–12, 16–19), with a large fresco of the Crucifixion, known as the 'Pianto degli Angeli', attributed to Nicola di Bonifazio (1384). Viale Vanni continues to the church and monastery of *Santa Lucia* surrounded by ilexes. The centrally-planned church (left unfinished) is by Clemente Moghini (1774).

Via Roma (see above) leads out through Porta Romana and past the interesting church dedicated to Beato Giacomo Villa (1687–1717) to the church of *Santa Maria dei Servi* (left; usually locked; for admission apply to the custodian of the Oratorio di Santa Maria dei Bianchi), founded in the late 13C and transformed in the 18C when it was decorated with stuccoes. It preserves remains of a Deposition by Perugino frescoed in 1517.

From Piazza Plebiscito Via Garibaldi leads SW past the grandiose *Palazzo della Fargna* (now the town hall), begun in the early 18C. In the piazza here is the *Teatro degli Avvaloranti* (being restored), built in 1830 by Giovanni Santini, with a backcloth by Mariano Piervittori (c 1870). Via Garibaldi continues past Palazzo Baglioni (1780) to the church of *San Pietro* (usually closed) founded in the 13C and restored in 1667. It contains a ruined fresco (detached and mounted on canvas), by Perugino and assistants, of St Anthony Abbot between Saints Paul the Hermit and Marcellus (to be restored). From the terrace here there is a fine view of the Val di Chiana.

Outside Porta Sant'Agostino (at the beginning of Via Vannucci) is the former church of *Sant'Agostino* with an interior dating from 1789, now used for conferences. It contains works by Salvio Savini and Nicolò Pomarancio. From the well in Via Vannucci, Via Santa Maria Maddalena leads N past the exceptionally narrow Vicolo Baciadonne to the church of *Santa Maria Maddalena* (1777, by Clemente Moghini) which contains a 14C fresco of the Crucifixion attributed to Jacopo di Mino del Pellicciaio.

To the S of Città della Pieve N71 leads to Orvieto via Monteleone d'Orvieto and Ficulle, described at the end of Rte 9.

FROM CITTÀ DELLA PIEVE TO PERUGIA, N220, 43km. This road is separated from Lake Trasimene by the low hills on its S shore, but it passes numerous small fortified villages whose histories are intimately connected with that of the lake. N71 leads S from Città della Pieve with a wide view over the Val di Chiana. After 2km, N220 diverges left for Perugia. The road winds down through woods with a good view of Città della Pieve on the left. 12km *Piegaro*, on a wooded hill to the right of the road above the river Nestore is of Roman origin. In the 13C Venetian exiles set up a glass industry here which flourished until the beginning of the 19C. 17km turning left for *Panicale* (5km; described above). 18km *Tavernelle*, has a pretty piazza and the church of the Santissima Annunziata (1578). Outside the village are lignite mines used for a large electrical plant which supplies energy to Rome. A by-road leads left to the *Santuario della Madonna di Mongiovino*, a centrally planned church begun in 1513 on a design by Rocco da Vicenza. It contains frescoes by Nicolò Pomarancio and Arrigo Fiammingo. Above is *Mongiovino Vecchio*, with a fine medieval castle (restored in 1968) on the site of a Roman castrum. Outside Tavernelle a by-road leads S to *Castiglion Fosco* with remains of its castle (1462). The church of Santa Croce (restored in 1823) contains 16C paintings and an 18C Crucifix, and the church of San Giovanni Battista a 16C painted wood statue of the Madonna and Child. A minor road leads E through Collebaldo to *Pietrafitta* with one tower left of its medieval castle, and the former *Abbazia dei Sette Frati*, a Benedictine foundation. To the SE is the abandoned castle of Cibottola.

The main road for Perugia continues from Tavernelle to a turning (24km; signposted) for *Fontignano* (1km left) with another castle, where Perugino died of the plague in 1523. The little church of the Annunziata contains his (modern) tomb and a fresco by him. 31km Turning for *Agello*, prominent on a hill to the left of the road. It is thought that some Roman soldiers fled here after Hannibal's victory on Lake Trasimene. It was famous for its castle, from which there is a fine view of the lake. The main road, now almost continuously built up, leads into (43km) Perugia (see Rte 1).

4

Città di Castello and the upper Tiber valley

Road (N3) from Perugia.—10km *Bosco*—35km **Umbertide.**—58km **Città di Castello.**—**71km** *San Giustino.*—75km **Sansepolcro** (described in *Blue Guide Tuscany*).

Railway. 'Ferrovia Centrale Umbra' from Perugia (Stazione Sant'Anna) to Sansepolcro, with stations at Umbertide and Città di Castello.

Information Office. 'APT dell'Alta Valle del Tevere', 2B Via Raffaele di Cesare (Tel. 075/8554817).

The road (N3) and railway from Perugia to Città di Castello and Sansepolcro follow the valley of the Tiber. The fast 'superstrada' (N3bis, now 'E45') to Cesena runs parallel to this route with exits at the main places, but in the description below the old road is described. From the tunnel under Perugia (see Pl. I;7) a winding narrow road descends and crosses the Tiber just before (10km) *Bosco*. Here the road (N298) for Gubbio begins, described in Rte 5. The road for Città di Castello continues up the left bank of the Tiber. 15km turning right for *Montelabate* (2km; 387m) dominated by the large church of Santa Maria built in 1325. It contains a fresco of the Crucifixion and saints by Fiorenzo di Lorenzo and a Madonna and Saints by Bartolomeo Caporali. The fine cloister dates from the 13C and the crypt from the 11C. The next by-road off the main road leads up to *Civitella Benazzone* (2km) with two paintings by Benedetto Bonfigli and Domenico Alfani in its church. To the NW are the remains of the medieval *Abbazia Celestina* (recently restored). This by-road continues towards Gubbio. Just before Santa Cristina, a signpost left indicates *Alcatraz*, a holiday centre in beautiful countryside, well worth a visit (hotel, restaurant, cottages to rent, campsite, etc.).

30km. A road leads across the Tiber to the *Badia di San Salvatore di Monte Corona* (1km) founded by St Romualdo c 1008. The Romanesque church (altered in subsequent centuries) has been restored. Here has been placed a lovely 8C ciborium. A road leads S to the Hermitage of Monte Corona (8km; 693m) erected in 1530 and now abandoned.

The main road passes numerous tobacco fields on the approach to (35km) **Umbertide**. Though heavily bombed in 1944, it is now a busy town (13,400 inhab.) with industrial outskirts.

Hotels. 3-star: 'Rio'; 2-star: 'Capponi'.

History. An important trading centre on the Tiber for the Umbrians and Etruscans, it was later the Roman *Pitulum*. It is traditionally thought to have been reconstructed by the sons of Uberto, who was son of Ugo, Margrave of Tuscany, and called *Fratta*. From the 12C it was under the control of Perugia and then ruled by the Papal States. In 1863 it changed its name to Umbertide.

The conspicuous church of *Santa Maria della Reggia* has a fine octagonal exterior by Bino Sozi (16C), which was completed by Francesco Laparelli. The crenellated towers (1385) of the *Rocca* (open for exhibitions) survive. Beyond is the piazza with Palazzo Comunale (which has a small collection of works of art) opposite the ex-Palazzo delle Poste with a clock, a neo-classical work by Giovanni Santini. Via Cibo, at the far end of the piazza, leads down to the main road. On the other side of the railway (crossed by foot) is the quiet Piazza San Francesco with three churches in a row. Santa Croce with a 17C interior (closed) and San Bernardino (also closed) stand on either side of the 14C church of *San Francesco* which has interesting 17C frescoes (very ruined) in the first N chapel, and on the left wall of the last N chapel is a Madonna and four saints by Nicolò Pomarancio (1577). A *Deposition by Luca Signorelli, formerly in Santa Croce, will probably be exhibited here after its restoratiA pretty road runs from Umbertide through typical Umbrian countryside to Lake Trasimene (28km). It passes beneath Monte Acuto (926m), and at 14km a by-road leads right to *Preggio*, a medieval village in a beautiful position with an interesting church. A chestnut festival is held here in the autumn. The road continues to Castel Rigone and Lake Trasimene, both described in Rte 3.

From Umbertide another beautiful road (N219) leads to Gubbio past the fine 16C castle of *Civitella Ranieri* (5km; no admission). In the wooded valley of the Assino is the Abbazia di Campo Reggiano (11C, with a fine crypt).

A road leads NE from Umbertide to **Montone** (8km) in a splendid position (482m) with fine views. Cars are parked outside the walls. 2-star hotel: 'Fortebraccio'; 1st class restaurant: 'Arte e Mestieri'. This was the birthplace of the famous condottiere Andrea Braccio Fortebraccio (1368–1424). It has imposing walls, and steps in one of the towers lead up to a terrace from which the remarkable view takes in: (to the W) the Sanctuary of Canoscio, Monte Santa Maria Tiberina, and La Verna; to the N, on a hill-top, the Rocca d'Aries (recently acquired by the Regione and to be restored as a study centre), and (behind) Monte Neroni, the valley of Carpina, and the high Monte Catria; to the E is Monte Subasio. Beside the terrace, beyond its 16C cloister (recently restored), is *San Francesco*, the most important church in the village, in which there are long-term plans to create a museum. The Gothic interior is closed during restoration work and most of its contents are stored in Palazzo Comunale. These include: the carved wood doors by Antonio Bencivenni (1518), *Madonna del Soccorso attributed to Bartolomeo Caporali or Benedetto Bonfigli, a 13C life-size wood group of Christ on the Cross with the Madonna and St John the Evangelist, an altarpiece of the Immaculate Conception with saints and sibyls (with a view of Lake Trasimene in the background) by Vincenzo and Valerio Mossi (1551), an interesting little Ecce Homo, and magistrates' stalls with intarsia work dating from 1505. In the Gothic apse are remains of frescoes and sinopie by Antonio Alberti of Ferrara (1422–23; very ruined). The damaged fresco of St Anthony Abbot between two saints is signed by Bartolomeo Caporali. In a higher part of the village is the *Collegiata* with a Last Supper by Calvaert. The church of *San Fedele* (usually closed; sometimes used for concerts) has an unusual relief above its portal of two flagellants. An Annunciation and saints by Tommaso Papacello and Vittore Cirello has been removed from the interior for restoration. Below the village is the *Pieve Vecchia* (ring at the house next door), a fine building of the 11C with very ruined frescoes.

The road leaves Umbertide and crosses the Tiber. At (40km) *Montecastelli* the faster road for Città di Castello forks right to recross the Tiber, while the more interesting road, described below, stays on the right bank of the river. At (47km) Trestina a by-road diverges left past numerous tobacco plantations for Morra.

The road passes close to the *Abbazia di Santa Maria di Petroia* (6km) with a crypt (11–12C). The village of **Morra** (10km), in a valley of chestnut woods, was the birthplace of Giuseppe Nicasi (1859–1915), a notable scholar of local history who discovered that the carbon signs made by the local millers on their sacks of flour derived from Arcaic Roman numerals, a theory confirmed by modern mathematicians. These signs, handed down over the generations, enabled the illiterate millers to keep count of their merchandise. Just beyond the village, on a little hill (signposted) is the *Oratorio di San Crescentino* (restored in 1974–76; the custodian lives in the modern house reached by a gravel road in front of the church). A confraternity was founded here c 1264 and the church dates from 1420. After 1507 Luca Signorelli and assistants painted frescoes on the upper parts of the walls: those at the E end are the only ones well preserved, with the Flagellation and a crowded Crucifixion scene. In the niche behind the high altar (with a pretty carved stone arch) are frescoes of Christ between two angels, thought to be by the hand of Signorelli, and Saints Mary Magdalene and Anthony Abbot. The frescoes of the Madonna of the Misericordia and the Madonna of Loreto in the two niches on the side walls are by the school of Signorelli. The former oratory (now the sacristy) preserves some interesting Late Gothic frescoes including San Crescentino on horseback.

From Trestina the road continues towards Città di Castello. On the left of the road at Fabbrecce is the *Santuario di Canoscio*, on a wooded hill, built by Emilio de Fabris in 1855–78. At (50km) San Secondo, a by-road leads left for *Monte Santa Maria Tiberina* (11km; Trattoria: 'Petralta') a well preserved medieval village in a beautiful position (688m) overlooking the upper Tiber valley. From the 11C this was the citadel of the Del Monte family whose burial chapel is in the Pieve of Santa Maria. A tower of the castle survives.

58km **CITTÀ DI CASTELLO** (38,000 inhab.), the most important town in the fertile upper Tiber valley. It flourished in the High Renaissance under the rule of the Vitelli, when it gave employment to many famous artists, among them Raphael, Signorelli, and the Della Robbia. It has been noted for its flourishing printing industries since the 16C.

Information Office. 'APT dell'Alta Valle del Tevere', 2B Via Raffaele di Cesare (probably to be moved to Via Sant'Antonio). Tel. 075/8554817.

Railway Station on the 'Ferrovia Centrale Umbra' line from Perugia to Sansepolcro. **Buses** to Arezzo.

Car Park on Viale Nazario Sauro, with escalators to the Cathedral.

Hotels. 4-star: 'Tiferno', 13 Piazza Raffaello Sanzio. 3-star: 'Hotel Garden', Via Aldo Bologni. 2-star: 'Umbria', Via dei Galanti. **Camping sites**. 3-star: 'La Montesca' (open May-October), and at Pietralunga and Monte Santa Maria Tiberina. Numerous holiday apartments for rent in the surrounding countryside (information from the APT).

Restaurants. 1st class: 'Il Bersaglio', Via Orlando; 'Adriano Due', Piazza Che Guevara; 'Il Fiore', Via Don Milani. Trattorie: 'La Carabiniera', Via San Florido; 'Da Lea', Via San Florido.

Annual **Chamber Music Festival** at the end of August and beginning of September.

History. In the Pleistocene era the valley was submerged by the great Lago Tiberino, a lake which stretched as far as Terni and Soleto. The region was later inhabited by elephants, hippopotamuses, and rhinoceros. The presence of man here has been traced since the Stone Age. The inhabitants are still called 'Tifernati' from the Umbrian town of *Tifernum* on this site. The Roman municipality of *Tifernum Tiberinum* was mentioned by Pliny the Younger who had a villa nearby, remains of which have been found in a locality called Colle Plinio. By the 6C it was the seat of a bishopric, and in the Middle Ages, as a free commune, it was contested between Perugia and the Church. The Vitelli family held the lordship in the 15C and 16C, and four of their palaces remain in the town. The firm of Scipione Lapi was famous for its book production here at the beginning of this century.

From the car park off Viale Nazario Sauro a path leads through the walls to two short flights of escalators which emerge in the public gardens on the site of a defensive tower destroyed in 1480. The monument to Vittorio Emanuele is by Vincenzo Rosignoli (1906). Beyond is the **Cathedral**, given a bizarre appearance by its half-finished façade begun in 1632–46. Of ancient foundation, it was rebuilt by St Florido who became bishop in 580, and again in the 11C and 14C. It had to be reconstructed after earthquake damage in 1458 and was consecrated in 1540. It is thought that Elia di Bartolomeo Lombardo and his son Tommaso were involved as architects. The splendid round *campanile (seen from behind) dates from the 11C, with a Gothic upper storey and conical roof. The Gothic N portal has two beautifully carved panels dating from 1339–59 representing Justice and Mercy.

The INTERIOR has fine Corinthian pilasters gilded in the 19C. The panelled wood ceiling was made by local craftsmen in 1697. It incorporates two paintings of angels by Tommaso Conca, and St Florido in Glory attributed to a follower of Giacinto Brandi. SOUTH SIDE. Third chapel, works by Giovanni Battista Pacetti ('Lo Sguazzino') born at Città di Castello in 1593, including a view of the town. In the fourth chapel, rebuilt in 1789 on a domed Greek-cross plan, is an *Altarpiece by Rosso Fiorentino, commissioned to show Christ in Glory between the Madonna and St Anne, Mary Magdalene, and Mary the Egyptian, and below a group of figures representing the populace. Although restored in 1983, the picture is very dark. In the fifth chapel are paintings by the local 17C painters Bernardino Gagliardi and Virgilio Ducci. The crossing and DOME are frescoed by Tommaso Conca (1795–97) and the four Evangelists in the spandrels are by Ludovico Mazzanti (1751). The two wood cantorie have 16C carving by Alberto di Giovanni Alberti (called 'Berto'). A door on the right leads into the SACRISTY (at present not open to the public), off which a little room contains a ruined fresco of the Ecce Homo and four saints by the school of Signorelli, discovered in 1968. The CHOIR is frescoed by Marco Benefial (1747–49) and the stalls (in very poor condition) are by Alberto di Giovanni Alberti on a design by Doceno and Raffaellino del Colle (1533 and 1540). The third N chapel is decorated by Bernardino Gagliardi, and the first chapel has works by Nicolò Pomarancio. In the LOWER CHURCH, on the site of the ancient crypt, are buried the patron Saints Bishop Florido and Amanzio in an ancient sarcophagus. There is a 15C fresco of St Florido in a side chapel.

On the right of the façade is the entrance (through an interesting 14C courtyard) to the *Museo Capitolare, beautifully arranged in fine 14–15C vaulted rooms and reopened in 1991 (admission 10–13, 15–17 except Monday). The case at the right-hand end of the SALONE displays the splendid silver *Treasure of Canoscio. This consists of 25 plates and utensils used during the celebration of the eucharist, found while ploughing a field near Canoscio (see above) in 1935. They are remarkable examples of paleo-Christian art of the 6C. The chronological order of the arrangement continues in the small room off the corridor ahead with a silver and gilded *altar-frontal with carvings showing the figure of Christ blessing surrounded by the symbols of the Evangelists and scenes from the life of Christ. According to tradition it was presented to the cathedral by Pope Celestine II in 1142. In the corridor is a wood statue of the seated Madonna and Child by a 14C Umbrian artist (removed for restoration). In the second small room off the corridor is an exquisite episcopal *crozier attributed to Goro di Gregorio (c 1324), and an unusual little marble basin dating from the 16C. The paintings include St Florido attributed to Giacomo di Ser Michele Castellano (1412), a Madonna enthroned in a Renaissance frame, dating from 1492 showing the influence of Signorelli, and an Annunciation by Francesco da Tiferno. The other cases in the SALONE display liturgical objects dating from the 12C–19C including processional crosses, thuribles, reliquary boxes, chalices, paxes, and an agate and silver gilt cross made by a Florentine goldsmith in the 15C. At the end of the Salone is a 16C painted wood reliquary and a Madonna and Child with the young St John by Pinturicchio. On the stairs is an unusual stone statue of St Sebastian (15C), two well-painted putti (fragments) attributed to Giulio Romano, and a fine Tuscan 15C wood Crucifix (removed for restoration). UPPER FLOOR. In the first room, a 17C painting of St Bonaventura, bozzetti by Ludovico Mazzanti, and Rest on the Flight into Egypt attributed to Tommaso Conca. In the second room, 16–18C liturgical objects, and bozzetti by Ermenegildo Costantini (1731–91). The third room has 18C reliquaries and 17–19C vestments.

In Piazza Gabriotti (where a market is held on Thursdays and Saturdays), beyond the flank of the cathedral, is the fine *Palazzo Comunale* (or 'dei Priori') begun by Angelo da Orvieto in 1322 but left unfinished. It is constructed in sandstone with lovely two-light windows. Beneath an archway a short alley leads to Via del Modello from which can be seen the round campanile of the cathedral (described above). Opposite Palazzo Comunale is the 14C *Torre Civica* which may be climbed (stairs only: 10–12.30, 15–18.30 except Monday). Corso Cavour, with some interesting palaces, leads out of Piazza Gabriotti beneath a pretty 14C loggia, and on the right is *Palazzo del Podestà* (now the seat of the Pretura), also by Angelo da Orvieto, and finished by 1368. The façade on Piazza Matteotti was rebuilt by Nicola Barbioni in 1687. From the piazza (with an elaborate 19C building, now the seat of a bank) there is a good view of the round tower of the cathedral.

Via Angeloni leads out of the piazza up to Piazza Raffaello Sanzio with a monument commemorating the fall of the Papal government in 1860 by Elmo Palazzi. Here is the church of *San Francesco*, built in 1273 with a fine 18C interior. The Vitelli chapel (off the N side) was built by Vasari and has an altarpiece by him. The beautiful entrance gate (1566) is by a local craftsman and the stalls date from the 16C. Beyond an altar with a very darkened terracotta of St Francis receiving the stigmata by the Della Robbian school, the fourth N altarpiece is a copy of Raphael's Marriage of the Virgin commissioned for the church in 1504 and removed by Napoleon in 1798 (now in the Brera gallery in Milan). Off the S side is a chapel with a carved wood 15C group of the Pietà.

From Piazza Raffaello Sanzio, Via degli Albizzini leads to Piazza Garibaldi with the large *Palazzo Vitelli a Porta Sant'Egidio*, now owned by a bank and used for exhibitions. It was built in 1540, perhaps on a design by Giorgio Vasari, for Paolo Vitelli, with decorations by Cristoforo Gherardi and Prospero Fontana. It has a beautiful garden façade overlooking a large garden with a grotto (in need of restoration), statues, and a little hillock grown with ilexes. At the far end of the garden (on Via San Bartolomeo) is a palazzina decorated with frescoes. Also on Piazza Garibaldi is the 15C *Palazzo Albizzini* with a collection of works donated to the city in 1982 by the local artist Alberto Burri (open 10–12, 15–17 except Monday). Via San Bartolomeo leads to Via Giulianelle in which is the new seat of the *Biblioteca Comunale*. Here is to be opened the Museo Civico with an archaeological collection relating to the Tiber valley (including fossils from the Pleistocene era), closed since 1988.

From Piazza Raffaello Sanzio (see above) Via XI Settembre leads down towards Santa Maria delle Grazie. On the corner of Via dei Lanari (right) is the Convent of the *Clarisse Murate* (a closed order) and the church of San Giacomo.

The garden façade by Vasari of Palazzo Vitelli alla Canonniera, now the Pinacoteca, Città di Castello

On the left, Via Sant'Andrea leads to the church of *San Giovanni Decollato* (closed) which contains frescoes by the school of Signorelli. In the road beside it is the church of *Santa Cecilia* (closed for restoration) with a large lunette of the Epiphany in enamelled terracotta by the Della Robbian school. Next door is the convent of the *Clarisse Urbaniste* with a 15C image of the Madonna and a 15C cloister. In Via Sant'Angelo, also off Via Sant'Andrea, is the church of *San Michele Arcangelo* with a high altarpiece of the Madonna and Child with saints by Raffaellino del Colle.

Via XI Settembre continues past the large 16C *Palazzo Vitelli a San Giacomo* (being restored) to the church of *Santa Maria delle Grazie*, with a square tower. It has a Gothic side portal next to a Renaissance doorway (No. 3). It was rebuilt in 1587 and contains a cast of the Assumption by Andrea della Robbia, and a fresco (much darkened) of the Transition of the Virgin attributed to Ottaviano Nelli. On the N side is an altarpiece known as the 'Madonna delle Grazie', the only known work signed and dated 1456 by Giovanni di Piamonte, who worked with Piero della Francesca. It is kept in an elaborate cupboard and exhibited only on 26 August and 2 February. Nearby at No. 21 Via XI Settembre is the Convent of the *Cappuccine* (closed order) where St Veronica Giuliani lived (1660–1727), with a small museum relating to her life.

From Piazza Raffaello Sanzio (see above) Via Angeloni and Corso Vittorio Emanuele II lead in the opposite direction to (500m) the church of *Santa Maria Maggiore* with an interesting vaulted interior. Dating from 1505 it is thought to be the work of Elia di Bartolomeo Lombardo. On the walls and in the niches remains of 15C frescoes alternate with modern works. Via Borgo Farinario and (right) Largo Monsignor Muzi lead to *San Domenico* a very dark Gothic church (1271–1424) which contains interesting 15C frescoes. On the right side of the nave in a chapel with two Gothic arches dedicated as a War Memorial, is a 15C Sienese fresco of the Crucifixion, and in the last chapel on the right are more 15C frescoes. At the E end of the nave, on the right and left side, are two Renaissance altars which used to contain a Crucifixion by Raphael (now in the National Gallery in London) and the Martyrdom of St Sebastian by Signorelli (now in the Pinacoteca). The fine choir stalls are by Manno di Benincasa (Cori; 1435). Via Borgo Farinario continues past the site of an old tobacco factory and under an archway. In Via della Cannoniera is the entrance to *Palazzo Vitelli alla Canonniera*, seat of the ***Pinacoteca Comunale** (ring the bell, 10–13, 15–18.30 except Monday), the most important collection of paintings in Umbria after the Pinacoteca in Perugia. The palace was built for Alessandro Vitelli in 1521–32 by Antonio da Sangallo the Younger and Pier Francesco da Viterbo. It was restored by Elia Volpi and donated by him to the town in 1912. The garden *façade has remarkable graffiti decoration by Vasari. The collection has been undergoing rearrangement and the palace has been in restoration for many years. Some of the rooms have 16C vault decorations by Cristoforo Gherardi, and on the stairs and in the Salone on the first floor are frescoes (recently restored) by Cola dell'Amatrice. When both floors are reopened the arrangement will be changed, but the most important works are listed below.

*Reliquary of St Andrew (1420), with two statuettes in gilded bronze by Lorenzo Ghiberti. Paintings of the Madonna and Child by Spinello Aretino, Antonio Vivarini and Giovanni d'Alamagna, Giorgio di Andrea di Bartolo, and Neri di Bicci. The striking *Head of Christ with signs of the Passion is variously attributed to Giusto di Gand or to a follower of Piero della Francesca of the late-15C Umbrian school. Works by Signorelli and his school include the *Martyrdom of St Sebastian, and a standard of St John the Baptist. The *Standard with the Creation of Eve and the Crucifixion of Saints Roch and Sebastian is a beautiful but very damaged work by Raphael. A *Maestà attributed to the 'Master of Città di Castello' (named from this work) has been removed for restoration for many years. Other paintings include works by Antonio da Ferrara, Raffaellino del Colle, Santi di Tito, Domenico Puligo and Francesco Tifernate. Among the sculptures are a Sienese marble relief of the 14C showing the Baptism of Christ and Della Robbian works. A sacristy cupboard in poplar wood with walnut inlay by Antonio Bencivenni (1501) was restored in 1987.

On the outskirts of the town, c 1.5km along the old road to Perugia, in a warehouse once used for drying tobacco, is another exhibition of works by Alberto Burri, donated by him to the city in 1990 (open 10–12, 15–17 except Monday). Beyond at *Garavelle* (2km from the town) is an interesting local ethnographical museum (open 9–12, 14–17 except Monday) in an old farmhouse. There is also an ornithological collection, model railways, and two steam engines built in 1930.

On the road to Fano (N257) the first turning on the right leads past the 19C cemetery designed by Emilio De Fabris to the *Terme di Fontecchio* (3km), a spa, whose alkaline sulphurous waters were known in Roman times. The 19C thermal building was designed by Guglielmo Calderini (season March–December). The Fano road now climbs the hill of Belvedere planted with cypresses and pine trees and passes the *Santuario della Madonna del Belvedere* (6km), a centrally planned building by Nicola Barbioni (1669) whose unusual semicircular façade has a portico and two cylindrical bell towers. The interior has numerous statues and stuccoes. The view of the Tiber valley is splendid.

Another road from Città di Castello leads across the Tiber towards the Eremo di Buonriposo. It passes *Villa La Montesca* (3km) surrounded by a fine park, built at the end of the last century by Baron Leopoldo Franchetti. A narrow road continues to the *Eremo di Buonriposo* (6km), traditionally thought to have been founded by St Francis. It is now privately owned (admission on request). Nearby is a spring.

Two roads continue from Città di Castello towards Tuscany. The road (and 'superstrada') to Sansepolcro traverse the wide valley. At (66km) a by-road leads right for Lama and Pitigliano near which is *Colle Plinio* where excavations begun in 1979 have revealed remains of the villa of Pliny the Younger (recognised as being his by the brick stamps found here in 1988). The site is not yet open to the public. Nearby are the 17C Villa Capelletti with a garden, and Villa Graziani dating from 1616. The main road continues to (71km) *San Giustino*, a busy little town, with the splendid Castello Bufalini, built in 1492 and altered by Vasari, with a delightful loggia, and frescoes by Cristoforo Gherardi. It is surrounded by a garden which has a maze. It has recently been sold to the State and may be opened to the public. There is an interesting medieval building beneath the priest's house near the modern church.

A very twisty mountainous road (N73bis) climbs from San Giustino through beautiful scenery via Bocca Trabaria (1049m), the pass between Umbria and the Marches, to Urbania (49km) and Urbino (66km), see *Blue Guide Northern Italy*.

The main road to San Sepolcro continues past *Cospaia* which became a tiny Republic in 1440 when it was omitted by mistake from the territory around Borgo San Sepolcro ceded by Pope Eugenius IV to the Florentine Republic. It remained independent up to 1826. This was the first place in Italy where tobacco was cultivated (in 1575). The road enters Tuscany just before (75km) **Sansepolcro**, described in *Blue Guide Tuscany*.

The road from Città di Castello to Monterchi and Arezzo (N221, 42km) passes Vingone (10km) where a road leads right to **Citerna** (14km), on a wooded hill-top on the border between Umbria and Tuscany. It was founded in Roman times, and reconstructed in the 7–8C. Damaged by earthquake in 1917 and in both World Wars, it is now a delightful peaceful village with brick buildings, well restored and well kept. Corso Garibaldi, named after the hero who spent three days here in 1849, leads up through the village from the entrance between two gate posts surmounted by fir cones. On the left, by No. 35, a yellow sign indicates a picturesque medieval passageway with a wood roof and arches which runs along the side of the hill. *Casa Prosperi* (No. 41), now the property of the Church (ask locally for the key), contains a monumental carved 16C fireplace in pietra serena. Opposite is *Palazzo Vitelli* (restored in 1975). Beyond the town hall is the church of *San Francesco* (1316; rebuilt in 1508). It contains delightful gilded wood altars. By the second right altar is a frescoed niche with the Madonna and Child with Saints Michael and Francis and two angels by Luca Signorelli and his workshop (in poor condition, but restored as far as was possible). It is thought to be a late work (1522–23), possibly with the help of Papacello. The two altars have a Della Robbian frieze with cherubs' heads, and Christ in glory with Saints Francis and Michael with six lovely angels, by Raffaellino del Colle. The Choir has pretty 16C stalls. Here are a Madonna and angels and saints by the 16C Umbrian school, a 14C statuette of the Madonna and Child in terracotta, and a crowded Deposition by a certain Alessandro Forzorio from Arezzo (1568; recently restored). In the left transept is a Deposition by Pomarancio, and in an elaborate wooden altar, *Madonna and St John the Evangelist, by Raffaellino del Colle, in a beautiful landscape on either side of a 14C wood Crucifix. Above are Saints Jerome and Francis and the Annunciation. In a niche, seated Della Robbian statue of St Anthony Abbot. The organ dates from 1828. A Holy Family attributed to the school of Raphael also belongs to the church.

On the opposite side of the Corso is another vaulted medieval passage-way. Beyond an arch over the road is the little Piazza Scipioni with a fountain and three lime trees, and a view over the Tiber valley. Above to the left is the church of *San Michele Arcangelo*, built in the 18C. It contains (third right chapel) a Crucifixion by Pomarancio and a bell dated 1269 and (second left chapel) a Della Robbian Madonna and Child with angels in polychrome terracotta. To the left of the church, by the bell tower of San Francesco, is the *Teatro Bontempelli*, a delightful little theatre, recently restored. Via della Rocca leads in the other direction past solidly built houses to the *Rocca*, destroyed in the Second World War, except for a fine circular brick tower. Within the damaged walls is a little fountain (1979) commemorating St Francis who probably came here in 1224. The view of the upper Tiber valley takes in Anghiari and La Verna, Sansepolcro, and Monte Subasio. A by-road leads from Citerna in less than 1km to the chapel of the Madonna del Parto (with Piero della Francesca's famous fresco) outside Monterchi, both in Tuscany and described in *Blue Guide Tuscany*.

5

Gubbio

Gubbio is reached from Perugia by the Strada Eugubina (N298), a beauti-ful road (40km). It leaves Perugia near the hospital, and descends to cross the Tiber before (10km) *Bosco*. Just beyond the fork at Bosco it passes *Pieve Pagliaccia* where the church has 13C frescoes. At 13km *Colombella Bassa* the 12C church of San Giustino has an interesting crypt. The road climbs to 662m and then descends to the *Abbazia di Vallingegno* (to the right of the road), a 13C Benedictine foundation, now privately owned (admission on request). The church has a Roman sarcophagus as its high altar in which are neatly preserved the bones of the martyr St Verecondo. The castle on a nearby hill is also privately owned. Beyond Mengara the road winds down, with splendid views ahead of Gubbio backed by the Apennines. Gubbio can also be approached from Umbertide (29km) along another beautiful road (see Rte 4).

GUBBIO a town of 31,400 inhabitants in an isolated position on the lower slopes of Monte Ingino, is one of the most beautiful and best preserved medieval towns in Italy, its lovely old buildings built of polished light grey stone quarried locally. Its main roads run parallel with each other following the contours of the steep hillside (529m) and between them towers the splendid Palazzo dei Consoli in Piazza Grande. The high green hillside, which forms a background above the town, and the wide plain at its foot are special features of Gubbio. Most of the buildings have been carefully restored since damage in an earthquake in 1982 which left 1500 inhabitants homeless.

Information Offices. 'APT', 6 Piazza Oderisi (Corso Garibaldi), Tel. 075/9220693; 'Gruppo Operatori Turistici Eugubini (G.O.T.E.)', 11 Via della Repubblica.

A **mini-bus service** runs every 20mins (except 14–15.00) from Loggia dei Tiratori (Piazza 40 Martiri) via Viale del Teatro Romano and Porta Castello up Via dei Consoli to Piazza Grande.

Country buses run by 'ASP' (information office, Via della Repubblica) to Perugia (1hr 10mins) (some with connections to Assisi), and to Città di Castello via Umbertide (1hr 30mins). Frequent service to Fossato di Vico (35mins), the nearest railway station. Some buses connect with trains to Ancona and Rome. On weekdays there is one bus a day to Florence (via Perugia, 3hrs 30mins) and to Rome (4hrs 30mins).

Cablecar (10–13.15, 14.30–17; closed on Wednesday in winter) from outside Porta Romana to Sant'Ubaldo (827m) on Monte Ingino (6mins).

Car parking. The centre of the town is closed to traffic. Free car parks off Viale del Teatro Romano (near the Roman Theatre); near San Domenico; and near the cablecar station outside Porta Romana. Car park with an hourly tariff in Piazza 40 Martiri.

Hotels in the historical centre. 3-star: 'Bosone', 22 Via XX Settembre. 2-star: 'Gatta-pone', 6 Via Ansidei; 'Grotta dell'Angelo', 47 Via Gioia (off Via Cairoli). On the outskirts. 4-star: 'Park Hotel ai Cappuccini', Via Tifernate, 1km along the road to Umbertide. 3-star: 'San Marco', 5 Via Perugina (corner of Viale Campo di Marte); 'Montegranelli', at Monteluiano, 4km SW. 2-star: 'Catignano', località San Marco, 3km SE.

Camping sites at Ortoguidone: 'Villa Ortoguidone' (4-star), and 'Città di Gubbio' (3-star).

Restaurants. Luxury-class: 'Alla Fornace di Mastro Giorgio', Via Mastro Giorgio (off Via Savelli Della Porta); 'Taverna del Lupo', Via Ansidei (off Via XX Settembre). 1st class: 'Grotta dell'Angelo' (see above); 'Fabiani', Piazza 40 Martiri; 'Dei Consoli', Via dei Consoli; 'Federico da Montefeltro', Via della Repubblica; 'Funivia' on Monte Ingino. Trattorie and Pizzerie: 'Picchio Verde', 65 Via Savelli Della Porta; 'Bargello Pizzeria', Via dei Consoli; 'Paninoteca La Lanterna', Via Gioia (off Via Cairoli).

Good places to **picnic** above the Duomo, near Sant'Ubaldo, or outside Porta Metauro.

Annual Festivals. The picturesque procession of the *Festa dei Ceri*, which may have a pagan origin, is held every year on 15 May, the vigil of the feast day of St Ubaldo (died 1160), the town's patron saint and bishop. At this ceremony three wax figures of saints (St Ubaldo, St George and St Anthony), on extremely heavy wooden 'candles', 4 metres high, are carried through the streets and up to the Basilica di Sant'Ubaldo at the double. The ten official bearers (who are replaced c every 10 metres) represent three confraternities: builders (St Ubaldo), peasants (St Anthony), and artisans (St George) in a demonstration of strength and ability. The first 'cera' to arrive at Sant'Ubaldo attempts to shut the church door in the face of the following 'cera'. On the last Sunday in May is held the 'Palio della Balestra', a crossbowmen's contest of medieval origin, against the citizens of Sansepolcro. On Good Friday there is a traditional procession.

History. The town was founded by the Umbri in the 3C BC, and its political and religious importance is attested by the famous Eugubian Tables (preserved in Palazzo dei Consoli) which are fundamental documents for the study of the Umbrian language. The Roman city of *Iguvium*, at the foot of the hill, flourished in the Republican era when the theatre was built. It had a celebrated temple of Jupiter. *Eugubium*, as it later came to be called, was sacked by the Goths but became a free commune in the 11C. With the help of the bishop saint Ubaldo Baldassini, born here in 1100, the town was saved from Barbarossa in 1155, when it was granted numerous priviledges. Although often at war with Perugia, Gubbio retained its independence, and its civic pride is represented by Piazza Grande and Palazzo dei Consoli, constructed in 1322. From 1387 to 1508 it came under the peaceful rule of the Montefeltro, counts of Urbino.

The frescoes and altarpieces in the churches of Gubbio are mostly by native artists.

The miniaturist Oderisio (who was born here, and died c 1299) is traditionally considered the founder of Gubbio's school of painting. In the 14C local artists included Guido Palmerucci and a certain 'Mello da Eugubio'. Ottaviano Nelli (c 1375–1444/50) was the most celebrated painter of Gubbio, and his beautiful frescoes survive in a number of churches in the town. His father Martino and brother Tommaso also worked here. In the 16C Benedetto and Virgilio Nucci painted numerous altarpieces, and in the 17C Francesco Allegrini and Felice Damiani were active here. The Maffei family of woodcarvers also produced fine work in the 16C. The greatest architect of Gubbio was Matteo di Giovannelli, called Gattapone, who died after 1376. The town has a number of churches with fine 17C and 18C interiors. Giorgio Andreoli ('Mastro Giorgio'), born at Intra c 1465–70, spent most of his life in Gubbio where he died in 1552. He discovered a particular ruby and golden lustre which reflects the light on majolica, but hardly any examples of his work survive in the city itself. The tradition of producing fine ceramics is carried on by a number of firms here, including 'Rampini' and 'Aiò'. Many of the old houses of Gubbio (as in other Umbrian towns) have the curious 'Porta del Morto' beside their principal doorway. This probably served to give access to the upper floors of the houses; it was formerly believed the small doorway was used when a coffin left the house.

The approaches from Perugia and Umbertide reach the town at *Piazza 40 Martiri*, planted as a public garden, from which there is a good view of all the main monuments of the town climbing the hillside. Here is the large church of **San Francesco**, formerly attributed to Fra' Bevignate of Perugia (1259–92). It has a fine exterior, especially the Gothic E end and octagonal campanile. INTERIOR. SOUTH SIDE. First altar, Antonio Gherardi, Immaculate Conception (in very poor condition); second altar, School of Virgilio Nucci, Crucifixion and saints; third altar, copy of Daniele da Volterra's Deposition in the church of the Trinità del Monte in Rome by his follower Virgilio Nucci. The chapel to the right of the apse (covered for restoration) has 14C frescoes of the life of St Francis. In the main chapel, high up, are very early frescoes of Christ enthroned with saints (13C). In the chapel to the left of the apse, complete fresco cycle of the *Life of the Virgin by Ottaviano Nelli (very ruined). On the altar is a venerated image of the Madonna of the Misericordia. NORTH SIDE. Third altar, Anna Allegrini, St Anthony of Padua (1673); second altar, Benedetto Bandiera, St Charles Borromeo; first altar, Imperiali, Madonna enthroned with Saints (early 18C). The SACRISTY is in part of a 14C house which belonged to the Spadalonga, friends of St Francis. In the CLOISTER are a 14C fresco of the Crucifixion and Roman polychrome mosaic pavement fragments (3C AD) found in Gubbio. In the CHAPTER HOUSE is another ancient fresco (detached from the cloister) thought to represent the Santa Casa of Loreto. A small MUSEUM has been closed since 1989. It contains a seal (the 'Sigillum Custodiae Eugubinae') with St Francis and the tamed wolf (1350), Crosses and liturgical objects, and paintings by Spagnoletto and Domenico Morelli.

The *Loggia dei Tiratori*, on the other side of the piazza, was built in 1603 and used for drying wool and hides. Beneath the 14C portico, with a fresco by Bernardino di Nanni, is a little fruit and vegetable market. At the left end is the entrance to the church of *Santa Maria dei Laici* ('dei Bianchi'; closed except when in use by a choral society). It was built in the 14C but the interior was transformed in the 17C. It contains 24 small paintings of the Life of the Virgin, by Felice Damiani. At the E end is a fresco of Paradise by Francesco Allegrini and on the left altar, the last work of Barocci (an Annunciation).

The characteristic Via Piccardi, with a good view of Palazzo dei Consoli, leads across the Camignano torrent (its paved bed dry for most of the year). On the right, in Via Cristini, is the little Romanesque church of **San**

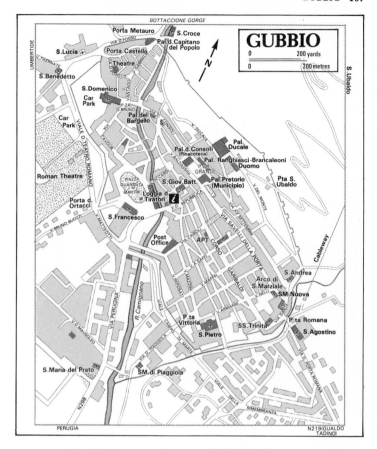

Giovanni Battista. On the first S altar, St Charles Borromeo by Claudio Ridolfi. In the baptistery is a varnished majolica font. A Baptism of Christ by the school of Perugino has been removed. On the first N altar, two paintings of saints by Benedetto Nucci.

The steep Via della Repubblica leads up to Via Savelli Della Porta. On the left is Via Baldassini from which can be seen the arches that support Piazza Grande and in which is the 14C *Casa di Sant'Ubaldo* (recently restored as the 'Centro di Studi Umbri'). It contains a fresco of St Anthony Abbot by Guido Palmerucci. Steps mount to Via dei Consoli, the main street of the city. To the left opens the splendid ***Piazza Grande** (or 'della Signoria') with a high balustrade overlooking the plain. In 1322 the 'Consiglio del Popolo' approved the construction of Palazzo dei Consoli and Palazzo del Podestà with the Piazza Grande between them at the centre of the town. Above the long neo-classical Palazzo Ranghiasci-Brancaleoni, designed by Francesco Ranghiasci in the early 19C, with tall columns decorating its façade, can be seen the Duomo and Palazzo Ducale on the hillside.

Palazzo dei Consoli, Gubbio

The superb ****Palazzo dei Consoli** is one of the most impressive medieval public buildings in Italy, begun in 1332. It towers over the city, and the SW side, which rests on massive vaulting, is 92m high to the top of the bell tower. It is usually attributed to the local architect Gattapone, although Angelo da Orvieto was also involved, but may only have designed the entrance door and the two Gothic windows on either side of it. It is approached by a delightful outside staircase. Above the Gothic portal is a lunette of the Madonna and Child with the patron saints of Gubbio, John the Baptist and Ubaldo, by Bernardino di Nanni.

In the interior is a MUSEUM AND PICTURE GALLERY (open every day, 9–12.30, 15.30–18; winter 9–13, 15–17). The arrangement is crowded and the labelling is erratic, and some of the paintings are in need of restoration. The huge barrel-vaulted HALL, where assemblies were held of the Comune, contains sculptural fragments, coats of arms, architectural fragments, an interesting Byzantine sarcophagus, Roman inscriptions, and sarcophagi. A few steps lead up to a small room with an eclectic collection of weights, glass, keys, architectural material, and coins. The room beyond, formerly the chapel, contains the seven celebrated *Eugubian Tables. These are bronze tablets found in 1444 near the city which were sold to the

Comune in 1456. They bear inscriptions in the Umbrian language, five in Etruscan and two in Latin characters. They record the rules of a college of priests, and date probably from 250–150 BC. They are the most important epigraphs in the Umbrian language known, and the most notable ritual texts to have survived from antiquity. More coins minted in Gubbio are exhibited here, and the fresco of the Madonna and Child with saints is attributed to Guido Palmerucci.

A very steep flight of stairs (constructed in 1488) leads up to the Picture Gallery (which also contains some furniture). R1 is on the extreme left and contains works by Guido Palmerucci, two 14C reliquaries, 13C Crosses, a Byzantine diptych, and an interesting little reliquary cupboard with 13C and 14C painted decoration. R2 has 14C frescoes mostly by 'Mello da Eugubio' (detached from Santa Maria Nuova) and a terracotta Pietà by the German school. R3 has a 16C doorway. The Madonna of the Pomegranate, attributed to Pier Francesco Fiorentino, is still missing after its theft in 1979. The MAIN HALL has a good brick vault and—an unexpected sight—a symbolic 14C fountain, now dry. The gonfalon of the Confraternity of the Madonna della Misericordia, a fine work by Sinibaldo Ibi, has been removed for restoration. Also here: 16C Flemish School, Deposition; Benedetto Nucci, Madonna of the Misericordia; Francesco Signorelli, Immaculate Conception. R5 contains 17C works, including paintings by Antonio Gherardi, Spagnoletto, and Rutilio Manetti. A door opens on to the LOGGIA with a splendid view: straight ahead is the church of San Francesco with the Loggia dei Tiratori, and below is the square campanile of San Giovanni. To the right is the Roman Theatre in a green field, and further right the medieval district of the town with several towers. On the left is the Piazza, and the Duomo can be seen above on the hillside.

Opposite Palazzo dei Consoli is *Palazzo Pretorio* (or 'dei Priori'; now the town hall), designed by Gattapone to pair with Palazzo dei Consoli, but left unfinished in 1350. Its interesting interior is constructed around a central pilaster which supports the Gothic vaulting on all floors. An L-shaped wing built in brick was added on the left in the 17C.

Beneath a narrow archway (signposted) the stepped medieval Via Galeotti leads up to Via Ducale. A steep climb continues up past the 14C Palazzo dei Canonici (with a huge 16C barrel in its cellars), to the 13C **Duomo** (open all day). The INTERIOR has remarkable stone vaulting and fine works of art in its chapels, most of them by local painters. SOUTH SIDE. First niche, Antonio Gherardi, Adoration of the Magi; second niche, Virgilio Nucci, Madonna of the Consolation. The fifth chapel (of the Holy Sacrament) is a splendid Baroque work of 1644–72 decorated by Francesco Allegrini, with the Birth of the Virgin on the left wall by Antonio Gherardi. Sixth niche, Benedetto Nucci, Christ with St Thomas; seventh niche, Dono Doni, Way to Calvary; eighth niche, Benedetto Nucci, Madonna and saints. In the PRESBYTERY is a fine carved episcopal throne by Girolamo Maffei. The stained glass dates from 1913, and the frescoes are by the local painter Augusto Stoppoloni. NORTH SIDE. Tenth niche, Benedetto Nucci, St Ubaldo, and, beneath the altar is a Roman sarcophagus; eighth niche, Sinibaldo Ibi, Madonna and Child with saints, signed and dated 1507; seventh niche, Timoteo Viti, St Mary Magdalene; sixth niche, Nativity by the school of Pinturicchio in a fine frame; fifth niche, Virgilio Nucci, Conversion of St Paul; fourth niche, Dono Doni, Pietà; third niche, Virgilio Nucci, Christ in the Garden; first niche, Antonio Gherardi, Nativity, and, above, an early fresco.

A MUSEUM (reached from the S side, but closed since thefts in 1990) has been arranged in the Refectory of the old convent. Its treasures include: a fresco of the Crucifixion and Saints and the Madonna and Child attributed to Guido Palmerucci (restored); detached frescoes by Giacomo di Benedetto di Beda (15C) from the crypt of Santa Maria dei Laici. Part of the celebrated Flemish *Cope, designed by a disciple of Justus of Ghent and presented by Marcello Cervini (Pope Marcellus II; 1555) was stolen in 1990.

A lane climbs the hillside planted with orchards and olive groves, along the N flank of the Duomo, with its fine arches. It continues up through the 13C walls to Sant'Ubaldo (see below).

Opposite the Duomo is the entrance (open 9–13.30) to the peaceful *COURTYARD of **Palazzo Ducale**. The palace was built for Federico da Montefeltro after 1470, in imitation of that at Urbino, and the design is attributed to Luciano Laurana or Francesco di Giorgio Martini. The beautiful Renaissance courtyard is built in pietra serena and red brick (recently restored). A delicately carved doorway leads off the courtyard to the main staircase, but at present the interior is not open to the public. Some carved doorways and fireplaces remain, but most of its contents were sold many years ago, including the intarsia studio of the Duke, now in the Metropolitan Museum of New York. The palace was built on the site of the Lombard 'Corte' and the 12C Palazzo Comunale, part of which still exists supported by a huge vaulted gallery, known as the *'Voltone'* (entered off Via Ducale below the entrance to the courtyard). From the gallery a delightful hanging garden is reached, near the former entrance to Palazzo Ducale.

From Piazza Grande (see above) the wide *Via dei Consoli** leads downhill past a series of lovely palaces and Via Gattapone from which the back and flank of Palazzo dei Consoli can be seen. Largo del Bargello has a pretty circular fountain. This is known as the 'Fontana dei Pazzi' as anyone may obtain a 'patente da matto' (a licence of madness) if he runs three times around the fountain while three native 'Eugubini' drench him with water. The Gothic *Palazzo del Bargello* built in 1302, was the first Palazzo Pubblico in Gubbio. Via San Giuliano on the left is an attractive road with a good view up of Palazzo dei Consoli. Via dei Consoli continues down past an ancient house with a tower to cross a bridge over the Camignano. The view right takes in the houses on the river front with the medieval tower of Palazzo Gabrielli on the left, and the Eremo di Sant'Ambrogio on the hillside of Monte Calvo. Via dei Priori ends in Piazza Giordano Bruno with the 14C church of **San Domenico**. The interior dates from 1765 and has niches decorated with stuccoes around the side altars. SOUTH SIDE. In the first two chapels, 15C frescoes; third chapel, Francesco Allegrini, Madonna and saints. The choir has stalls dating from the 16C. The *lectern, with intarsia attributed to Terzuolo has been removed. NORTH SIDE. Seventh chapel, seated 16C statue of St Anthony in varnished terracotta; sixth chapel, Giovanni Baglione, Mary Magdalene; fifth chapel, Tommaso Nelli, St Vincent Ferrer; fourth chapel, Raffaellino del Colle (attributed), Madonna and Child; second chapel, Tommaso Nelli, Scenes from the Life of Saints Vincent Ferrer and Peter Martyr. The first chapel, with 15C frescoes, is covered for restoration.

Just out of the piazza, at the beginning of Via Cavour, is the 15C Palazzo Beni (being restored). The medieval district can be explored by taking Via Cleofe Borromei on the right of San Domenico (with a view of the hillside) and then Via del Popolo left past the *Teatro Comunale*, built in 1727 by Bartolomeo Benveduti, to Porta Castello. Outside the gate, beyond Santa Lucia and on the corner of Viale del Teatro Romano, is the church of *San Benedetto*, with a fine 18C interior by Bartolomeo Benveduti. Beyond, in

Largo del Bargello, Gubbio

Via Tifernate, is the Gothic church of *San Secondo* which contains (second S altar) Stefano Tofanelli (19C), Martyrdom of St Secondo and (second N altar) Bernardino di Nanni, Madonna and Child with angels. In the little cemetery, beyond the fine cloister, is a chapel with frescoes by Giacomo di Benedetto di Beda (1457). Inside the gate, the pretty Via Capitano del Popolo, with 13C houses leads to the 13C *Palazzo del Capitano del Popolo* with a private museum of instruments of torture and modern sculpture (open 10–20). *Porta Metauro* retains its wood doors. Outside the gate, in a picturesque corner of the town, a lane (right) leads over a bridge, with views, to the church of *Santa Croce* (being restored), with gilded wood decoration of the 17C, a 16C ceiling, and paintings by Virgilio Nucci and Francesco Allegrini. In Via Gabrielli, which returns to Piazza Giordano Bruno, is the entrance (not at present open) to a park laid out in the early 19C by the Ranghiasci (approached by a picturesque covered bridge) which extends as far as Palazzo Ducale. At No. 25 is Palazzo Gabrielli, next to its tower. Numerous alleys lead down to the pretty river-front.

Via XX Settembre leads out of the other side of Piazza Grande and steps descend to Via Savelli Della Porta (with a fine doorway at No. 16). At the end of this street is the former 13C church of **Santa Maria Nuova** (ring at No. 66 Via Dante for the custodian) which has a fresco known as the

*Madonna del Belvedere, a very beautiful work by Ottaviano Nelli, perhaps his masterpiece. There are also other frescoes here by his pupils, 16C carved wood altars, and church vestments. Above Via Dante (left) is the 15C *Arco di San Marziale* on the site of the Porta Vehia of the Umbrian era. Beyond the arch is the simple church of *Sant'Andrea* with two naves (recently restored), perhaps dating from the 11C. Via Dante leads down to *Porta Romana*, outside which is the church of **Sant'Agostino**, a 13C church with the triumphal arch and apse entirely frescoed by Ottaviano Nelli and his pupils (1420). On the fifth S altar, fresco of St Ubaldo and two saints with scenes from the life of St Augustine, also by Nelli. The altarpiece of the Baptism of St Augustine is by Felice Damiani. Near the church is the station for the cablecar which climbs the hillside to Sant'Ubaldo (see below). Via di Porta Romana leads out of the town into attractive countryside.

Inside Porta Romana Via Dante (with a fountain and a fresco) leads down left. On the corner of Corso Garibaldi is an unexpected large tabernacle with a statue of St Ubaldo erected in 1761. Opposite is the church of *Santissima Trinità* (closed) next to its monastery with an interesting wall. Corso Garibaldi, in which is the 16C *Palazzo Accoromboni* where Vittoria Accoromboni (the model for Webster's heroine in 'The White Devil') was born in 1557, continues downhill and Via Vincenzo Armanni diverges left for the large church of **San Pietro**. It has four worn Corinthian columns on its façade, perhaps dating from the 11C. The 16C INTERIOR was decorated with stuccoes in the 18C. SOUTH SIDE, first altar, Rutilio Manetti, Martyrdom of St Bartholomew; fourth altar, Giannicola di Paolo, Visitation; fifth altarpiece and frescoes by Raffaellino del Colle. SOUTH TRANSEPT, Agostino Tofanelli (1770–1834), Death of St Romualdo. NORTH TRANSEPT, venerated wooden Crucifix. NORTH SIDE, third altar, Francesco Allegrini, St Michael Archangel; second altar, Virgilio Nucci, St Sebastian. The splendid Baroque organ is carved by Antonio and Giovanni Battista Maffei (1598).

Outside Porta Vittoria, Via della Piaggiola leads to the church of **Santa Maria della Piaggiola** (see the Plan) with a beautiful Baroque interior (1613–25), with fine stuccoes and statues (if closed, ask at San Pietro). It contains a Pietà by Domenico di Cecco, and on the high altar a Madonna and Child by Ottaviano Nelli (repainted and restored), and paintings by Annibale Beni (1764–1845). Across the Camignano, on the main road to Perugia, is the church of *Santa Maria del Prato* (see the Plan; being restored). It was built in 1662 on a plan taken from San Carlino alle Quattro Fontane by Borromini in Rome. The interior, with fine stucco work, has an elliptical dome frescoed by Francesco Allegrini. The altarpieces are by Allegrini (Martyrdom of St Stephen) and Ciro Ferri (St Ubaldo and Frederick Barbarossa). Via della Piaggiola (see above) leads SE across the Avarello to Via Frate Lupo (15min walk) and the little *Chiesa della Vittorina*, a chapel in an isolated position. Built in the 13C, it has a Gothic vault. It was transformed in the 16C when the frescoes were painted (attributed to Virgilio Nucci). In a wood near here, St Francis is traditionally thought to have tamed the wolf of Gubbio (commemorated in front of the church in 1973 by a bronze bas-relief by Francesco Vignola).

Via Reposati leads from San Pietro back down across the Camignano to Via Matteotti and Piazza 40 Martiri. Beyond Porta degli Ortacci is Viale di Teatro Romano, off which are the extensive remains of the exceptionally large *Roman Theatre* (restored) of the 1C AD. It was ruined by the Lombards and used as a quarry in the Middle Ages. Classical plays are sometimes performed here in summer. There are remains of a *Roman Mausoleum* further E (off Via Bruno Buozzi). It is 9m high and has a well-preserved burial chamber (no admission).

Environs of Gubbio

A cablecar (see above) mounts in 6min from outside Porta Romana to the basilica of **Sant'Ubaldo** (827m) on Monte Ingino, with a superb panorama. It can also be reached by a steep serpentine path above the cathedral, or by road (7km) from Porta Metauro via the Bottaccione gorge (see below) and the recreation area of *Coppo*. The church was rebuilt in 1514 and above the high altar is buried St Ubaldo. The three 'Ceri' are kept here (see above). On the hillside above (903m) are remains of the 12C *Rocca* (excavations in progress).

The **Gorge of Bottaccione** (3km) is reached outside Porta Metauro by the road for Scheggia. It ascends the pretty valley of the Camignano between Monte Ingino (right) and Monte Calvo (or 'Foce'; left), on which is the *Hermitage of Sant'Ambrogio* (1331), near a prehistoric site. It passes several old water mills and on the right of the valley is a 14C aqueduct, still in use. At Bottaccione (585m) a dam was built in the 14C across the river to supply the water mills in the valley, but the basin is now covered over. The valley is of great interest to geologists who have found in a thin layer of sedimentary rocks here a high concentration of minerals (including iridium) which may help to prove that the extinction of dinosaurs and most marine life sixty-five million years ago was caused by the impact on earth of a huge meteorite, which created an explosion of dust in the high atmosphere, big enough to have blocked out the sun's rays.

The road from Gubbio to Umbertide (N219; 29km) is described in Rte 4. At 11km it passes a turning right for *Pietralunga* (12km), a pretty medieval village (3-star hotel: 'Candeleto'; 2-star camping site 'Pineta'; and Trattoria 'Della Pace').

FROM GUBBIO TO GUALDO TADINO VIA THE VIA FLAMINIA (N298, N3, 36km). Outside Porta Metauro the road leaves Gubbio and climbs up the Bottaccione gorge (see above), reaching a summit level of 777m at the *Passo di Gubbio* with fine views of the Apennines. 12.5km *Scheggia* was a Roman station on the Via Flaminia.

N360 continues NE around the base of Monte Catria (1700m). At Isola di Fossara (9km) a by-road leads left for the abbey of *Santa Maria di Sitria* (12km) founded by St Romualdo in the 11C, with a fine Romanesque church. This road winds on to the Eremo di Fonte Avellana in the Marches, see *Blue Guide Northern Italy*. N360 continues along the Sentino valley through a protected area down to Sassoferrato in the Marches.

The Via Flaminia (N3) leads S from Scheggia. 19km *Costacciaro*, is an old village with the interesting church of San Francesco. 2-star camping site 'Rio Verde', and a Youth Hostel 'Villa Scirca' at Scirca on the road to Sigillo. At (22km) *Sigillo*, the church of St Anna has frescoes by Matteo da Gualdo, and the Palazzo Comunale has a neo-classical façade. Nearby is Ponte Spiano, the remains of a Roman bridge. A by-road (9km) climbs the slopes of **Monte Cucco** (1566m) which has caves of great interest to speleologists, including the 'Grotta di Monte Cucco', 922m deep. Interesting walks can be taken in this protected area of natural beauty, frequented also by hang-gliders (information at Costacciaro, where there is also the 'Centro Nazionale di Speleologia'). 28km *Fossato di Vico* (2-star hotel, 'Camino Vecchio'), on the railway line from Ancona to Rome. In the upper medieval town is the Cappella della Piaggiola with frescoes by Ottaviano Nelli and his school. The church of San Pietro has an interesting 11C interior.

36km **Gualdo Tadino**, a small town noted for its ceramic production. It has a fine castle, enlarged by Frederick II. The painter Matteo da Gualdo, active in the late 15C, was born in Gualdo and the Pinacoteca here has many of his works, although it has been closed for years.

Information Office, 'Pro Tadino', 39 Via Calai.

Hotel 'Gigiotto' (2-star). **Trattorie**: 'Clelia', 'Dal Bottaio', and 'Gigiotto'.

History. The town stands near the site of the ancient *Tadinum* on the Via Flaminia where Narses routed the Goths and killed Totila in 552. In the 13C Gualdo became a free commune and its castle was strengthened by Frederick II. 'Tadino' was added to its name in 1833.

In the central Piazza Martiri della Libertà are the 18C *Palazzo Comunale* and the *Duomo (San Benedetto)*, with a lovely rose window. The Gothic building of 1256 was transformed by Virginio Vespignani at the end of the 19C, when the pictorial decoration was carried out by Ulisse Ribustini. The cathedral owns a precious collection of works of art, at present not on view. On the exterior of the wall of the Duomo (on Corso Italia) is a wall fountain attributed to Antonio da Sangallo the Elder. Opposite Palazzo Comunale, a passageway leads out on to a terrace with a view. From here can be seen the fine apse of San Francesco (see below). On the right is the ex-*Palazzo del Podestà* (recently restored) with its 13C tower, lowered and surmounted by a Baroque lantern. A fine coat of arms from Palazzo Comunale has been placed on the façade. Beyond a pretty Art Nouveau chemist's shop, is the church of *San Francesco* (key at the Vigili Urbani in the piazza), now deconsecrated and used for exhibitions. The exterior has a handsome N flank with tall cylindrical towers. The beautiful light INTERIOR, has a Gothic E end. Over the W door, story of St Julian, a fresco by the school of Nelli (recently restored). Other frescoes in the church have been ruined by the infiltration of water. On the S side, high up, is a huge lunette of the Dormition of the Virgin (almost totally destroyed), an extremely intresting 14C work. In the chapel beneath is a lavabo and 16C altarpiece in enamelled terracotta of local workmanship (recently restored). In the apse are various frescoes including a Crucifixion by Matteo da Gualdo, and the 14C Gothic high altar. On the N side, Roman sarcophagus front with two figures of winged Victories, and a large 14C pulpit on two columns. On the pilaster between the first and second arches, Madonna enthroned with the colossal figure of St Anne behind, interesting for its iconography.

The works of the *Pinacoteca Comunale* have been in store for many years and it is not known where they will be housed. The fine collection includes numerous paintings by Matteo da Gualdo, a polyptych by l'Alunno (1471), a painted Crucifix by a follower of the 'Master of San Francesco', and a Coronation of the Virgin by Sano di Pietro.

In Piazza XX Settembre is the church of *Santa Maria* (recently restored) with a 16C fresco outside (behind glass). Lower down the hill is the church of *Santa Chiara* (formerly 'Santa Maria di Tadino'), thought to be the earliest church in the town, now deconsecrated and restored. Beyond the Duomo, Via della Rocca (partly stepped) leads up to the **Rocca Flea* which may date from before 1000. It was restored and enlarged by Frederick II who surrounded it with a wall. The interesting interior, with fine vaulted rooms, is being restored and is at present closed to the public.

A minor road to Perugia from Gualdo (30km) runs through a pretty wooded valley and passes *Casa Castalda* (14km), with medieval walls and a triptych by Matteo da Gualdo in its church. *Valfabbrica* (23km) preserves two towers of its medieval castle. Outside the village is a huge dam above the Chiascio river.

From Gualdo a by-road (8km) climbs NE to *Valsorda*, with a magnificent view. 3-star hotel 'Stella' and 1-star camping site. Delightful walks can be taken in this area. Near here is the church of Santissima Trinità on Monte Serra Santa (1348m) dating from the 12C. The altarpiece is a copy by Giuseppe Pericoli (1928) of the glazed terracotta altarpiece now in San Francesco in Gualdo.

Nocera Umbra, described in Rte 6, is 14km S of Gualdo Tadino, reached by the Via Flaminia.

The direct road back to Gubbio (N219; 24km) passes close to *San Pellegrino* (6km), a pretty little hill village. In the church, with frescoes by Matteo da Gualdo, is a triptych by Girolomo di Giovanni da Camerino (1465), recently refound after its theft. The 11C *Castel d'Alfiolo* (19km), in the middle of tobacco plantations, has an attractive frieze on its façade dating from 1224.

6

Spello, Foligno, and Trevi

These three small towns are situated close together in the wide alluvial plain known as the 'Valle Umbra' SE of Perugia. They are all just off the fast **Road** (N75, N3) from Perugia to Spoleto. The 'superstrada' (N75) runs from Perugia past the turning for Assisi (see Rte 2) to (31km) *Spello*. Beyond Spello N75 links up with N3 for (39km) *Foligno* and (50km) *Trevi*. It continues past (54km) the temple and spring of *Clitunno* into (68km) *Spoleto* (described in Rte 11).

Railway. The Terontola–Foligno branch line has services from Perugia to *Spello* (40mins) and to *Foligno* (45mins), with connections from Florence and Rome. *Foligno* is also on the Rome–Ancona line, with stations at *Trevi* and *Campello sul Clitunno* (slow trains only).

Buses connect Perugia with Spello and Foligno.

Information Office 'APT del Folignate e Nocera Umbra', 12 Piazza Garibaldi, Foligno (Tel. 0742/350493).

SPELLO is a beautiful little medieval town (8000 inhab.), well preserved, and charmingly situated on the southernmost slope of Monte Subasio (314m). The Roman 'Hispellum' it is particularly interesting for its Roman remains. The buildings are built of pink-and-white stone, quarried locally, and are well kept and decorated with colourful flowerpots. The hillside is planted with olives.

Information Office, 'Pro Loco', Via Cavour (next to the church of Sant'Andrea).

Railway Station on the Terontola–Foligno line, c 1km from Porta Consolare.

Car parking. It is best to park outside the walls, although there is a car park behind the church of Sant'Andrea. There are plans to close the centre to traffic and build a car park (provided with escalators) below Sant'Andrea.

Hotels. 3-star: 'La Bastiglia', 17 Via dei Molini (off Piazza Vallegloria). 2-star: 'Il Cacciatore', 42 Via Giulia. **Camping site**: 'Internazionale Umbria', località Chiona (2-star).

Restaurants. 1st class: 'Il Molino', 6 Via Cavour, 'Il Cacciatore', Via Giulia; 'La Bastiglia' (see above). Trattoria: 'La Cantina', 2 Via Cavour, 'Il Pinturicchio', Largo Mazzini. Places to **picnic** outside Porta Montanara.

Annual Festival, 'Infiorate' on Corpus Domini when the streets are carpeted with fresh flowers in numerous different designs.

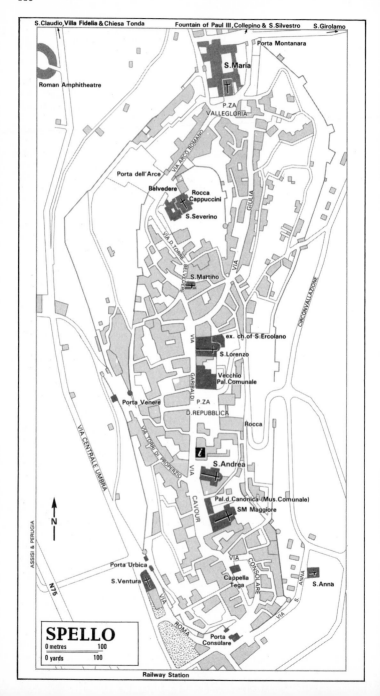

S.Claudio, Villa Fidelia & Chiesa Tonda

Fountain of Paul III, Collepino & S.Silvestro   S.Girolamo

Porta Montanara

S.Maria

Roman Amphitheatre

P.ZA
VALLEGLORIA

VIA ARCO ROMANO

Porta dell'Arce

VIA GIULIA

Belvedere   Rocca
Cappuccini

S.Severino

VIA D. TORRE BELVEDERE

S.Martino

CIRCONVALLAZIONE

ex. ch. of S.Ercolano

VIA GARIBALDI

S.Lorenzo

Vecchio
Pal. Comunale

Porta Venere

P.ZA
D.REPUBBLICA

Rocca

VIA TORRI DI PROPERZIO

VIA CAVOUR

S.Andrea

Pal. d. Canonica (Mus. Comunale)

SM Maggiore

VIA CENTRALE UMBRA

N

ASSISI & PERUGIA

N75

Porta Urbica

VIA CONSOLARE

S.Ventura

VIA ROMA

Cappella
Tega

VIA S. ANNA

S.Anna

Porta
Consulare

SPELLO
0 metres   100
0 yards   100

Railway Station

History. On the site of a settlement of the Umbri, it was a Roman Municipium and then the 'Splendidissima colonia Iulia Hispellum' flourished here. Constantine named Hispellum the religious centre of Umbria. After destruction by the Lombards, it became part of the Duchy of Spoleto. In c 1238 it was destroyed by Frederick II and then came under the dominion of Perugia.

The main entrance to the town is through the 14C *Portonaccio*. Beyond is *Porta Consolare, a fine Roman gateway with three arches. The ancient Roman road has been revealed here. On the upper part of the façade, rebuilt in the Middle Ages, are three Republican statues found near the amphitheatre, and placed here at the end of the 17C. The gate is flanked by medieval buildings including a tower, on Roman foundations. On the left Via Roma skirts a fine stretch of Augustan walls, built in pink-and-white stone from Monte Subasio, as far as *Porta Urbica* (or 'Santa Ventura'), flush with the walls, also of the Augustan period. Here is a small door through a tower in the walls (recently reopened; steps lead up to Via del Tempio di Diana). The medieval church of *Santa Ventura*, outside the walls, has a 13C fresco fragment and an interesting high altar.

From Porta Consolare the steep and winding Via Consolare and Via Cavour, on the line of the ancient 'cardo maximus', climb to the centre of the town. At the beginning are a number of picturesque medieval streets. The 14C *Cappella Tega* has 15C frescoes by Nicolò Alunno and Pietro di Mazzaforte (attributed). At the beginning of Via Cavour is the Collegiata of **Santa Maria Maggiore** (closed 12.30–14). Founded in the 12C it was reconsecrated in 1513. The FAÇADE was rebuilt in 1644 by Belardino da Como incorporating Romanesque carving traditionally attributed to Binello and Rodolfo (12–13C). The carved wood doors date from the 17C. At the foot of the Romanesque campanile are two Roman columns made from Luni marble.

The large INTERIOR was transformed in 1656–70 when it was decorated with fine stuccoes attributed to Agostino Silva. The funerary altar of Gaio Titieno Flacco (60 AD), one of the best pieces of Roman carving found in the city, is now used as a stoup; an unfinished marble Corinthian capital serves as the other stoup. SOUTH SIDE. The altarpieces date from the 17C. The font is by Antonio di Gasparino (1509–11). SOUTH TRANSEPT. The altar of the Madonna of Loreto is perhaps the best work of Agostino Silva in the church. The Cappella del Crocifisso (at present covered for restoration) contains detached frescoes. EAST END. The delightful baldacchino over the high altar was carved by Rocco da Vicenza (1512–15). It has eight terracotta heads of prophets by Gian Domenico da Carrara (1562). On the triumphal arch is a small stained glass tondo attributed to Tommaso Porro (1538). On the two pilasters flanking the apse are two very late frescoes by Perugino (1521), a Pietà and a Madonna and saints. The Choir stalls are by Pier Nicola da Spoleto (1512–20). NORTH TRANSEPT. In the Cappella del Sacramento is a tabernacle carved in 1562 by Gian Domenico da Carrara. Above a lavabo is a painting of an angel attributed to Pinturicchio. The intarsia bench dates from the 16C. In the little adjoining room can be seen a fresco of the Madonna and Child also attributed to Pinturicchio (but largely repainted). The altar in the transept is decorated in stucco by the 17C Lombard school. Above the sacristy door, in a fine frame, is an altarpiece by the local painter Carlo Lamparelli (late 17C). NORTH SIDE. The pulpit is a good work by Simone da Campione. The *frescoes (restored in 1978) in the *CAPPELLA BAGLIONI (light; fee) were commissioned from Pinturicchio by Troilo Baglioni, prior of the church, in 1500. They are among his best works, and he may have been helped by Giovanni Battista Caporali and perhaps also Eusebio da San Giorgio. The three large lunettes, which incorporate numerous classical details, represent the Annunciation, the Adoration of the Shepherds, and Christ among the doctors, and in the vault are four sibyls. In the Annunciation scene, beneath a shelf, hangs a self-portrait of the artist. In the scene of Christ among the doctors the figure in a black habit on the left is a portrait of Troilo Baglioni. The majolica floor dates from 1566 (perhaps of Deruta manufacture).

The MUSEO COMUNALE is to be housed in the adjoining *Palazzo della Canonica* which is being restored. Works of art from the church to be exhibited here include: a precious enamelled 14C Cross by Paolo Vanni, and the bell from the campanile, signed and dated 1209 by Bencivenni da Pisa. A Madonna and Child attributed to Pinturicchio and stolen in 1970 has still not been refound. The collection formerly in the Vecchio Palazzo Comunale includes two Roman marble portrait heads, a 15C stone and terracotta Pietà, and a diptych by Cola Petruccioli (1391). On the right of the church is *Palazzo Priorale*.

Farther up on the right is the church of **Sant'Andrea**. In the INTERIOR there are lights for the frescoes. SOUTH SIDE. First niche, Tommaso Corbo, Madonna and Saints (1532); second niche, Dono Doni, Mary and Joseph (1565). Beyond, in a smaller niche, 14C fresco fragment of the Madonna and Child. The E end is being restored: in the right arm of the crossing there is a large altarpiece of the *Madonna and Child with saints (light on the door to the right) by Pinturicchio and Eusebio da San Giorgio, and a tondo of the Redeemer, also by them (restored in 1979). The pretty high altar has 14C columns. The large *Crucifix is attributed to an Umbrian master of the late 13C (a follower of Giotto, perhaps the 'Maestro di Farneto'). NORTH SIDE. On the pulpit, Resurrection, attributed to Pinturicchio; 14C Crucifix; and (in a chapel at the W end), 15C frescoes by a local master.

In front of the church, Via Torri di Properzio descends to the *Porta Venere*, of the Augustan age, the best preserved of the Roman gateways. It is flanked by two handsome pink 12-sided towers.

A short way beyond Sant'Andrea opens Piazza della Repubblica. In the atrium of the *Vecchio Palazzo Comunale* an archeological collection is provisionally arranged (open Monday, Wednesday, Friday, and Saturday, 8–14) including Roman fragments, sarcophaghi, and inscriptions. On the upper floor (where some of the rooms are frescoed) are works by Emilio Greco. Other works of art will eventually be displayed in the Museo Comunale next to Santa Maria Maggiore (see above). Still higher is the Romanesque church of **San Lorenzo**, traditionally thought to have been founded in 1120. The interesting façade preserves Roman and medieval fragments. INTERIOR. On the W wall, fresco of St Bernardine of Siena, and the Madonna and Child with St Catherine. SOUTH SIDE. On the first pilaster is a well carved 15C tabernacle. The second chapel dates from 1793; the tabernacle is by Flaminio Vacca (1589). On the next altar, St Catherine of Alexandria with Christ and the Virgin by Fran van de Kasteele of Brussels (1599), and at the end of the S aisle, Christ and the Virgin receiving Souls from Purgatory, a very unusual painting also by Kasteele. The baldacchino over the high altar dates from 1631 and on the high altar is a gilded silver Cross of 1820. The choir stalls were carved by Andrea Campano da Modena (1530–34) who also carved the fine intarsia furniture in the Sacristy. Also here is a 15C lavabo. The pulpit in the left aisle was carved by Francesco Costantini (1600).

Via di Torre Belvedere (keep left) leads up past the little Romanesque church of *San Martino* (usually closed) to the top of the hill. The Belvedere

Borgo dell'Arco d'Augusto, Spello

provides a fine view: to the left is Montefalco and the plain in front of the hills of Bettona and Perugia, and to the right Santa Maria degli Angeli, Assisi and Monte Subasio. Below the hill of Spello, the overgrown Roman amphitheatre is clearly seen beyond the main road next to the modern sports stadium. Nearby are the church of San Claudio and the Villa Fidelia with its garden. The Roman arch here ('Porta dell'Arce') probably dates from the Republican era (part of it is underground). Remains of the *Rocca* are incorporated in the convent of the Cappuccini, and the church of *San Severino*, one of the oldest in the town. Via Arco Romano descends to Piazza di Vallegloria with the church and monastery of *Santa Maria*, founded c 1320. The road to the right leaves the town by the 18C *Porta Montanara* on the site of a medieval gate. Here can be seen remains of the Roman aqueduct (reused in the Middle Ages) from Monte Subasio. Viale Poeta, with fine views, leads into the country past the Fountain of Paul III, incorporating a medieval sarcophagus.

Via Giulia returns from Piazza di Vallegloria towards the centre of Spello. It passes the 18C theatre, a round tower of the Rocca, and (near the remains of a Roman gate), the characteristic Borgo dell'Arco d'Augusto. Just before rejoining Via Garibaldi an alley on the left leads to the former church of Sant'Ercolano of ancient foundation.

The road below the town on the W (parallel to the 'superstrada' and railway) passes the ruined and overgrown **Roman Amphitheatre** (closed for restoration), dating from the 1C AD. It could hold some 15,000 spectators. On the other side of the road is the charming little 12C church of *San Claudio* (usually closed), with a bell-cote. Just beyond is the conspicuous **Villa Fidelia**, on the site of a Classical sanctuary dating from the Republican era. At the beginning of the 18C a villa was constructed here by Donna Teresa Pamphili Grillo, modelled on the Villa Madama in Rome, and the garden laid out. The present building dates from the late 18C or early 19C and is attributed to Giuseppe Piermarini. It is surrounded by a terraced garden with fine cypresses.

Since 1985 Villa Fidelia has housed the STRAKA-COPPA COLLECTION (open Thursday, Saturday, and Sunday, 10–13, 15–18) of Italian art (well labelled). On the *ground floor* is an interesting display of early 20C works and documents relating to the Futurists. The *first floor* has contemporary works. On the *top floor* are early paintings including (R1) Diana and a warrior by Lodovico Carracci, and the Portrait of a Gentleman by Carlo Ceresa. R6 has Venetian paintings including a Madonna and Child by Vincenzo Catena and the copy of a portrait by Titian of Laura de' Dianti with a boy. The collection also includes silver, ceramics, porcelain, and furniture. Nearby, right on the 'superstrada', is the **Chiesa Tonda** (1517–39), an attractive centrally planned Renaissance church. It is now deconsecrated and privately owned (closed).

From outside Porta Montanara (see above), a by-road leads up to **Collepino** (6km), a medieval walled village (600m) with fine views. (Restaurant, 'Taverna di San Silvestro'.) Above the village, on the slopes of Monte Subasio, is the Romanesque church of *San Silvestro*. The abbey here was founded by St Romualdo in 1025. It has a Roman sarcophagus as its altar and a fine crypt. This beautiful unsurfaced road continues across Monte Subasio towards Assisi (21km from Collepino; see Rte 2E).

Outside Porta Montanara (see above), another road leads to the church of *San Girolamo* (1km), next to the cemetery. Founded in 1474, it is preceded by a fine portico beneath which are frescoes of the Epiphany by a follower of Pinturicchio and of St Francis by Mezzastris. Inside is a fine carved Crucifix and another fresco by a follower of Pinturicchio.

The 'Circonvallazione' (see the Plan) runs outside the walls on the E side of Spello, and passes several gates. The church of *Sant'Anna* contains numerous frescoes by local 13–16C artists. Via Sant'Anna returns to Porta Consolare.

FOLIGNO, with a number of industries, is the third largest town in Umbria (after Perugia and Terni) with 50,000 inhabitants. It is situated on the river Topino and has numerous interesting palaces and some churches with good 18C interiors.

Tourist Offices. 'APT' Information Office, Porta Romana (Tel. 0742/60459); 'APT del Folignate-Nocera Umbra', 12 Piazza Garibaldi (Tel. 0742/350493).

Railway Station on the branch line from Terontola and Perugia, and on the main line from Ancona to Rome.

Buses to Montefalco, Bevagna and Todi; to Perugia direct and via Assisi, and to Rome.

Car parking near Porta Firenze and Porta Todi (with hourly tariff).

Hotels. 4-star: 'Nuovo Poledrini', 3 Viale Mezzetti. 3-star: 'Italia', 12 Piazza Matteotti; 'Le Mura', 29 Via Bolletta. 2-star: 'Roma', 10 Viale Mezzetti; 'Nunziatella', 3 Via Pagliarini. *On the outskirts*: 'Villa Roncalli', 25 Viale Roma (1km from the centre), with a 1st-class restaurant (3-star). **Youth Hostel** 'Fulginium', Piazza San Giacomo.

Restaurants. 1st-class: 'Villa Roncalli' (see above); 'Da Remo', 49 Viale Cesare Battisti. Trattorie and Pizzerie: 'Dei Franceschi', Via dei Franceschi; 'La Taverna', 9 Piazza Branducci; 'La Tartuga', 19 Via Corso Nuovo; 'Al Griffo', Piazza San Domenico; 'Del Corso', Corso Cavour; 'La Brocca', Via XX Settembre; 'Marechiaro', 58 Via Piermarini.

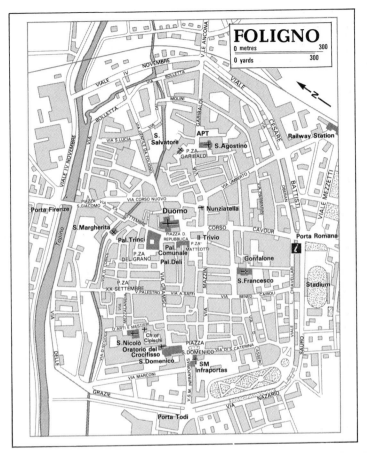

FOLIGNO

On the outskirts (on the road to Bevagna): 'Lu Centru de lu Munnu', 8 Via Lago di Cecita, Fiamenga.

Annual Festival. The 'Giostra della Quintana', a joust dating from 1613, was reinstated in 1946 and is held in the stadium on the second and third Sundays of September, and there are celebrations in 17C costume in various districts of the town and in Piazza della Repubblica. Large fairs are held in September, and for 3 days around 26 January (San Feliciano), where typical local products can still be found.

History. Foligno was the *Fulginia* of the Romans and absorbed the population of *Forum Flaminii*, another Roman town 3.5km W. Long a free commune, latterly under the rule of the Trinci family, it passed to the States of the Church in 1439. Here was born Angela of Foligno (1248–1309), who became a Franciscan tertiary, and one of the most famous mystics of Europe. Its school of painting was largely indebted to Nicolò da Foligno, or Nicolò di Liberatore, called l'Alunno (c 1430–1502), who has a very unusual style. Printing was introduced at Foligno in 1470, only six years after the first book printed in Italy had appeared at Subiaco. The first edition of Dante's *Divina Commedia* was published here in 1472. Vernon Lee took a 17C palace in Foligno as the setting for her story 'The Doll' (1927). Serious damage was done to the town by bombing in 1943–44. Raphael's Madonna di Foligno is now in the Vatican.

Lion at the south-west portal of the Duomo, Foligno

The centre of the town is **Piazza della Repubblica**. Here is *Palazzo Comunale* with a neo-classical façade by Antonio Mollari, with decorative bronze lamps. A medieval tower of the earlier town hall protrudes above the façade. Next to it is the Renaissance *Palazzo Orfini* (with traces of external painted decoration), which may have been the seat of the first printing house in the town (see above), and remains of *Palazzo Pretorio* with a large arch. At the far end of the square is the neo-classical façade (1841–47) of **Palazzo Trinci** which is undergoing a lengthy restoration. Its fine Gothic exterior (1389–1407) can be seen from Piazza del Grano. It has a restored brick courtyard and Gothic stair. The interior, with the **Pinacoteca Civica** is at present not open (for information ring at the Biblioteca Comunale). The chapel and hall contain paintings by Ottaviano Nelli. The Sala delle Arti Liberali o dei Pianeti, and the Sala dei Giganti contain interesting faded mural *paintings of the 15C. Here also are exhibited paintings by the native artist Pierantonio Mezzastris, detached frescoes by Bartolomeo di Tommaso, works by Lattanzio, son of Alunno, and Dono Doni, and a fresco of the Annunciatory Angel from the deconsecrated church of San Domenico attributed to Benozzo Gozzoli.

On the last side of the square is the magnificent secondary (N) façade of the **Duomo** (1133–1201). The beautiful portal (covered for restoration) was carved by Rodolfo and Binello. Between the N façade and W entrance of the Duomo is the pink-and-white *Palazzo della Canonica* with Gothic two-light windows (reconstructed in 1926). The main façade of the Duomo, also pink-and-white, with a rose window, was restored in 1904.

The huge ornate INTERIOR, reminiscent of St Peter's in Rome, was decorated by the native architect Giuseppe Piermarini in the 18C on a design by Luigi Vanvitelli. SOUTH SIDE. First altar, Enrico Bartolomei, Death of Messalina (1860); second altar, Giovanni Andrea Lazzarini, Holy Family (18C). In the SACRISTY is a fine painting (in very good condition) of the Madonna and St John by Alunno, on either side of a 14C sculpted wood Crucifix. Two busts here of Bartolomeo and Diana Roscioli have recently been identified as works by Gian Lorenzo Bernini. In a little room off the S transept (unlocked on request) is all that remains of a life-size 18C silver statue of St Feliciano by Giovanni Battista Maini, seated on a throne by Andrea Pozzo. Much of it was dismantled and stolen in 1982; some parts have been remade, but the scene of the saint's martyrdom on the back of the throne was recovered. When the statue is taken in procession on 24 January, 16 men are needed to carry it. There are also three 18C Crucifixes here. Between the first and second altars on the N side is a detached 16C fresco.

Via Gramsci, with the finest palaces in the town, leads out of Piazza della Repubblica past Palazzo Trinci (see above). It is adjoined by the graceful *Palazzo Deli* or *Nuti* (16C; beautifully restored in 1989), with a fine portal and incorporating a medieval tower. The large *Palazzo Alleori Ubaldi* has a neo-classical façade and contemporary painted decorations inside by Marcello Leopardi. Since 1986 it has been restored as a cultural centre. Via Gramsci continues past (right) Via della Scuola di Arti e Mestieri.

Beyond the tiny church of *San Tommaso dei Cipischi* (1190; closed) is *San Nicolò* which conserves two fine paintings by Alunno: a polyptych of 1492 and a Coronation of the Virgin (c 1489). Via Mezzalancia leads from here to Piazza XX Settembre with the 17C Palazzo Barnabò with a good staircase. Via Giovanni dell'Acqua leads up to the picturesque Via della Conce on a canal with the old porticoed tanneries (a district particularly animated during the 'Quintana' celebrations in September). In this area, near remains of a Roman bridge, is the church of *Santa Margherita* (or San Giuseppe) with a rococo interior (key at San Giacomo).

Via Gramsci ends by the huge 18C *Palazzo Candiotti* (now a school). Its chapel, called the *Oratorio del Crocifisso* has a 17–18C interior (key at Santa Maria Infraportas). In the adjoining piazza is the church of *San Domenico*, deconsecrated and being restored as an auditorium. Important medieval frescoes have recently been discovered here. Also in the piazza is **Santa Maria Infraportas**, a Romanesque basilica with an interesting exterior and an ancient bell tower. It contains 12–14C frescoes, some by Pier Antonio Mezzastris. Via Mazzini, with 16C palaces, leads back to the centre past (right) Via Cesare Agostini with a flying arch and *Palazzo Pandolfi Elmi*, still owned by the family and beautifully maintained. To the S is the church of *San Francesco* with early frescoes, next to the oratory of the *Gonfalone* (1735). In the medieval district here is the house of Beata Angela where interesting 13–14C frescoes were discovered in 1989. Via Mazzini meets Corso Cavour, the main shopping street of the town, at a crossroads called 'Il Trivio'. Via Garibaldi continues past the *Nunziatella* an oratory (open in summer on request at the town hall) which contains a fresco by Perugino, and the deconsecrated church of the *Suffragio*, with a Greek-cross interior of 1728–35. In Piazza Garibaldi is the church of *Sant'Agostino* with an 18C interior. An early 18C wood statue of the Madonna, fully robed, is exhibited on 12 January and 31 May. Opposite is *San Salvatore* with a 14C façade. The restored 18C interior contains beautiful fragments of 16C Flemish tapestries illustrating the Story of Joseph.

FROM FOLIGNO TO COLFIORITO, 25km, N77. At (4km) a by-road (signposted) leads through the village of Uppello (keep right) and under an archway and then left (signposted Casale); a rough road continues up to the **Abbey of Sassovivo** in an isolated position on the beautiful wooded slopes of Monte Serrone. A Benedictine foundation of the 11C, it is now occupied by a religious community. The church (rebuilt in 1851) and the delightful little *cloister (1229–32, by Roman sculptors) may be visited. The main road continues through Colle San Lorenzo with fine views ahead. 7km **Pale** lies at the bottom of a valley, wedged in between two rock faces. It has been noted for its paper mills since the 13C and one large old mill survives here. Beyond it (keep left) are remains of 14C walls. The short street beyond the arch ends at the church of San Biagio, with a pyramidal tower (key at No. 4 Via della Mura). It contains (S side) a lovely painted wood *statue of the Madonna and Child enthroned, by the 14C Umbrian school. On the N side are two paintings by Felice Damiani. From the steps of the church can be seen the Hermitage of Santa Maria Giacobbe high up on the rock face (approached by a path on the other side of the valley). It contains 14–15C frescoes (ask for the key locally). The main road continues along the floor of the valley. It passes *Scopoli* (Luxury-class restaurant 'Sette Mari') with a 15C castle. At (10km) *Casenove* the road for Norcia (see Rte 12) diverges right, while this route ascends, in places steeply, through the wooded river valley, with splendid views right, to the *Valico Colfiorito* (821m). To the N, Monte Pennino (see below) is seen beyond Monte Acuto, while to the right of the road rises Monte Profoglio (1322m). There is a pretty cultivated and marshy upland plain on the borders of Umbria and the Marches just after (25km) **Colfiorito** (3-star hotel: 'Villa Fiorita', Via del Lago). The attractive villages are built of the light local stone, and the plain is interesting for its vegetation. Beyond the watershed where the river rises the road descends along the Chienti in a deep enclosed valley towards Camerino in the Marches (see *Blue Guide Northern Italy*).

FROM FOLIGNO TO NOCERA UMBRA, 22km, N3 (Via Flaminia). The road ascends the *Valtopina* with some remains of medieval castles and a number of churches, including the *Rocca di Postignano*, once a castle of the Trinci. 22km **Nocera Umbra**, is a rather grim little town (6300 inhabitants) in a fine position. Two 2-star hotels, and 2-star camping site 'La Valle'. The Nuceria Camellaria of Pliny, it was later a lordship of the Trinci family. The waters of the Sorgente Angelica at *Bagni* (4km SE) are bottled and sent all over Italy. The key of the Pinacoteca is kept by the 'Vigili Urbani' (No. 21) on the other side of the main road at the entrance to the town. Beyond Viale Matteotti, an avenue with a War Memorial, Porta Vecchia leads into the Corso. On the right a portico leads to the church of *San Filippo*, built in 1886 by Luigi Poletti. The Corso continues up past *Santa Chiara* (closed for restoration) with three altarpieces by Carlo Maratta and a fine cantoria, and then winds left to Piazza Caprera. Here the church of *San Francesco* is the seat of the *Pinacoteca* (key at the 'Vigili Urbani', see above). It contains frescoes and paintings by Matteo da Gualdo, a polyptych of the Nativity and saints by Nicolò Alunno, and a 13C Crucifix. It also includes a collection of sculpture and some archaeological material. Opposite is a building (recently restored) with Gothic elements. Beside an unusual church (being restored) Via San Rinaldo continues up to the side door of the *Duomo* with an 18C interior with a barrel vault, neo-classical pilasters. and four columns in each side chapel. The last chapel on the right side has good paintings of the Life of the Virgin by Giulio Cesare Angeli (1619) and stuccoes by Francesco Silva di Morbio. Opposite the façade of the Duomo is a tall 11C tower of the Rocca and a terrace with a fine view of the Topino valley. From Piazza Caprera a road descends to *San Giovanni* with a carved door and attractive interior with a 16C altarpiece of the Birth of the Virgin.

A road runs E from Nocera Umbra to *Bagnara* (7km) at the foot of *Monte Pennino* (1571m; winter sports facilities), with the Trattoria 'Pennino'.

The valley now widens out and the main road (N3) continues N towards Gualdo Tadino (38km from Foligno). It passes close to *Boschetto* (right) where the church, by a stream, has a chapel at the W end with frescoes by Matteo da Gualdo. Other works from the church have been removed for safety. *Gualdo Tadino* is described in Rte 5.

The road from Foligno to Bevagna (9km) is described in Rte 7.

TREVI is a pretty, well-preserved little town (6500 inhabitants) in a delightful position on a hill covered with olive groves. Of Roman foundation, it became part of the Duchy of Spoleto. It has brick and cobbled lanes and many of its old houses are decorated with pots of flowers.

Information Offfice. 'Pro Loco', Piazza Mazzini. 2- star **Hotel** 'Cochetto' (with restaurant), 13 Via Dugali. **Youth Hostel** 'Casa San Martino', 4 Viale Ciuffelli. In early October the 'Palio dei Terzieri' takes place here.

The prettiest approach from the Foligno road is by the turning for Santa Maria in Valle, just after the tall medieval *Torre Matigge* conspicuous on the main road. There is a splendid view of Trevi before the road reaches the church and monastery of *San Martino*, built on a rock and surrounded by cypresses. In the lunette over the door is a fresco by Tiberio d'Assisi. In the two tabernacles either side of the presbytery are frescoes by Mezzastris (Madonna and Child) and Tiberio d'Assisi (St Martin and the beggar). To the left of the church is a little chapel (1512; unlocked on request at the monastery) with an *Assumption and saints by Lo Spagna and *St Emiliano by Tiberio d'Assisi. There is a fine view of the plain from the 'belvedere'. An avenue continues up to Piazza Garibaldi (car parking) at the entrance to Trevi. Via Roma leads past a little piazza (left) with the orange-coloured *Teatro Clitunno* built by Domenico Mollaioli in 1874 (restored in 1991) with a back-cloth painted by Domenico Bruschi in 1877. Beyond the church of San Giovanni (open only for services at weekends) is *Piazza Mazzini* with the 15C town hall, with a tall tower. The Pinacoteca here has been closed indefinitely awaiting removal to Palazzo Lucarini (see below). In front of the town hall the stepped Via Placido Riccardi leads up to the *Duomo* (Sant'Emiliano). Founded in the 12C, it preserves Romanesque elements on the exterior. The 15C portal has a charming relief of St Emiliano between two lions and is flanked by two Roman capitals. The three original apses survive, as does another door with a statue of St Emiliano. The centrally planned interior was reconstructed in 1775 and again in 1893 by Luca Carimini. The *Altar of the Sacrament was beautifully carved by Rocco di Tommaso (1522). The two statues are by Mattia di Gaspare da Como. On the opposite side of the nave is a statue of the Redeemer by Cesare Aureli and a seated wood processional statue of St Emiliano. At the W end of the church is a large cupboard (kept locked; sometimes opened on request by the sacristan) which protects another wood statue of St Emiliano by a German sculptor (1751).

Beside the Duomo is the fine old *Palazzo Lucarini*, destined to become the seat of the Pinacoteca Comunale. The works it contains include a large altarpiece of the Coronation of the Virgin by Lo Spagna and other 15C Umbrian paintings, and archaeological material. Steps lead down beside the palace to Via Dogali, a pretty old street, which leads left to the medieval *Portico del Mostaccio*, once the main gate of the town. It continues up left and back to Piazza Mazzini. Via San Francesco (on the opposite side of the square) leads past the fine 16C Palazzo Valenti to the Gothic church of *San Francesco*, the W end of which has been concealed. It contains various fresco fragments and scagliola altars. At the W end, in a semicircular niche with a fresco of the Madonna and saints and Christ carrying the Cross (1577) is the sarcophagus (3C or 4C), used as the tomb of St Ventura (died 1310).

In the nave is an interesting organ of 1509 by Pietro di Paolo of Montefalco with a wooden gallery decorated with paintings in the 17C. Over the high altar is a fine 14C Crucifix. In the chapel to the right of the apse, 15C votive frescoes and an 18C wood altar with a statue of the Madonna. In the chapel to the left of the apse, tomb of Ottavia Attavanti and her son Alessandro Valenti (1576–77) with two fine busts, and the pavement tomb (set into the wall) of Valente Valenti (1357) and an 18C wood altar with a statue of St Anthony. From the 13C walls nearby there is a good view.

1km below the town, on the hillside, reached by the direct road back to the main road is the church of the *Madonna delle Lacrime*, a Renaissance church by Antonio Marchisi (1487). The lovely portal (1495) is by Giovanni Giampietri da Vicenza. In the interior on the S side, the first altar has 16C frescoes and the second altar an *Epiphany by Perugino with a delightful background. In the S transept, in an altar of 1621, is a lovely fresco of the Madonna and Child (1483). Behind the high altar is a worn detached fresco of the Crucifixion with the Marys at the foot of the Cross, between a Madonna and Child and an Annunciation. In the left transept chapel are *frescoes by Lo Spagna. The church also has particularly fine 16–17C funerary monuments, many with busts, of the Valenti family.

Another road leads S to (3km) *Bovara* where the church of *San Pietro* has a conspicuous campanile, heightened in 1582. The interesting façade dates from the 12C. The Romanesque interior (ring for admission at the priest's house on the right) preserves a 14C wood Crucifix. On the other side of the Foligno road, 5km N of Trevi, the 14C church of *Santa Maria di Pietrarossa* has numerous 15C votive frescoes.

Two kilometres from Trevi on the main road from Foligno to Spoleto, in the scattered comune of Campello sul Clitunno (Residence 'Vecchio Mulino') is the little *Tempietto del Clitunno, on the right behind railings in a group of pine trees above the Clitunno river. Although adjacent to the road, it is easy to miss: there is a lay-by beside it with a path to the temple, or it can be approached from the old road which runs parallel to the fast road. Ring for the custodian at the gate (9–12, 15–18; summer 9–12, 16–19; Sunday and fest. 9–12; closed Monday; tip expected). The temple is thought to have been erected in the 4C or 5C using antique fragments from the pagan edifices which once lined the river here (see below). It has a beautiful exterior with handsome classical columns and carved palaeo-Christian friezes in the pediments. The charming little interior has faded frescoes of the greatest interest (thought to date from the 7–8C) of Saints Peter and Paul and God the Father.

About 1.5km farther on along the main road (well signposted; also on the right) is the entrance to the *Fonti del Clitunno, a green oasis at the spring of the river Clitunno, the classical Clitumnus. The park (now disturbed by the main road), laid out in 1852 by Paolo Campello with weeping willows and poplars surrounding a lake inhabited by swans, is open every day 9–12, 14–17.30 (14–20 in summer).

These cool crystal clear waters were famous in antiquity and the abundant spring was dedicated to the god Clitumnus, a famous oracle whose temple was erected here. White sacrificial oxen were bred on its banks. The beauty of this sacred spot was celebrated by Propertius, Virgil, and Pliny the Younger. Soon after the Roman era the waters diminished considerably, but it continued to capture the imagination of the Romantic poets. Byron visited the river in 1817 and includes a description of it in 'Childe Harold's Pilgrimage' (Canto IV). Carducci composed a famous ode to the Clitunno in 1876. On the hillside above the main road can be seen the medieval village of *Pissignano* with a fine castle built c 1000.

About 500m beyond the lake, on the left of the main road, is the tiny chapel of *San Sebastiano* (in need of restoration) surrounded by poplars. Inside (key at the house above the road) are lovely frescoes by Lo Spagna and votive figures of St Sebastian. Just beyond in a field can be seen the little 12C church of *San Cipriano e Giustina* (ruined in the 19C). The main road now runs straight towards Spoleto. A by-road leads left to the village of *Campello sul Clitunno*. Trattoria 'Pettino'. 3-star hotel 'Benedetti' at Settecamini, and 'Le Casaline' restaurant (with some rooms), 3km E of Campello. A small antiques fair is held here on the first Sunday of each month. The church of the Madonna della Bianca here was built in 1514 and has a fine classical portal by Cione di Taddeo. The interior with an elaborate high altar was designed by Valadier. The fresco in the apse is by Fabio Angelucci (1574). In the sacristy are two frescoes by the school of Lo Spagna. Higher up on the hillside is the church of *San Lorenzo a Lenano* with 15C frescoes. Above, the ruined castle of *Campello Alto* was built in the 10C. Here is the church of San Donato with an 18C organ and a font of 1610. In the convent is a fresco of the Crucifixion and Saints by the 15C Umbrian school.

Beyond, on low ground to the right of the Spoleto road is *San Giacomo di Spoleto*. The church of San Giacomo has interesting 16C frescoes (in poor condition) by Lo Spagna (in the apse and left niche of the presbytery), a Deposition by Fabio Angelucci, and a Madonna with angels and saints by Dono Doni and Bernardino d'Assisi. Opposite the church is a rectangular castle with four angle towers built by Cardinal Albornoz, interesting for the double street of little houses inside its walls.

The main road continues to *Spoleto*, described in Rte 11.

7

Bevagna and Montefalco

These two lovely small towns are situated 6km apart close to Foligno (see Rte 6). They are in an area which produces excellent red wine (including the strong 'Sagrantino'). By car Bevagna is reached from Foligno in 9km by a straight road, the old Roman Via Flaminia, along which (right) are the conspicuous remains of two Roman tombs. Montefalco is signposted from Foligno outside Porta Todi. The road (12km) passes beside the massive square medieval *Torre di Montefalco*, overgrown with vegetation. A pretty little hamlet here, with an old mill, lies at the confluence of several rivers and canals.

Buses run from Foligno to Bevagna and Montefalco.

Information Office 'APT del Folignate e Nocera Umbra' (Tel. 0742/350493).

BEVAGNA is a charming ancient little town (4700 inhab.) on low ground (295m) surrounded by a fertile plain watered by numerous rivers including the Topino, Clitunno, and Teverone. It has considerable Roman remains and a beautiful medieval central piazza. Its walls are well preserved: the medieval circuit in places incorporates Roman fortifications of the 1C BC.

Information Office. 'Pro Loco', Piazza Silvestri.

Bus services from Foligno.

Car parking outside the walls.

Camping site 'Pian di Boccio' (3-star).

Trattorie. 'Da Nina', Piazza Garibaldi; 'La Taverna Ottavi', off Piazza Silvestri. Pastry shop and bakery: Pasticceria Polticchia', Corso Matteotti. Good places to **picnic** outside the walls.

An annual **fair** called 'La Gaite' is held here in spring.

History. Bevagna was the Roman 'Mevania' on the Via Flaminia to Narni, opened here in 220 BC. It became a Roman Municipium by 90 BC, but had lost importance by the 3C AD when the new Via Flaminia was diverted through Spoleto and Terni. Later part of the Duchy of Spoleto, Bevagna was ruled by the Trinci from 1371–1439. Hemp and flax were formally cultivated in the surrounding countryside, and the craft of rope-making is still carried on by a few inhabitants who work near Porta Guelfa or in Via Porta Molini.

The centre of the town is *Piazza Silvestri, one of the most harmonious squares in Umbria. The Roman column has a Corinthian capital and the handsome fountain dates from 1896. The 13C **Palazzo dei Consoli** has Gothic two-light windows and a wide outside stair. After the palace had been damaged by earthquake, the charming *Teatro Torti (now being carefully restored) was built inside the Gothic shell in 1872–86. The painted decoration was carried out by Domenico Bruschi and Mariano Piervittori. The stage extends above three Gothic arches towards the restored two-light windows on Largo Gramsci next to the apse of San Silvestro.

An arch (built in 1560) connects the palace to the church of *San Silvestro, with an unfinished façade and no campanile. It was built in 1195 by Maestro Binello. The beautiful *INTERIOR has a raised chancel and fine columns with double Corinthian capitals. The apse can be seen from Largo Gramsci. Opposite is *San Michele Arcangelo, the most important church in the town, built in the late-12C or early 13C. The FAÇADE has a fine 14C campanile and a *PORTAL signed by Rodolfo and Binello beneath the relief of the dragon beside the bust of St Michael on the left impost. Opposite is a flying angel. The door posts are made up of reworked Roman friezes. The wooden doors date from the 16C. The INTERIOR (restored in 1957) is similar to that of San Silvestro, with a raised chancel. SOUTH SIDE. The first chapel is a neo-classical work by Vincenzo Vitali, decorated by Traversari. Between the first and second chapels is a processional painted wood statue of St Vincent enthroned (1638). The second chapel has very ruined frescoes by the native artist Andrea Camassei (early 17C). On the NORTH SIDE is a 15C Crucifix between paintings of the Madonna, St John the Evangelist, and Mary Magdalene. A silver processional statue of St Vincent by Peter Ramoser (1785) also belongs to the church. The CRYPT is noteworthy. The exterior, with an interesting flank and beautiful apse, can be seen from Via Marconi. Near the E end is the church of *San Filippo*, built in 1725 (closed).

Also in the piazza, beyond Palazzo dei Consoli, is the church of **San Domenico**. In the INTERIOR the 18C side altars have been eliminated in recent restoration work. On the SOUTH SIDE are scagliola altar frontals. The paintings include works by Giovanni Battista Pacetti (St James, 1642), Andrea Camassei (Madonna and saints, surrounding a St Dominic by Pacetti), and the native artist Fantino (c 1557–1646; Madonna of the Rosary). The tomb of Vincenzo Antici (died 1552) bears his bust. Above the 17C HIGH ALTAR is a bronze urn containing the body of the Blessed Giacomo Bianconi (1220–1301) who founded churches and convents in the town after its destruction by Frederick II in 1249. In the CHOIR are remains of interesting early frescoes including the figure of the Madonna (from an Annunciation scene). In the chapel to the right of the Choir is a 13C wood Crucifix, and in the chapel to the left of the Choir is a 13C wood statue of the Madonna and Child. On the NORTH SIDE are more 18C scagliola altar frontals, a Madonna in Glory by Fantino, and the tomb of Properzio Antici with his bust (died 1596). The church also owns a Roman sarcophagus which was used as the first tomb of the Blessed Giacomo Bianconi.

Via del Gonfalone leads down past the side door of the church (with a

Portal of San Michele in Bevagna

tabernacle above with traces of a 14C fresco) to the church and oratory of the Gonfalone. On the left, Vicolo del Gonfalone leads beneath four arches to remains of a *Roman Edifice* (unlocked on request at the Comune). Formerly identified as baths, it is now thought this may be part of a port built on the river Clitunno. The walls are decorated with opus reticulatum.

Corso Matteotti, on the line of the old Via Flaminia, leads out of Piazza Silvestri. At No. 107 is the entrance to the *Cloister* (1629–32) of San Domenico (ring for admission at the convent) with very worn frescoed lunettes by Giovanni Battista Pacetti. On the left (No. 72) is the **Municipio** in Palazzo Lepri, with a neo-classical façade (1787). On the stairs is the MUSEO ARCHEOLOGICO, a collection formed in 1787 by the local historian Fabio Alberti, and arranged here in the 19C. The interesting Roman material, all of it found in Bevagna or its vicinity, includes architectural fragments from the Roman theatre, inscriptions, sepulchral stelae, cinerary urns of Etruscan type, fragments of reliefs and statues, and a fine portrait head of the Republican era. The PINACOTECA (admission on request at the Library) contains an Adoration of the Magi by Corrado Giaquinto, and paintings by Fantino, Giovanni Battista Pacetti, and Andrea Camassei (many of them in poor condition). The SALA CONSILIARE has wall paintings (1867) of famous natives of the town by Mariano Piervittori. The BIBLIOTECA COMUNALE and archives preserve interesting volumes and documents.

Farther on in the Corso is a little piazza with the attractive 13C façade of the former church of *Santa Maria in Laurenzia* (now a shop) with a relief of the Madonna nursing the Child. On the left is the church of the *Consolazione*, with an 18C interior decorated with stuccoes. The high altarpiece of the Holy Family is by Etienne Parrocel (1738). A statue of the Risen Christ (late 16C) is exhibited at Easter. A road on the right leads down from the Corso to the church of *Santa Margherita* (ring for admission at the convent on the left), rebuilt in 1640. The high altarpiece of the Martyrdom of St Margaret is by Andrea Camassei. In a niche behind the altar (seen through a grille) is a good fresco of the Madonna and Saints by Fantino (1592). Farther along the Corso is the church of *Santa Maria del Monte* (ring for admission at the monastery at No. 15). It contains (right altar) a fine bronze altar frontal. Near the end of the Corso (left) is the interesting façade of the former church of *San Vincenzo*, partly faced in travertine, with four Roman fluted pilasters on either side of the portal. *Porta Foligno* (restored in 1797) leads out through the Roman and medieval walls to a park with ilexes, a War Memorial by Vincenzo Jerace, and fragments of Roman buildings (1C AD). Inside the gate, Via Francesco Torti leads up under a passageway to Via dell'Anfiteatro, with pretty houses which follow the curve of the *Roman Theatre* built on this site in the 1C AD. A yellow sign marks the entrance to part of the barrel-vaulted corridor which supported the cavea of the theatre (later used as a wine cellar). On the left the road emerges beneath an arch in Via Dante Alighieri. Here a fine Roman frieze of bucrania has been set into the wall of the Casa Andreozzi. The road continues right beneath an arch supporting a terrace and emerges above Piazza Garibaldi and a Roman temple (described below). The church of *San Francesco* is at the highest point of the town. The interior dates from 1746–50. On the S side is a chapel attributed to Galeazzo Alessi, with terracotta decoration in the cupola attributed to Sante Buglioni, and a 15C carved tabernacle in the last chapel. The church also contains works by Fantino.

Steps, lined with rose bushes, descend to Piazza Garibaldi. On the right is the 13C *Porta Cannara*, the best preserved gate in the walls (outside of which a path leads left along a fine stretch of walls). At the opposite end of the square, standing on a high basement, is a *Roman Temple*, later converted into a church. The exterior preserves some semi-columns and pilasters (with fragments of stucco fluting). It is thought to date from the 2C AD. In Via Porta Guelfa is the entrance to a building which protects a *Roman Mosaic (the custodian lives at No. 2), with beautiful marine creatures, including octopus, lobsters, and dolphins, in a symmetrical design. It was made from black-and-white tesserae at the beginning of the 2C AD. Discovered before the 17C, it decorated part of a thermal building, more of which can be seen beneath the modern grid. A walkway is to be built above the mosaic, which has recently been restored. From Piazza Garibaldi, Via Crescimbeni returns to the Corso.

From Piazza Silvestri (see above) the Corso Amendola continues the line of Corso Matteotti in the opposite direction. It passes a number of interesting palaces before reaching the church of *Sant'Agostino*, just inside the walls, with a 15C fresco of the Madonna over the door. It contains numerous ruined 15–16C frescoes. The pretty Via Santa Maria leads round to the left past the ex-church of Santa Maria. Beyond the house at No. 1 a road leads out to *Porta Molini* an impressive 15C gate flanked by a tower with a semicircular wall, in a fine stretch of Roman walls. Beyond a mill here is a public wash-house on the Clitunno in use since c 1900. Via Porta Molini leads back up to Largo Gramsci with the apse of San Silvestro and the back of Palazzo dei Consoli, adjoining Piazza Silvestri.

Just outside the town, off the road to Foligno, and behind the little octagonal church of the *Madonna della Rosa* (1691) the elliptical form of the Roman *Amphitheatre of Mevania* can be seen in a field.

Two km N of the town, on the road for Cannara and Bettona, is the **Convento dell'Annunziata**. In the interior, the first S altar, a fine 16C work in wood, contains a painting of the Incredulity of St Thomas by Fantino. The first N altar, also dating from the 16C, has a sculpted Crucifix with painted mourners by Fantino. The beautiful terracotta high altarpiece of the Annunciation is attributed to Sante Buglioni. Below the convent (reached from the right of the main road) is a picturesque little lake surrounded by poplars known as *L'Aiso*, some 13m deep and fed by an abundant spring. A local legend relates how a rich and miserly peasant was drowned in his house on this spot for attempting to thresh his grain on a feast day. His pious wife who tried to escape saving her child was submerged by another spring now called 'Aisillo'. The main road continues to **Cannara** (9km), on the Topino river. In the church of San Francesco is a painting of the Madonna and Saints by Nicolò Alunno. There is an interesting collection in the Municipio of detached frescoes and fragments from excavations of *Urvinum Hortense*, 7km W, beyond Collemancio. This was a Roman municipium and a Republican temple basement and baths have been found here. Nearby is *Limigiano* with remains of a castle and the Romanesque church of San Michele. *Bettona*, 7km N, is described in Rte 1E.

Another road from Bevagna, to the SW, leads up to the *Santuario della Madonna delle Grazie* from which there is a fine view. It was begun in 1583 by Valentino Martelli, with an octagonal drum surmounted by a lantern. In the interior (N transept) is a 15C sculpted Crucifix. The high altar of 1641 protects a venerated image of the Madonna. In the S transept is a 15C fresco of the Madonna and Child. The altarpieces in the nave are by Fantino, including the Byzantine Madonna of Constantinople (1603).

Gualdo Cattaneo, a tiny medieval town (1-star hotel, 'Marinangeli') lies in a beautiful position 8km W of Bevagna. Of ancient foundation, its name derives from the Saxon 'Wald' from the forests which were once here. In the piazza is a fine circular tower of 1494 and a War Memorial. Just out of the square is the *parish church*. Inside, on the left wall, Madonna by 'Bastiano', dated 1350. The two scagliola altars date from 1732. In the apse is a fine Last Supper by Fantino. The chapel to the left of the apse was decorated in 1608 with stuccoes and paintings by Ferrau' Ferroni da Faenza. The crypt (1220) has pretty vaulting and columns. To the left a passageway and steps lead down to Piazza Mazzini from which a long flight of steps continues down to *Sant'Agostino* which contains (in a niche on the left) a fresco of the Crucifix and four saints (1482) by the school of Alunno. **Collazzone**, 21km W of Gualdo Cattaneo, is a medieval town surrounded by its walls, amidst olive groves and oak and pine woods. In the convent of San Lorenzo here Jacopone da Todi died in 1306. In the parish church is a wood tabernacle with a 14C polychrome seated statue of the Madonna and Child. Seven kilometres S is *San Terenziano* with a Romanesque church (3-star hotel 'Dei Pini'). Nearby, at *Grutti*, is the Trattoria 'La Noci'.

FROM BEVAGNA TO MASSA MARTANA, N316, 27km. This route traverses the delightful hills known as the **'Monti Martani'** which separate the Valle Umbra from the Tiber valley. They are particularly beautiful in autumn when the oak trees are red. The highest peak is Monte Martano (1094m). From Bevagna the road climbs, and beyond some lignite mines passes the 'Ponte del Diavolo' a Roman bridge on the old Via Flaminia from Bevagna to Narni. 11.5km *Bastardo*, has a huge electricity plant. 14km A pleasant road diverges left for San Felice and Giano. Beyond *Castagnola*, with a

13–14C castle, there is a good view of the attractive 19C sanctuary of the *Madonna del Fosco*, in the valley below. Beyond, a road (left) leads along a pretty wooded ridge for *San Felice*, a 12C Benedictine abbey in red stone, restored in 1957. It is now the seat of a missionary college (and is being restored again). *Giano dell'Umbria* is a medieval walled village with some interesting churches. 2-star hotel (and restaurant) 'Park Montecerreto', and 2-star camping site 'Pineta di Giano'.

N316 continues S past (right) *Montecchio* with remains of old walls and (19km) *Viepri* (1km right), a lovely old group of buildings around a church in the valley. 27km **Massa Martana** in wooded hilly country has remains of its walls with a round tower, and a fine 10C gate. The road continues S for another 5km to join the superstrada from Todi to Terni, just N of Acquasparta (see Rte 10). Just outside Massa Martana a secondary road (right; signposted Todi) winds down to another junction, and off the Foligno road which continues right, is a by-road (signposted) for the 12C church of *Sant'Illuminata* (no admission) with frescoes of 1430. Beyond, on the opposite side of the road (unsignposted) is the Abbey of *Santi Fidenzio e Terenzio*, dating from the 11C, with an interesting interior (also closed). N316 continues S from Massa Martana and passes *Santa Maria in Pantano*, next to the road on the site of the Roman Vicus Martis on the old Flaminia. It has a rose window in its façade and pretty apse, and beside it stands a medieval tower to which has been added a belfry. Of ancient foundation, it has interesting architectural features in the interior (key at the house on the right). A column in the sanctuary is partly made out of a huge Corinthian capital. A Roman altar serves as high altar. It has remains of primitive frescoes and Roman fragments. Just before reaching the slip-road for the 'superstrada' a by-road (right) leads to the attractive walled village of *Villa San Faustino*, outside which is the 12C *Abbey of San Faustino* (key at the house next door), with fragments of a Roman freize on its façade. It is surrounded by interesting old buildings. Below can be seen the factory which bottles the mineral water from the spring of San Faustino.

MONTEFALCO lies in a panoramic position (427m) just over 6km S of Bevagna. A delightful little hill town with splendid views, it is known as 'the Balcony of Umbria'. It has numerous interesting frescoes in its churches. It is surrounded by extensive olive groves and its water tower is conspicuous for miles around.

Hotels and Restaurants. 2-star hotels: 'Santa Chiara', 18 Via De Cuppis; 'Ringhiera Umbra', Via Mameli. On the outskirts (at the Bevagna turning): 'Nuovo Mondo', 7 Viale della Vittoria. These last two have restaurants. Another restaurant is 'Coccorone' in Largo Tempestivi.

History. Called *Coccurione* in the Middle Ages, the town was a free commune by the 12C. After its destruction by Frederick II in 1249, Montefalco adopted its new name. From 1383–1439 it came under the rule of the Trinci family. Frescoes carried out in the town in 1450–52 by Benozzo Gozzoli had a wide influence on the Umbrian school of painting. Other artists who worked here include Pier Antonio Mezzastris and the native artist Francesco Melanzio.

Several roads lead up to the charming circular **Piazza del Comune** with a medley of buildings, at the highest point of the town. The tower of *Palazzo Comunale* can be climbed on request to see the panoramic *view which takes in Perugia, Assisi, Spello, Trevi, and Spoleto. On a very clear day, beyond the Monti Martani, can be seen the sea. On the left (No. 18) is the former church of *San Filippo Neri* converted into a theatre in 1895 (recently restored; when closed ask for the key at the Vigili Urbani in Corso Mameli). The Oratory of *Santa Maria di Piazza* (closed) has a terracotta door. The 15C *Palazzo Senili* (No. 12) is next to the 16C *Palazzo Camilli* (No. 9). On the last side of the piazza is a small neo-classical palace (No. 6) next to a portico (being restored).

Via Ringhiera Umbra leads downhill from the square past a neo-Gothic covered passageway to the ***Museo di San Francesco** which consists of a frescoed church, a pinacoteca, and a lapidary collection (open 10–13, 15–18; July and August, 10–13. 16–19; closed Monday). The CHURCH was built in 1335–38 and contains frescoes of the greatest interest (most of them recently restored; others are in the process of being restored). In the 15C chapels on the SOUTH SIDE: first chapel, *frescoes by Benozzo Gozzoli (1452); second chapel, frescoes by the 15C Umbrian school; third chapel, painted Crucifix, an Umbrian work dating from the late 13C or early 14C; fourth, fifth and sixth chapels (partly in restoration), frescoes by Giovanni di Corraduccio of Foligno. In the chapel to the right of the main apse are some very ruined 15C Umbrian frescoes. The MAIN APSE has a well preserved *fresco cycle of the Life of St Francis by Benozzo Gozzoli, one of his best works. In the chapel to the left of the main apse are more frescoes by Giovanni di Corraduccio. On the NORTH WALL is a niche with a lunette fresco of the Madonna between St Louis of Toulouse and an angel by the school of Perugino. The square domed CAPPELLA BONTADOSI dates from 1589 with stuccoes and paintings by Fantino. Beyond are two niches, one with frescoes of the miracles of St Anthony of Padua by Jacopo Vincioli, and the other with a fresco of the Madonna enthroned between two saints by Tiberio d'Assisi. On the WEST WALL is a semicircular fresco of the *Nativity (with Lake Trasimene in the background) by Perugino (1503). Beneath the cantoria (1644) is a detached fresco of c 1471 attributed to Cristoforo di Jacopo of Foligno.

Stairs lead up to the PINACOTECA, a municipal collection founded in 1870, which has recently been arranged here and is well labelled. The works by Francesco Melanzio include the *Madonna del Soccorso, and the *Madonna enthroned between six Saints (1498), the town standard, and detached frescoes. Beyond are a 13C painted Crucifix, a lovely Madonna and Child by the bottega of Melozzo da Forlì, and Stories of the life of Christ by a painter from Foligno (c 1450–60). Also here, frescoes by the 14C Umbrian school and Mezzastris. Beyond a Crucifix in relief (removed for restoration), between Mourners and St Francis of Assisi by the circle of Alunno (from the church of San Fortunato) is a *painting of three saints by Antoniazzo Romano, and small 16C works. At the end of the room are 16C and 17C paintings, church vestments and silver, ex-votos, etc.

The MUSEO LAPIDARIO is arranged in well-vaulted rooms downstairs. The sculptural fragments dating from the 9C–15C include a stone lion (1270) and a marble 16C statue of a river god, a statue of Hercules (1C AD, probably restored in the 17C), Roman funerary altars (1C AD) and a Corinthian capital. A slab decorated with acanthus leaves in the 1C AD was re-used as an altar in the Middle Ages. At the bottom of Via Ringhiera Umbra there is a splendid viewpoint.

Corso Mameli, the main street of the town, leads down from Piazza del Comune to the 14C castellated *Porta Sant'Agostino*. On the right (No. 51) is Palazzo Pambuffetti, with a 15C façade. On the left is the 16C Palazzo Tempestivi. Farther down is the church of *Sant'Agostino* (1279–85; enlarged in 1327) which contains numerous interesting frescoes (14–16C), many of them showing the influence of Benozzo Gozzoli. Roman fragments decorate the façade of *Casa Angeli* the last house on the left, just before the gate. Outside the gate, Borgo Garibaldi leads round left to Via Verdi on the corner of which is **Santa Chiara** with a 17C interior. The *Cappella di Santa Croce* (ring at the convent door at the end of the left aisle, 9–11.30, 15.30–18.30) has interesting Umbrian frescoes of 1333, including a crowded Calvary scene, and Evangelists with animal heads in the vault. The convent is also of interest, with a 14C cloister, a collection of 16C marriage chests, a 14C Crucifix, and a fresco of St Chiara by Benozzo Gozzoli. Via Verdi continues to **Sant'Illuminata** with a fresco of the Madonna of the Misericordia by Francesco Melanzio over the door. The interior has three large semicircular chapels on either side of the nave decorated with more early 16C frescoes by the native artist Francesco Melanzio and by Bernardino Mezzastris. Opposite, with two Renaissance portals, is the church of *San Leonardo* (if closed, ring at the convent at No. 1) which has a Madonna enthroned by Francesco Melanzio over the high altar, and a detached 15C fresco of the Madonna and Child (N wall). About 1km beyond Porta Spoleto is the church of San Fortunato, described below.

From Via Verdi, Piazza del Comune is reached by Porta Federico II (right; 1244) which has a relief of the Imperial eagle, and the steep Vicolo degli Operai. On the left is the apse of the 11–12C church of *San Bartolomeo* (with 17C paintings including the high altarpiece of the Madonna and Child with saints by Giacinto Gemignani), and the ancient church of *Santa Maria Maddalena*, with 15C frescoes in the 18C interior (often closed). The medieval district to the right, with the church of Santa Lucia, Porta Camiano, and Vicolo del Monte, is worth exploring.

*San Fortunato** (open all day), outside Porta Spoleto (and just over 1km from the centre) is in a beautiful position surrounded by ancient ilex trees. It was founded in the 5C. Off the 15C cloister, which incorporates four antique columns, is a chapel (left) with *frescoes of the life of St Francis (1512) by Tiberio d'Assisi with a charming vault. In the *lunette over the door into the church, Madonna with saints and angels, frescoed by Benozzo Gozzoli. On the right of the door, St Sebastian, a fresco by Tiberio d'Assisi. In the CHURCH (if closed, ring at the monastery on the right of the entrance to the cloister), on the S altar, St Fortunato enthroned, also by Gozzoli, and on the right, Adoration of the Child, a fragment by Gozzoli. On the N side, 18C painting of St Michael Archangel, and in a little chapel off this side, is the sarcophagus of St Severus with three very worn frescoed tondi by Gozzoli.

To the S of Montefalco a by road runs via *Turrita* with an interesting parish church with votive frescoes (14–16C) to the sanctuary of the *Madonna della Stella* (8km), an elaborate work by Giovanni Santini (1862–81) with painted decoration by Cesare Mariani. S side: first altar, Enrico Pollastrini, Holy Family; third altar, Giuseppe Mancinelli, Santa Chiara. The church was built in honour of the miraculous 16C fresco fragment on the high altar. N side: third altar, Giuseppe Sereni, Madonna and Saints; first altar, Friedrich Overbeck, Visitation.

Castel Ritaldi, is c 5km farther S. Its 13C castle is being restored. Inside the gate is the portico (right) of the church of Santa Marina. In the presbytery (behind a curtain) in a niche on the right is a Madonna with angels and Saints, an extremely worn fresco by Tiberio d'Assisi.

8

Todi

TODI is a beautiful old town (16,000 inhab.) in a delightful position on an isolated triangular hill (410m) some 40km S of Perugia. It preserves many interesting medieval buildings and steep old streets. The surrounding countryside is particularly lovely and unspoilt. The terrain is subject to landslips and work is being carried out to shore up the hill. In recent years Todi has become a fashionable place to have a house.

Information Office. 'APT' Information Office, 38 Piazza del Popolo (Tel. 075/8943062); the headquarters of the 'APT del Tuderte' is at No. 6 Piazza Umberto I (Tel. 075/8943395).

Railway Station at *Ponte Rio*, 2km N of Porta Perugina on the 'Ferrovia Centrale Umbra' line from Perugia to Terni (bus in connection with trains).

Buses from Piazzale della Consolazione to Perugia (six times a day) and to Terni (six times a day). Once a day from Piazza Jacopone to Rome via Massa Martana (except Sunday) and to Orvieto.

Car parking. The centre has not yet been closed to traffic, but it is best to park outside the walls. There is a small car park outside Porta Perugina, and a larger car park in Piazzale G. Fabrizio Atti (with a mini-bus service to the centre). There are plans to build a car park off Viale della Consolazione with an escalator to the Rocca. In the centre (limited space) there is a car park in Foro Tempio di Marte (or Piazza del Mercato Vecchio).

Hotels. There are no longer any hotels open in the centre of the town. 4-star: 'Bramante', Circonvallazione Orvietana (near Santa Maria della Consolazione). 3-star: 'Villa Luisa', Viale A. Cortesi (outside Porta Romana). 2-star: 'Zodiaco', Via del Crocifisso (outside Porta Romana). 2km S of the town, in Località Fiore, is a 5-star hotel: 'San Valentino'.

Restaurants. Luxury class: 'Umbria', Via San Bonaventura. Trattorie: 'Jacopone', 3 Piazza Jacopone; 'Cavour', 23 Corso Cavour. At Izzalini-Asproli, 10km outside the town: 'La Palazzetta' restaurant.

Pleasant places to **picnic**: on the Rocca hill or outside Porta Perugina.

An **Antiques Fair** is held here in April.

History. Todi was founded by the Umbri, and later absorbed Etruscan influence. By 42 BC it had become the Roman colony of 'Tuder'. One of the first free communes in the Middle Ages, by the early 13C when the Palazzo del Popolo was built, it was at the height of its power (with Terni and Amelia under its rule). Todi was the birthplace of Jacopo de' Benedetti (c 1230–1306), called Jacopone da Todi, poet and mystic, the reputed author of the 'Stabat Mater'. In 1523 more than half the population died of the plague. In the 19C numerous unsystematic excavations took place in Todi and its surroundings; nearly all the remarkable Etruscan and Roman finds made then now belong to the Museo Archeologico in Florence or to the Villa Giulia in Rome. The famous bronze statue of Mars dating from the beginning of the 4C BC, found here in 1835, is now in the Vatican.

The prettiest approach (unsignposted) from Perugia is by the country road which leads right up to the *Porta Perugina* (described below). The central ***Piazza del Popolo**, one of the finest in Italy, is bordered by well-proportioned Gothic buildings. It is built above a series of Roman cisterns, and is on the site of the Roman Forum. Opposite the cathedral stands the battlemented **Palazzo dei Priori** (now used as civic offices) which dates from 1293–1337. The bronze eagle, coat of arms of the town, was put up here in

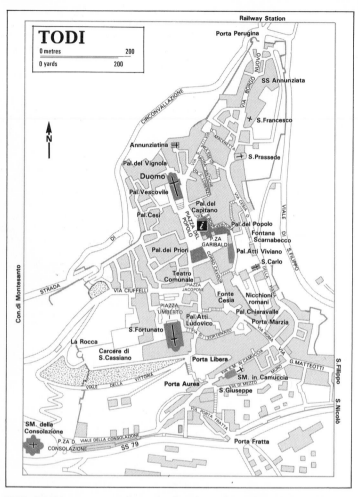

TODI

| 0 metres | 200 |
| 0 yards | 200 |

Railway Station

Porta Perugia

VIA BORGO NUOVO

SS Annunziata

CIRCONVALLAZIONE

✝ S.Francesco

N

Annunziatina ✝

✝ S.Prassede

Pal.del Vignola

VIA S.LORENZO

Duomo

VIA S.ANTICHE

VIA CESIA

Pal.Vescovile

Pal.del Capitano

PIAZZA DEL POPOLO

🄸

Pal.del Popolo

Pal.Cesi

VIA CAVOUR

Fontana Scarnabecco

VIALE DI S.FILIPPO

P.ZA GARIBALDI

Pal.dei Priori

CORSO CAVOUR

Pal.Atti Viviano

✝ S.Carlo

Teatro Comunale

PIAZZA JACOPONE

Fonte Cesia

Nicchioni romani

VIA CIUFFELLI

STRADA

Con.di Montesanto

PIAZZA UMBERTO

Pal.Atti Ludovico

Pal.Chiaravalle

Porta Marzia

S.Fortunato

VIA ROMA

La Rocca

Carcere di S.Cassiano

P.ZA S.FORTUNATO

Porta Libera

VIA S.M.IN CAMUCCIA

G.MATTEOTTI

S.Filippo

MURO

VIALE DELLA VITTORIA

Porta Aurea

SM. in Camuccia

VIA DI MEZZO

S.Giuseppe

S.Nicolò

VIA PORTA FRATTA

SM. della Consolazione

P.ZA D. CONSOLAZIONE

VIALE DELLA CONSOLAZIONE

SS 79

Porta Fratta

1339. Additions were made to the façade in the 16C, and the 14C tower had to be lowered for reasons of stability. A monumental flight of steps (1267) provides an entrance to the PALAZZO COMUNALE which occupies the Gothic **Palazzo del Popolo** (1213), one of the oldest town halls in Italy (the battlements were added in 1901) and the adjoining **Palazzo del Capitano** (c 1290) which has two orders of elegant three-light windows, those on the first floor beneath pretty foliated triangular frames. The PINACOTECA here was closed many years ago for restoration. It contains a large polyptych by Lo Spagna, a bronze Crucifix attributed to Giambologna, frescoes, terracottas, and Etruscan bronzes. The 17C paintings include Christ and the Virgin and souls of Purgatory by Ferraù Fenzoni, and a Presentation in the Temple by Andrea Polinori.

The **Duomo** (closed 12–15) is approached by an imposing flight of steps

(1740). The FAÇADE (covered for restoration) was altered in the early 16C when the three rose windows and the portal were decorated. The carved door is by Carlo Lorenti (1639; the four highest panels survive from the earlier door of 1513 by 'Maestro Antonio'). The lovely INTERIOR has superb Corinthian *capitals, a raised presbytery and a semi-dome in the apse. On the WEST WALL is a Last Judgement fresco (c 1596) inspired by Michel-angelo's famous work, by Ferraù Fenzoni (covered for restoration). On the SOUTH SIDE a pretty Gothic arcade with graceful little columns was added in the 14C as a fourth aisle. The stained glass is by 19C local craftsmen. Beneath the arcade is a detached fresco fragment of the Trinity by Lo Spagna (1525; temporarily removed). Beyond the beautiful font (1507) is a 14C *Madonna and Child, partly in relief. At the end of this aisle is an altarpiece by Giannicola di Paolo. At the end of the two main aisles are gilded wood organs (that on the right dates from 1765 and that on the left from 1852). The HIGH ALTAR has little Gothic columns (14–15C). In the APSE are carved and inlaid *stalls by Antonio Bencivenni da Mercatello and his son Sebastiano (1521–30). A Crucifix (late 13C) hangs in the apse (temp-orarily removed). On either side of the presbytery, Saints Peter and Paul, small paintings by Lo Spagna (also temporarily removed). On the left of the choir is the CAPPELLA CESI (covered for restoration) built in 1605. The tombs of Angelo and Giovanni Andrea Cesi have portraits attributed to Annibale Carracci. At the end of the NORTH AISLE steps lead down to the CRYPT with fine vaulting, and a LAPIDARY MUSEUM with miscellaneous fragments including numerous pavement tombs. On the wall of the aisle have been placed three mutilated statue groups, which may have belonged to a funerary monument, attributed to the school of Giovanni Pisano.

Via Mazzini leads out of the opposite end of the piazza past the handsome façade of the *Teatro Comunale*, a fine theatre enlarged in 1872 by Carlo Gatteschi (being restored) to *San Fortunato, in a raised position with steps above a garden laid out with box hedges at the beginning of this century. The unfinished FAÇADE was begun c 1415–58, and the campanile with its cusped top dates from 1460. The *portal has exquisite carving with saints beneath baldacchini and curious figures entwined with leaves. On either side are statues of the Annunciation; the angel, with her robes flowing over her wings, is particularly fine and is attributed by some scholars to Jacopo della Quercia. The exceptionally light *INTERIOR (closed 12.30–15.30) is typical of German late-Gothic hall churches, with all three naves of equal height, clustered pilasters, and a polygonal apse. It was begun in 1291 at the E end but not completed until 1459. The attractive tiled brick floor dates from 1463. The grey stone brackets have been installed to counteract the outward lean of the pilasters. The two stoups may have belonged to an earlier church on this site. Many of the chapels have 14–15C fresco fragments. SOUTH AISLE. Fourth chapel, *Madonna and Child with two angels by Masolino (restored in 1987). The late-14C frescoes in the sixth chapel include damaged fragments with scenes from the life of St Francis. The seventh chapel is a fine domed Baroque work, decorated with stuccoes. At the end of the S aisle is the CHAPEL OF THE SACRAMENT. High up on the outside is a 14C stone pulpit. The chapel (closed for restoration) has a large wood altar (1758), and fresco fragments by Niccolò Vannucci da Todi. The 14C HIGH ALTAR has little Gothic columns (in between which figures of saints were painted in 1860). Above it is a statue of St Fortunato (1643). The choir stalls were carved in 1590 by Antonio Maffei. In the CRYPT are preserved the remains of Fra Jacopone (see above) with a monument erected by Bishop Angelo Cesi (1580). NORTH AISLE. Fifth chapel, 14–15C

Todi

fresco fragments of the Banquet of Herod. The third chapel (being restored), with a dome, was well decorated by the local painter Andrea Polinori (1586–1648).

Beside the church is the 16C *Palazzo Ludovico Atti* attributed to Galeazzo Alessi, and, at the bottom of the steps, a monument to Jacopone del Todi, made up from antique fragments and with a bronze statue (1930). To the right of the church is Piazza Pignattaria laid out as a garden. Here is the entrance to the ex-convent of San Fortunato (now a school), with a large 15C cloister. A lane leads up from here to the top of the hill, with the large round tower of the ruined *Rocca*, surrounded by a delightful public garden with lovely views above Santa Maria della Consolazione. The so-called *Carcere di San Cassiano* is a ruined Roman cistern, later converted into a chapel.

On the left of the church of San Fortunato, *Via San Fortunato* leads down to an archway (right) on Via Lorenzo Leoni which diverges right to the edge of the hillside, just above the ruined Porta Libera, a gate in the inner Etruscan walls. The dome of Santa Maria della Consolazione can just be seen from here, as well as crumbling steps descending through orchards to the old borgo di Porta Fratta, and another gate, the Porta Aurea, in the Roman walls, near the church of Santa Maria in Camuccia (described below), and farther downhill the Porta Fratta, in the third circle of walls (c 1244).

The charming old stepped Via San Fortunato continues down through an interesting medieval district to *Corso Cavour*. Here is the *Porta Marzia*, a medieval archway constructed with Roman material in the first circle of walls. It is surmounted by an elegant balcony. From here it is worth following Via Roma downhill to the first road on the right which leads to the 13C church of **Santa Maria in Camuccia**. On either side of the door are two handsome Roman columns. The church owns a precious 12C wood *statue of the seated Madonna and Child (the 'Sedes Sapientiae') which is being restored since its theft in 1988. In the first N chapel is the font and a 15C fresco of the Madonna and Child. Roman remains have been found beneath the church. The church of *San Giuseppe*, just before the gate, contains a Holy Family considered to be one of the best works of Andrea Polinori (1623). Outside Porta Aurea (from which there is a fine view) Via di Mezzo Muro (left) has notable traces of the Roman walls.

Via Matteotti continues the line of Via Roma down to the 16C *Porta Romana* (c 500m from Porta Marzia). Just inside the gate (left) is the church of *San Filippo* which contains a marble statue of St Filippo Benizi attributed to the Paolo Naldini, or the school of Lorenzo Bernini. Opposite is the Gothic church of *San Nicolò*. Via del Anfiteatro Antico on the left passes scant remains of the Roman amphitheatre of Todi.

From Porta Marzia (see above) Corso Cavour leads back up to the centre. On the left (No. 58) is the 13C *Palazzo Chiaravalle*. Higher up, in front of a group of palm trees, is the *Fonte Cesia*, erected in 1606 by Bishop Angelo Cesi. On the right the stepped Via del Mercato Vecchio leads under a passageway down to Piazza Mercato Vecchio (or Foro Tempio di Marte) with four remarkable tall *ROMAN NICHES, with semi-domes, from a Roman building. Below the piazza is the Romanesque church of *Sant'Ilario* (or San Carlo) with a charming façade and bell-cote. In the interior (usually closed) is a fresco of the Madonna of the Misericordia by Lo Spagna. Nearby (left) is the *Fontana Scarnabecco* (1241) with a pretty portico.

The Corso ends in **Piazza Garibaldi** with a monument to the hero by Giuseppe Frenguelli (1890). Here is the handsome *Palazzo Viviano Atti* (1552). There is a superb view of the countryside beyond a tall cypress (supposed to have been planted in 1849 to commemorate Garibaldi's visit to Todi) and a small garden; below can be seen the centrally planned church of the Crocifisso (described below).

At the upper end of Piazza del Popolo, Via del Duomo skirts the flank of the Duomo past the campanile and an outside stair. In Via del Seminario is the 16C *Palazzo del Vignola* (heavily restored after a tragic fire in 1982), named after its architect, which ingeniously fits its corner site. Beyond is the church of the *Annunziatina* (or 'Nunziatina'), built in 1609, which contains two frescoes by Andrea Polinori. Via del Vescovado skirts the beautiful apse of the cathedral. From Via Paolo Rolli (named after the translator of Milton, 1687–1765, who was born in Todi) can be seen *Palazzo Vescovile* (1593), with a portal by Vignola. On the right is *Palazzo Cesi* (1547), attributed to Antonio Sangallo the Younger. The medieval district to the S is well worth exploring.

From Via del Duomo (see above) Via San Prassede descends past an old arch and fragments of the earliest walls built into the houses (right; plaque). Via delle Mura Antiche, a lane beneath a low arch, leads right to emerge beside the walls. Via Santa Prassede, a peaceful old street, continues right (at the end of Via della Maleretta a stretch of medieval walls may be seen) and descends steeply to the 14C church of *Santa Prassede* (if closed, ring for the priest). It contains two late-16C wood statues, and two 17C paintings: Mourning over the dead Christ by Hendrick de Clerck, and St Teresa of Avila by Andrea Polinori. Beyond Porta Santa Prassede is the monastery of *San Francesco*, with its arch over the street. The interior of the church was decorated in 1860 by the Agretti brothers. The 16C high altarpiece is by Livio Agresti. On the left of the altar can be seen an interesting large 14C fresco representing an allegory of Salvation. Via Borgo Nuovo continues out of the town through the double *Porta Perugina*, with its round tower in the medieval circle of walls (begun c 1244), beyond which is beautiful countryside.

Outside the walls to the SW (best reached on foot from San Fortunato along Via Ciuffelli, or from a path which descends from the Rocca), on a busy road (and beside a bus park) is the church of ***Santa Maria della Consolazione** (closed 13–15), a masterpiece of the Renaissance. A domed church on a Greek-cross plan, it clearly shows the influence of Bramante. Begun in 1508 and finished in 1607, it is thought to have been built by Cola da Caprarola, and perhaps completed by Ambrogio Barocci and Francesco da Vita. In the interior the vault decoration dates from 1579–82.

Beyond Santa Maria della Consolazione the Orvieto road leads in c 2km to the church and convent of *Montesanto* on a little hill and approached by an avenue. In front of the church is an ancient lime tree. Inside is a 16C fresco of the Nativity and a Crucifixion attributed to Alunno.

Outside Porta Romana (see above) and c 1.5km from the centre, reached by Viale Cortesi and (left) Viale del Crocifisso is the Greek-cross church of *Santissimo Crocifisso* in brick and marble. It is attributed to Valentino Martelli (1591).

FROM TODI TO PERUGIA. A 'superstrada' (N3bis; 46km) leads along the Tiber valley passing close to Deruta and Torgiano (described in Rte 1E). The more interesting and prettier alternative route (N397; 49km) is described below.

Beyond *Montemolino* the road crosses the Tiber and at 10km a by-road leads left to **Montecastello di Vibio** (3km), a medieval hill town (423m) dominating the Tiber valley. Of ancient foundation, its name is derived from the Roman family 'gens Vibia'. In the Middle Ages it came under the dominion of Todi. It has remains of its walls. In 1808 the *'Teatro della Concordia'* was built in honour of the French Revolution. This remarkable little theatre is to be restored. 13km **Fratta Todina** was important in the Middle Ages when its *Castle* was contested between Todi and Perugia; remains of its walls survive. The 16C *Palazzo Vescovile* was enlarged by Cardinal Giovanni Battista Altieri in the following century (with an interesting courtyard and garden). The 19C *Parish Church* was built by Giovanni Santini. 20km **Marsciano** is a busy little town with some remains of a feudal castle. The church has a campanile by Giovanni Santini. The charming road (N317) continues along a ridge of hills towards Perugia through beautiful countryside. At (27km) *Cerqueto* the parish church contains a fresco fragment of St Sebastian, the earliest dated work of Perugino (1478). 10km W is *Monte Vibiano* with a small hotel and restaurant, and an exclusive 4-star hotel in the castle.

38km *San Martino in Colle* is a medieval village with another church by Giovanni Santini. 49km **Perugia**, see Rte 1.

FROM TODI TO ORVIETO. The fastest route (43km) is by N448 which skirts the Tiber and the artificial *Lago di Corbara*, created to regulate the flow of the Tiber and to supply a hydroelectric station (3-star camping site 'Orvieto'). A good white wine is produced in this area. The road passes close to *Civitella del Lago*, with a famous luxury-class restaurant 'Vissani', and another restaurant 'Da Peppe'. Nearby is the hill town of *Baschi*, conspicuous from the Florence–Rome motorway. The prettier, but longer route (N79bis; 48km) climbs over the hills to the N of Lago di Corbara with superb views. Beyond (6km) *Pontecuti*, an old walled village which was almost totally destroyed in the last War, it climbs to a height of 637m. It then descends steeply to the Paglia bridge by Orvieto station.

A road leads S from Todi towards Massa Martana and the Monti Martani (described in Rte 7). On this road (11km) is *Colvalenza* with the large 'Santuario dell'Amore Misericordioso' by Julio Lafuente (1955, enlarged in 1965).

The area to the S of Todi around Acquasparta and Amelia is described in Rte 10.

9

Orvieto

ORVIETO (23,600 inhab.) built on a precipitous tufa crag (315m) dominating the valley is famous for its splendid position (it is especially well seen from the Bolsena road to the SW). It is a city of great antiquity, with notable Etruscan remains, preserving its medieval aspect with numerous narrow streets with many arches. The oldest buildings are built in a rich golden-coloured tufa. It is renowned for the beauty of its cathedral, which, at the highest point of the town, stands out on the skyline. New building has taken place around the station (*Orvieto Scalo*) leaving the old town and the cultivated fields beneath its rock remarkably unchanged. Landslips here in recent years have caused much alarm and funds have been designated by the State and work has been in progress since 1980 to consolidate the rock on which the town is built. It is the centre of a famous wine-growing area and local crafts include lace-making and pottery.

Information Office, 'APT', 24 Piazza Duomo (Tel. 0763/41772).

Railway Station at Orvieto Scalo at the bottom of the hill, on the main line from Florence to Rome (but served by only a few slow trains a day).

Funicular Railway from the Railway Station to Piazzale Cahen in (just over 2 min) every 15 minutes. Built in 1888 when it was operated by water, it was reopened (powered by electricity) in 1990. It ascends through an avenue of trees and then tunnels beneath the Fortezza (see below). The ticket includes a minibus service from Piazzale Cahen to Piazza Duomo or Piazza Garibaldi (see below).

Town Buses. Minibus A (every 15 min) from Piazzale Cahen via Via Postierla to Piazza Duomo. Minibus B (every 20 min) from Piazzale Cahen via Piazza XXIX Marzo, Piazza della Repubblica, Via Alberici, and Via Maitani to Piazzale Duomo. Bus No. 1 from Piazza Cahen or Piazza XXIX Marzo (c every hour) for the Crocifisso del Tufo necropolis and the Railway Station.

Country Buses run by 'ACOTRAL' from Piazzale Cahen (except on Sundays) via Montefiascone and Bagnoregio to Viterbo; to Bolsena (twice a day), and to Narni, Terni, and Todi (once a day).

Car parking. The centre is closed to traffic. Visitors are strongly recommended to leave cars at the free car park beside the Railway Station and take the underpass to Piazza

Stazione for the Funicular (see above). Other car parks at Piazzale Cahen, or off Via Roma.

Hotels. 4-star: 'Maitani', 5 Via Maitani; 'Aquila Bianca', 13 Via Garibaldi; in the environs below the town: 'La Badia', 8 Località La Badia (in a beautiful position); 'Villa Ciconia', 69 Via dei Tigli. 3-star: 'Reale', 25 Piazza del Popolo; 'Virgilio', 5 Piazza del Duomo. 2-star: 'Duomo', 7 Via Maurizio. At Orvieto Scalo at the bottom of the hill near the Station (in a much less pleasant position): 'Europa', 'Kristal' (3-star). 2-star: 'Umbria', 1 Via Nibbio. **Camping Site** (3-star) open April–September at Lago Corbara, Baschi.

Restaurants. Luxury-class: 'Il Giglio d'Oro', 8 Piazza Duomo. 1st-class: 'Etrusca', 10 Via Lorenzo Maitani; 'Maurizio', 78 Via del Duomo; 'Monaldo', 1 Piazza Sant'Angelo; 'Antico Brigattiere', 16 Via Quattro Cantoni; 'Dell'Orso', 18 Via della Misericordia; 'La Grotta', 5 Via Luca Signorelli. Trattorie: 'Sciarra', 26 Via della Cava; 'La Palomba', 16 Via Cipriano Manente; 'Della Mezza Luna', 3 Via Ripa Serancia; 'La Volpe e l'Uva', 1 Via Ripa Corsica. The Fortezza public gardens are a pleasant place to **picnic**.

Annual Festival. Procession in period costume on Corpus Domini (in June) starting in Piazza del Duomo.

History. The rock of Orvieto was already occupied in the Iron Age, and an important Etruscan city grew up here in the 7C BC, usually identified as *Volsinii Veteres*, one of the chief cities of the Etruscan Confederation. The town was destroyed in 265 BC by the Romans, and the inhabitants resettled at a spot on the NE side of Lake Bolsena which developed into the town of Bolsena (Volsinii Novi). In the Middle Ages the commune of *Urbs Vetus* (from which the modern name is derived) was important, and it became especially powerful in the 13C. Pope Gregory X here received Edward I of England on his return from the Crusades. The rivalries between the Guelf Monaldeschi and the Ghibelline Filippeschi dominated events in the town during the 14C, and later Alexander VI and Clement VII were to take refuge here from revolts in Rome. The architects Angelo da Orvieto (14C), Ascanio Vittozzi (died 1615), and Ippolito Scalza (c 1532–1617) were born here. There are now several military barracks in the town.

In Piazzale Cahen, with the funicular terminus and where the main road enters the town, is the *Fortezza* (1364), the grounds of which are now a pleasant public garden with fine views of the valley. An avenue to the left of the new Funicular Station descends to the •**Pozzo di San Patrizio** (open daily 8 or 9–18 or 19), built by Antonio da Sangallo the Younger (1527–37) to provide an emergency water supply in the event of a siege, by order of Clement VII, who fled to Orvieto after the sack of Rome. The well, surmounted by a low tower, is 63m deep, and is encircled by two spiral staircases each with 248 wide steps and lit by 72 windows. It is called 'St Patrick's Well' because it is supposed to be similar to St Patrick's cavern in Ireland. In the public gardens above the well are conspicuous remains of an Etruscan Temple, known as the *Tempio del Belvedere*.

From the piazza, Corso Cavour (open to access traffic only) ascends gently towards the centre of the town at Piazza della Repubblica. It passes the flank of the Romanesque church of *Santo Stefano* in yellow tufa, with a vaulted interior and a fragment of a 14C fresco of the Madonna and Child. Beyond, in a small square, is the church of *San Michele Arcangelo*, with a relief of a classical temple on its façade (1832). By the *Teatro Mancinelli* (1844–55; to be restored), on the left, is a good view of the Duomo. Opposite the theatre is Palazzo Urbani (Petrucci) by Michele Sanmicheli. Ahead there is a view of the tall *Torre del Moro* (12C). Opposite the tower, Via del Duomo leads left past numerous ceramics shops for tourists. In a little piazza is a Baroque octagonal church and a palace by Simone Mosca with a doorway by Ippolito Scalza. In Piazza Scalza, off the other side of Via del Duomo is Palazzo Clementini, also by Ippolito Scalza. •**Piazza del Duomo**

La Pergola – up side alley on W side of
Via del Duomo.   (Via dei Magoni – 9)

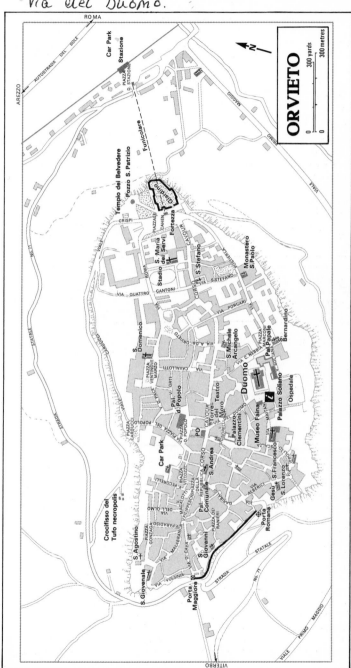

ORVIETO

is dominated by the magnificent exterior of the cathedral. At the entrance to the square is a clock tower called the *Torre del Maurizio*, surmounted by a bronze figure known as 'Maurizio' (1351) which strikes the hours. A row of simple low houses lines the N side of the piazza, and opposite the façade of the cathedral is the palace housing the Museo Civico Faina (see below), and the Opera del Duomo (covered for restoration; with the Tourist Office). On the S side of the square is a neo-classical church façade (1835; in very poor repair), and a hospital with a small park of pine trees from where there is a splendid view of the valley with the Badia di Santi Severo e Martirio. The fine Palazzo Buzi, on the corner of Via Soliano, is the work of Ippolito Scalza. The two monumental buildings in yellow tufa which house the Museo dell'Opera del Duomo and the Museo Nazionale Archeologico are described below. The ****Duomo** is one of the most striking buildings of its period in the country. It dominates the view of the city for miles around.

The construction of the Duomo was ordered by Urban IV to commemorate the miracle of Bolsena (1263). The first stone was laid on 13 November 1290, when it was blessed by Nicholas IV. The church was begun to a Romanesque plan, perhaps by Arnolfo di Cambio, but continued in the newly arrived Gothic style by Lorenzo Maitani, who took over in 1310. He was followed by his son Vitale; Nicolò and Meo Nuti (1331–47); Andrea Pisano (1347–48); Nino Pisano (1349); Andrea di Cecco da Siena (1356–59); and Andrea Orcagna (1359). Michele Sanmicheli became master in 1509–25, and the façade was not completed until the early years of the 17C.

The church stands on a plinth of seven steps, alternately red and white, surrounded by a lawn on the S side. The two beautiful flanks built in horizontal bands of white travertine and grey basalt are decorated with the exteriors of the tall semicircular side chapels and handsome Gothic windows. On the N side are the Porta di Canonica, with a fresco by Andrea di Giovanni, and the Porta del Corporale (three statues by Andrea Pisano have been removed from the lunette for restoration). On the S side is the Porta di Postierla, probably the oldest doorway. The two statues of Sibyls at the foot of the façade are by Fabiano Toti (1588) and Antonio Federighi.

The huge ***FAÇADE**, designed and begun by Lorenzo Maitani, which covers the W end, is one of the finest Italian Gothic works and has been compared in design to a painted triptych in an elaborate frame. In fact it is chiefly remarkable for its sculptural details rather than for its harsh polychrome mosaics, mostly remade in the 17–19C. Four elegant spires with high crocketed turrets divide the façade vertically: on the pilasters at their bases are superb marble ***bas-reliefs** (c 1320–30) ascribed to Maitani, his son Vitale, and Nicolò and Meo Nuti. They depict the story of the Creation to the time of Tubal Cain, the stories of Abraham and David, scenes from the Life of Christ, the Last Judgement, Hell, and Paradise. Above them are bronze symbols of the Evangelists, also by Maitani. The Madonna by Andrea Pisano and bronze angels by Maitani, formerly in the lunette above the main door, have been removed and may be replaced here by copies; they will be exhibited in the museum after their restoration. The bronze doors are by Emilio Greco (1964–70). The great rose window (covered for restoration), surrounded by statues in niches, is Orcagna's work.

In the uncluttered ***INTERIOR** (closed 13–14.30) the fine architectural lines can be appreciated to the full. The walls are lined with horizontal bands of white and grey. The columns of the nave, with fine capitals, carry round arches, over which a graceful triforium, with a clerestory above it, runs all round the church, except in the transepts. The semicircular side chapels are particularly graceful (and many of them have interesting fresco frag-

Detail of a relief of the Damned in Hell by Lorenzo Maitani on the façade of the Duomo, Orvieto

ments of the 14–15C). The lower panels of the stained glass windows are made of alabaster. In the NAVE are a stoup by Antonio Federighi (1485) and a font of 1390–1407. The fresco of the *Madonna and Child is by Gentile da Fabriano (1425; beautifully restored in 1987). By the doors of the church are three more stoups, attractive works of the 16C. NORTH TRANSEPT. Pietà by Ippolito Scalza (1579) and a carved altar and altarpiece by Simone Mosca and Raffaello da Montelupo. Here is the CAPPELLA DEL CORPORALE. On the walls are restored frescoes illustrating Miracles of the Eucharist by Ugolino di Prete Ilario (1357–64). On the right wall is the story of the miracle of Bolsena; on the altar wall, the Crucifixion; and on the left wall are more scenes of miracles involving the Holy Sacrament. In the vault, symbols of the Eucharist and saints. The huge panel of the *Madonna dei Raccomandati by Lippo Memmi (1320), usually displayed in the Gothic recess here, has been removed for restoration.

Over the altar, incorporated in a large tabernacle, designed by Nicolò da Siena (1358) and continued by Orcagna, is the *Reliquary of the Corporal, a superb work in silver-gilt with translucent enamels, by the Sienese Ugolino di Vieri (1337; removed for restoration). This contains the corporal (linen cloth) of the miracle of Bolsena, and is displayed only on religious festivals. The corporal is taken in procession on Corpus

Domini, but since 1979 it has been exposed in a subsitute reliquary for this occasion. On either side of the altar are statues of angels by Agostino Cornacchini (1729).

Above the entrance to the chapel is the huge colourful organ (1584, by Ippolito Scalza). The CHOIR, at present covered for restoration, is decorated with frescoes by Ugolino di Prete Ilario and his assistants; the carved and inlaid stalls are the work of Giovanni Ammannati and other Sienese artists (1331–41; being restored). The restored stained glass of the great E window is by Giovanni di Bonino (1325–34). On either side of the sanctuary are statues of Christ: Ecce Homo by Ippolito Scalza (1608), and Christ at the Column by Gabriele Mercanti (1627). The SOUTH TRANSEPT contains the Altare dei Magi (begun 1514), a good early work of Sanmicheli, with bas-reliefs by Raffaello and Francesco da Montelupo. In neo-classical niches here are statues of Adam and Eve by Fabiano Toti. The *Cappella della Madonna di San Brizio, or *Cappella Nuova* contains famous *frescoes by Signorelli, one of the most remarkable fresco cycles of the Italian Renaissance. They are suffering from humidity and restoration work has been in progress for several years. At present they are completely covered.

In 1447 Fra Angelico, with the help of Benozzo Gozzoli, began the decoration of the chapel: he had completed just two sections of the vault over the altar (the Saviour in Glory and the Prophets) before he was recalled to Rome. At the end of the century Luca Signorelli was commissioned to complete the frescoes (1499–1504). They are particularly important for their beautiful nude figure studies. On the LEFT WALL (near the entrance) is the Sermon of Antichrist, with Fra Angelico and Signorelli as two solemn bystanders, and the figure of Dante as one of the crowd; on the ENTRANCE WALL, the day of Judgement; on the RIGHT WALL the Resurrection of the Body, and the Casting out of the Wicked; and on the ALTAR WALL, Angels drive the sinners into Hell and guide the elect to Paradise; on the adjacent half of the LEFT WALL, the Blessed entering Heaven. The exquisite decoration on the lower part of the walls is also by Signorelli and includes medallion portraits of Homer, Dante, Virgil, Ovid, Horace, Lucan, and Empedocles, and scenes from classical myth and from Dante's 'Divine Comedy'. The Pietà in the recess on the right is also the work of Signorelli. On the Baroque altar is a local 14C painting called the 'Madonna di San Brizio'. The CRYPT, with traces of frescoes and part of the substructure of the Duomo, can be seen outside the East End (reached along the N flank).

Opposite the façade of the cathedral is **Palazzo Faina** (adm. 9–13, 14.30–16.30; summer 9–13, 15–18.30; closed Monday). Part of the archaeological collection of the **Museo Civico** is displayed on the ground floor (in need of restoration), including a tomb with bas-reliefs (4C BC), polychrome terracotta decorations from the Belvedere Temple (4C BC); the so-called 'Venus of Cannicella', a statue probably representing a female goddess of fertility made from Naxos marble and thought to be an Archaic Greek original of the 6C BC; and the colossal stone head of a warrior from the Crocifisso del Tufo (6C BC). The **Museo Claudio Faina** (founded in 1864 by Mauro Faina) is haphazardly arranged in old fashioned show-cases in four frescoed rooms on the piano nobile. The collection includes fine Attic red- and black-figure vases, and Etruscan ceramics, found in Etruscan tombs (the best ones are in the last room). The top floor is being restored to display more of the collection.

The battlemented **Palazzo Soliano** (or dei Papi), begun in 1297 for Boniface VIII is built in tufa, typical of Orvieto, with arches and an outside staircase. It houses the *Museo dell'Opera del Duomo** which has been closed for several years for rearrangement and restoration (entrance at the top of the stairs). In one huge hall is a miscellany of works of art (mostly from the cathedral). The contents include: *statues of the Madonna in marble by Andrea Pisano and his school, by Nino Pisano (1349), and (in wood), by Giovanni Pisano. The Madonna and angels by Pisano and Maitani from the central door of the Duomo may be exhibited here after their restoration. Among unfinished works by Arnolfo di Cambio are two damaged angels. The wooden statue of Christ blessing is attributed to an assistant of Maitani (1330). The paintings include parts of a fine polyptych by Simone Martini, a self-portait and other works by Signorelli, and a Madonna by Coppo di Marcovaldo (1268). Outstanding among the metal work is the Reliquary of the Head of San Savino, by Ugolino di Vieri; and the collection of vestments is notable. Displayed are two sketches for the façade of the cathedral; as built with three gables (by Maitani), and with only one gable, now thought to be by Arnolfo di Cambio. The colossal figures of the Apostles (16–18C) which formerly lined the nave of the cathedral, and two *statues of the Annunciation by Francesco Mocchi formerly on either side of the high altar may be returned to the Duomo. In a room below is a gallery of works left to the city in 1980 by Emilio Greco (open 10.30–13, 14 or 15–18 or 19; closed Monday).

*Palazzo Papale**, by the E end of the cathedral, is also built in tufa, with three large Gothic arches and fine windows. This splendid 13C building has recently been restored. It houses the **Museo Archeologico Nazionale** (9–13.30, 15–17; summer: 9–13.30, 15–19; fest. 9–13; closed Saturday and Monday). So far four huge rooms with fine vaults on the ground floor have been opened. The most notable exhibits include: Etruscan material from the Cannicella necropolis at the foot of the rock of Orvieto (see below; from excavations in 1900, 1936, and 1971) dating from the late 7C to the early 6C BC. Finds (1982–83) from the Crocifisso del Tufo necropolis and material (including armour) from the tomb of a warrior (4C BC) at Settecamini. Two painted tombs discovered in the 19C at Settecamini have been reconstructed and their original paintings displayed (detached in 1951). There is also a fine collection of Greek red- and black-figure vases (4C BC), bucchero ware, and bronze mirrors.

Via del Duomo (see above) returns to Corso Cavour which leads left to PIAZZA DELLA REPUBBLICA, the centre of the life of Orvieto. Here is the church of **Sant' Andrea** (closed for restoration; normally entered from the portico on the N side, under which flowers are sold), a 12C building with remains of 14C and 15C frescoes, and a fine twelve-sided campanile (over-restored in 1928). Here in 1281 Martin IV was crowned in the presence of Charles of Anjou. The sacristan (who lives at No. 17 Via Cipriano Manente, through the archway to the S of the church) will normally admit visitors to the excavations beneath the church. Here a 6C pavement from the primitive basilica overlies Etruscan and Roman remains. Here, also, are pieces of relief sculpture (8–9C?) from a choir screen, embedded on the reverse side with Cosmatesque mosaic work (other pieces have been reused for a pulpit in the upper church). In the piazza is *Palazzo Comunale*, first built in 1216, with a façade (c 1580) by Ippolito Scalza, opposite a neo-classical palace by Virginio Vespignani.

Via Garibaldi leaves the piazza beneath an arch under Palazzo Comunale. Via Alberici then continues left past the church of the *Gesù* (1618), with Baroque stucco work inside, to the Romanesque church of **San Lorenzo de Arari** (or *dell'Ara*) over-restored at the beginning of this century. It takes its name from an Etruscan altar beneath the altar-table. Above it is a pretty little 12C ciborium. The apse fresco of Christ enthroned with four saints in the Byzantine style and the frescoes illustrating four episodes in the life of St Lawrence (1330) in the nave were all poorly restored in 1919. On the columns are 14–15C fresco fragments. Via Ippolito Scalza leads on to the large church of *San Francesco* in Piazza dei Febei, with a 13C façade and a white interior (altered in 1773). The wood Crucifix is attributed to Lorenzo Maitani. Here, in the presence of Edward I of England, took place the funeral of Prince Henry of Cornwall, murdered at Viterbo in March 1271; here also Boniface VIII canonised St Louis of France. Via Maitani leads back to Piazza Duomo.

From Piazza della Repubblica, Via Loggia dei Mercanti, with several towers characteristic of the old city, leads past the roofless 14C church of the Carmine to Piazza de' Ranieri. To the N is the church of **San Giovanni Evangelista** with views of the valley and sheer rock face on which the town is built (being shored up). Founded in 916 the church was rebuilt in 1687 on an octagonal plan. It contains a detached fresco of the Madonna and Child of 1356. The cloister (restored) dates from 1513 with a fine well-head of 1526. In Via della Cava, farther NW, beside a restaurant at No. 28 is an interesting well excavated for Clement VII in 1527 (see the Pozzo di San Patrizio). Admission is freely granted to see the well, and the remains of a pottery found beside it, thought to have been active from the 13C to the 16C. From Porta Maggiore, one of the oldest city gates, Via Volsinia leads along the top of the walls above the tufa cliff to the church of **San Giovenale** with a square bell tower. It stands in a beautiful position on the edge of the rock, with orchards below. The church, of ancient foundation, contains interesting frescoes by local artists (13–16C). Pleasant walks may be taken in this old part of the town. Nearby is the former church of *Sant'Agostino* with a Gothic façade, and an 18C interior, being restored as a museum. Beside it a huge Gothic arch is now incorporated in a modern restaurant. Calle Paradiso (see the Plan) leads back towards (left) Piazza della Repubblica.

From Corso Cavour, Via Palazzo del Popolo leads to Piazza Capitano del Popolo dominated by the unusual *Palazzo del Popolo**, restored in 1990 as a conference centre. The splendid exterior built in tufa, with decorated arches and windows, was probably begun in 1157, and later altered. Excavations beneath the building have revealed Etruscan remains and a medieval well filled with ceramics (13–16C). A market is held in the surrounding piazze on Thursdays and Saturdays. To the NE, in a less attractive part of the town, is **San Domenico**, thought to be the first church dedicated to St Dominic, built in 1233–64. In its former convent St Thomas Aquinas taught theology. The church, of which only the transept remains, has a pretty exterior. In the interior are the *tomb of Cardinal de Braye (died 1281), by Arnolfo di Cambio, and the Cappella Petrucci (below the main church, entered from a door in the S wall unlocked by the sacristan), an interesting architectural work by Sanmicheli. It also has various mementoes to St Thomas Aquinas.

At the foot of the rock to the N, and just off the road to the station (reached on foot from outside Porta Maggiore, or by Bus No. 1 from Piazza XXIX Marzo or Piazzale Cahen) is the Etruscan necropolis of '**Crocifisso del Tufo**' (admission daily 8.30–dusk) of the 4C BC, with small but well-preserved chamber tombs.

At the foot of the rock to the SW of the town, next to a hotel and restaurant, is the Premonstratensian abbey of *Santi Severo e Martirio*, also known as *'La Badia'*, dating from the 12C. It can be reached by road (2.5km), or in 20min by footpath from the Porta Romana. The most interesting of the ruined buildings are the abbot's house, the former refectory (now the chiesa del Crocifisso), and the original church with its twelve-sided campanile. About 1km farther on, at *Settecamini*, is another 4C Etruscan burial-ground.

On the road (N71) towards Bolsena in Lazio (see *Blue Guide Northern Italy*) is the *Convento della Trinità* (5km) with interesting 17C frescoes, and 15C frescoes attributed to Pastura.

Another road runs S to *Porano* (9km) a picturesque little village with an interesting church. A by-road runs to *Castel Viscardo* (13km) with a 15C castle and church.

FROM ORVIETO TO CITTÀ DELLA PIEVE, N71, 47km. From Orvieto Scalo N71 crosses the motorway and Paglia river and, with fine views, it winds up to (21km) a summit level of 544m at the Valico di Monte Nibbio. The road descends to (25km) *Ficulle*, founded in the 8–9C, and still surrounded by its medieval walls. The 17C Collegiata was designed by Ippolito Scalza. The road continues through *Fabro* (with an entrance to the motorway) (3-star hotel and restaurant 'Bettola del Buttero') to (40km) *Monteleone d'Orvieto*, an attractive little hill town. To the E are the interesting villages of Montegabbione and Montegiove. 47km Città della Pieve, see Rte 3.

The road (N79bis) from Orvieto to Todi is described in Rte 8. Off this road at (10km) Colonnetta another fine road diverges N (N371) towars Marsciano. It traverses lovely deserted countryside around *Monte Peglia* (837m) with a nature reserve (Youth Hostel 'Centro Turistico Giovanile' at San Venanzo).

10

Terni, Narni, and Amelia

These three towns are situated close together in the SW corner of Umbria. They are reached from Perugia by a 'superstrada': to Terni, 81km; to Narni, 84km; and to Amelia, 91km.

TERNI (130m) is the second largest town in Umbria and capital of its second province. It faces the broad plain of the Nera river, and the presence of abundant water here has led to its expansion as a thriving industrial centre, particularly important for plastics and machinery. Its population (106,000 inhab.) has trebled since the beginning of this century. Badly damaged in the Second World War, it was reconstructed with pleasant residential suburbs, under the guidance of the architect Mario Ridolfi (1904–1984), who lived here at the end of his life.

Information Office. 'APT del Ternano', 5 Viale Cesare Battisti (Tel. 0744/43047).

Railway Station, Piazza Dante Alighieri. Services on the Rome–Ancona line, and the Rieti–Aquila line. The 'Ferrovia Centrale Umbra' has services to Perugia, Umbertide, and Sansepolcro.

Buses ('ATC') from Piazza Dante Alighieri to Narni, Acquasparta, the Cascata delle Marmore, Piediluco, Sangemini, and Otricoli.

Hotels. 4-star: 'Valentino', 5 Via Plinio il Giovane. 3-star: 'De Paris', 52 Viale della Stazione. Outside the historic centre: 'Garden', 4 Via Bramante (4-star); 'Allegretti', 76 Strada del Staino (3-star). **Camping sites** (both 2-star and open in summer) at the Cascata delle Marmore and Lago di Piediluco (see below).

Restaurants. 1st class: 'Alfio', Via Galilei; 'La Fontanella', 3 Via Plinio il Giovane; 'L'Erba Dolce', 2 Via Castello. The 'Caffè Pazzaglia', Corso Tacito, has good pastries.

History. The valley was inhabited in the Iron Age as finds from an important necropolis here testify. The city was founded by the Umbri in 672 BC and called 'Interamna' from its position between the two streams (inter amnes) Nar and Serra. Conquered by the Romans in the 4–3C, it became an important Municipium on the Via Flaminia. The emperor Gallus was murdered here in 253. Just outside the city a basilica was built above the tomb of the martyr saint Valentino, beheaded in 273 AD. In 1174 Bishop Cristiano di Magonza destroyed much of the city by order of Frederick Barbarossa because it had taken the side of Pope Alexander III. In 1798 the French, under General Lemoine, won a victory here over the Neapolitans.

The centre of the city is the busy **Piazza della Repubblica** and the adjoining Piazza Europa, now little more than an area at which numerous roads converge. Beside Palazzo Comunale there is a niche in which has been placed a 15C terracotta statue of the Madonna and Child from the Duomo. In Piazza Europa is the huge **Palazzo Spada** (its façade is on Via Roma) an unusual fortress-like building of the late 16C, once attributed to Antonio Sangallo the Younger. It was altered in the 17C and 18C. Nearby, raised and surrounded by a little garden, is the church of **San Salvatore**. The 11–12C façade and nave precede an interesting domed *rotonda, with a central oculus, once thought to have been a Temple of the Sun. On the site of a Roman house, this was probably built as a little oratory in the 7C. At the E end is a Roman altar, and a fresco of the Crucifixion. In a chapel off the left side are 14C frescoes (in very bad condition).

Via Roma, the old main street, leads out of Piazza Europa past the façade of Palazzo Spada and a medieval tower. On the right Via del'Arringo leads to the **Duomo**, thought to have been founded in the 6C. It was reconstructed in the 12C, and again in 1570, and decorated in the 17C. The 17C portico was crowned with a balcony and statues by Corrado Vigni in 1933–37. The main portal has fine classical decorations dating from the late 12C; the other door was carved in 1439. In the INTERIOR, on the W wall, is a Circumcision painted in 1560 by Livio Agresti. The high altar is by Antonio Minelli (1762). The splendid *Organ is thought to have been designed by Lorenzo Bernini. The Choir is by Domenico Corsi (1559). In the sacristy are fragments of sculptures and a 16C wood statue of St John the Baptist. The crypt dates from c 1000. In the piazza is a fountain (being restored) also by Corrado Vigni. Adjacent are the ruins of the Roman *amphitheatre* built in 32 AD by a certain Fausto Tizio Liberale. Part of the wall in opus reticulatum survives. Built at the SW corner of the Roman city, it could hold up to 10,000 spectators.

Via XI Febbraio leads out of the piazza in front of the Duomo to the Romanesque church of *Sant'Alò*, in the road (left) of the same name. It has interesting Roman and medieval sculptural fragments on the exterior. The interior, with remains of frescoes, has been closed. Across Via Cavour (where on the right is the 16C *Palazzo Mazzancolli*), in Via Fratini the 17C Palazzo Fabrizi houses the **Pinacoteca Comunale** (open 10–13, 16–19, except Monday). The collection is well labelled. In the first room: L'Alunno, Standard with the Crucifix and Saints Francis and Bernardine (1497). In the room to the left: Benozzo Gozzoli, small painting of the Marriage of St Catherine (signed and dated 1466); Pier Matteo d'Amelia (formerly known as the 'Master of the Gardner Annunciation'), triptych with the Madonna enthroned between two saints, and large triptych of the Madonna with four saints, complete with predella and painted frame, dated 1485. The other rooms contain 17–18C works, including some by Gerolamo Troppa (c 1636–after 1706), and an 18C Visitation. The modern collection has graphic works, and paintings by the local painter Orneore Metelli.

At the end of Via Fratini Via Nobili leads left to a piazza in front of the church of **San Francesco**, first built in 1265. The elegant campanile is by Antonio da Orvieto (1345). The PARADISI CHAPEL at the end of the S aisle (light on right) was frescoed in the mid-15C by Bartolomeo di Tommaso of

Foligno with unusual scenes of the *Last Judgement, inspired by Dante's 'Divina Commedia'. They are among the most interesting works in Umbria of this date (restored in 1988). On the N side of the crossing the sacristy occupies the ex-Cappella della Croce Santa with remains (high up) of stucco decoration by Sebastiano Fiori (1575).

From Piazza della Repubblica (see above) the Corso Vecchio leads NE. In a little square on the right rises the church of *San Pietro*, rebuilt in 1287 and restored after the Second World War. On the façade is a 15C relief of Christ blessing. Among the 14–15C frescoes inside is a Transition of the Virgin (almost totally ruined). In the first niche on the N side is a 14C fresco by a painter from Spoleto. Nearby is *Palazzo Carrara* where part of the archaeological collection of the Museo Civico is kept, including local Iron Age finds (but at present they are not on view). The Corso continues past the *Teatro Verdi* (now also used as a cinema) built in 1849 by Luigi Poletti with a neo-classical portico (reconstructed after the War) to *San Lorenzo*, with an unusual interior with two naves, one much lower than the other. It has two Roman columns and a painting of the Martyrdom of St Biagio (late 16C). To the W is Corso Tacito laid out in the 19C to connect Piazza della Repubblica to the station. Here the Caffè Pazzaglia, still famous for its pastries, was opened in 1913.

On the outskirts of the town, across the railway (reached by Viale di Porta Sant'Angelo; 2km), in the cemetery, is the church of *Santa Maria del Monumento*, enlarged in 1474, named after a Roman funerary monument (part of which is inserted into the façade). On the S wall are interesting 15C votive frescoes of uncertain subject matter.

Two kilometres S of the centre, reached by Via Roma, and beyond the river Nera, by Via Mentana, is the 17C Basilica of *San Valentino*, on the site of a cemetery with the tomb of the martyr St Valentino, beheaded in 273 AD. The first basilica here was probably built in the early 4C, and reconstructed in the 7C.

The *Cascata delle Marmore, 6km SE, are reached either by the Rieti road (Via Garibaldi) or the Ferentillo road (Piazza Dante). A bus runs from Piazza Dante along the Valnerina road (10min). This waterfall, 165m long and on three levels, is one of the most spectacular sites in Italy, and a famous tourist excursion. The falls have been diverted entirely for industrial purposes, but are released to their original channels on certain days throughout the year. The times vary but at present they can be seen as follows. In winter: fest. 15–16; mid-March–April, and September and October: fest. 10–12, 15–21, Saturday, 18–21; May–August: fest. 10–13, 15–22, Saturday, 17–21; 15 July–31 August, also on weekdays, 17–18.30. In great measure they are the work of man, for Curius Dentatus, conqueror of the Sabines (271 BC), was the first to cut a channel by which the river Velinus (Velino) was thrown over a precipice into the river Nar, to prevent floods in the plain of Reate (Rieti). Another channel was cut in 1400 and a third (draining the plain of Rieti without flooding Terni) in 1785. Among the many travellers who have admired the falls are Galileo, Charlotte of Brunswick (wife of George IV), Corot, and Byron (who stayed here in the Villa Graziani Pressio in 1817 and describes them in 'Childe Harold's Pilgrimage'). They are surrounded by poplars, elms, pine trees and ilex woods: a path leads to the best viewpoint (and it continues to the station of Marmore, on the railway to Rieti). In recent years landslips have threatened the stability of the travertine rock.

The road continues from Marmore to (13km) **Piediluco**, a charming little resort on the beautiful **Lago di Piediluco**, the second largest lake in Umbria (with a perimeter of 17km). 3-star hotel 'Casalago', and 2-star hotel 'Lido', and 2-star camping site. The irregular fingers of the lake reach up into pretty woods. The attractive long main street of Piediluco runs parallel to the lake past the flank of the church of *San Francesco* (1293) approached by a wide flight of steps and entered by its side door. It contains a stoup made out of an Antique capital and (on the S wall) two paintings of prophets (1581) on either side of a niche decorated with stuccoes and a statue of St John the Baptist. To the left is a niche with a Roman *Statue of a lady, a remarkable work and an unexpected sight. The frescoes include works by Marcantonio di Antoniazzo. A lane leads up from the church to the ruins of the *Rocca* (542m) built by Cardinal Albornoz in 1364. N79 continues into Lazio towards Rieti, see *Blue Guide Northern Italy*.

Nine kilometres S of Terni is the hill town of *Stroncone* which preserves part of its medieval walls and several churches. 3-star camping site 'I Prati', and Trattoria 'Taverna di Portanova'. One kilometre outside is the church of San Francesco with interesting frescoes (one by Tiberio d'Assisi) and a wood statue of St Sebastian.

Collescipoli, an interesting little village, lies 4km SW of Terni. The church of Santa Maria has a 16C portal, 17C stuccoes and frescoes, and a striking painting of the Death of St Joseph, by an unknown 17C painter. Outside, in the cemetery, is the church of *Santo Stefano*, with an interesting relief of the Crucifixion above its portal, and an inscription describing the donation in 1093.

FROM TERNI TO SAN PIETRO IN VALLE, N209, 23km. The road follows the Valnerina (the upper part of which is described in Rte 12). 13km On the right is the village of **Arrone**. (1st class Restaurant 'Grottino del Nera', and 2-star hotel with restaurant at Castel del Lago 'Rossi'). The church of Santa Maria is on a by-road for Piediluco. In the interior, in the apse on the right of the main altar, is a fresco of the Madonna of the Misericordia (1544) by Jacopo Siculo. In the main apse are frescoes by Vincenzo Tamagni and Giovanni di Spoleto (derived from the frescoes by Filippo Lippi in the Duomo of Spoleto). In the apse to the left of the main altar are three fine terracotta statues of the Madonna and Child seated in a niche flanked by two saints. On the left wall is a small painting in a pretty frame which is an early 20C copy of a painting by the school of Perugino.

A by-road continues through woods to *Polino* (11km) in a lovely position, above which is Colle Bertone (1232m) with the 1-star hotel 'La Baita'. 18km **Ferentillo** is situated on both sides of the main road, and has recently expanded. On the left of the road is Santa Maria with a tall campanile with a pyramidal top. Inside (usually closed) are 16C works. On the right of the road is the church of *Santo Stefano* (also usually closed), in the crypt of which is a bizarre Museum of Mummies (ring for custodian). Here are shown some 20 mummified corpses, the exceptional preservation of which is probably due to the ventilation in the rock and the composition of the earth in which they were buried. The frescoes date from the 15C.

The main road continues and there is soon a good view (left) of San Pietro in Valle. Just before (23km) Sambucheto there is a yellow sign (left) for *San Pietro in Valle. A narrow road (nearly 2km long) leads up past the custodian's house (indicated with a yellow sign; ring) just over 1km before the abbey, which is in a splendid position enclosed amidst woods and fields. From the terrace there is a view of the beautiful unspoilt countryside. The domed church, founded in the 8C, preserves its triapsidal plan, and contains remarkable though damaged mural *paintings of scriptural scenes (c 1190). These are among the most important works of this era to have survived in Italy; they are being restored. The high altar has a very unusual medieval altar frontal with decorations in bas-relief signed by 'Ursus'. Among other interesting sculptural fragments in the church are five sarcophaghi, including the so-called sarcophagus of Faroaldo (3C) with Dionysiac scenes. The charming two-tiered cloister and the campanile are of 12C workmanship. The main road continues up the pretty Valnerina, described in Rte 12.

FROM TERNI TO ACQUASPARTA, N397, 23km. 4km turning right for **Cesi** (7km), an interesting little medieval town which preserves an altarpiece of the *Madonna and Child with saints and angels of 1308. The artist, known from this work as the 'Maestro di Cesi' shows the influence of the Spoleto school. 13km **Sangemini** is a small town famous for its mineral water (see below). 3-star hotel 'Duomo'. A local festival, the 'Giostra dell'Arme', is held here in late September when numerous 'taverne' are open which offer good meals. At the entrance to the town (left) is Piazza San Francesco with a fountain and gardens above it. Here is Palazzo Comunale with its clock and *San Francesco* with a pretty vaulted interior, and interesting frescoes (15–17C). Via Roma, left of the church, leads to the newer part of the town with a 19C Duomo. Outside a gateway (1723) is the church of *San Nicolò* (privately owned) with Roman and medieval remains and a fresco of 1295. From Piazza San Francesco, Via Casventino, a lovely narrow old street leads through the medieval gateway to the little piazza in front of the picturesque *Palazzo del Popolo*. Across the road is the oratory of *San Carlo* with frescoes of the 14–15C in the interior (closed). The road continues to *San Giovanni*. The mosaics of its Cosmatesque portal have virtually disappeared. The inscription above gives the date (1199) and architects of the church. The oddly-shaped interior has two octagonal pilasters and four gilded wood altars. An archway nearby leads out to a terrace with a view.

The main road continues to (16km) a crossroads near the spa buildings of *San Gemini Fonte* (2-star hotel and restaurant 'All'Antica Carsulae'). The road to the right (signposted for San Gemini Fonte) leads past the spa and hotel and then left for the Roman remains of *Carsulae (3km; the shorter, signposted road is unsurfaced and not easy to follow). The ruins are preceded by a map of the site, which is unenclosed and surrounded by lovely countryside. This was an important Roman station on the Via Flaminia, on the site of the Umbrian town of Carseoli. It was abandoned after an earthquake. The little medieval church of *San Damiano* was built from Roman materials. It faces the Via Flaminia, with its ancient paving stones, which leads right to the area of the Forum, with remains of a basilica on the right, and on the left, behind a restored arch, steps lead up to a piazzale once surrounded by public buildings. The Via Flaminia continues to the limit of the town, marked, just over the hilltop, by the Arch of St Damiano. Outside the arch is a large circular sepulchre and other funerary monuments. On the other side of the approach road are the remains of the amphitheatre and theatre. At *Portaria*, 3km N is the Trattoria 'Pesciaioli'.

The main road continues and crosses under the 'superstrada' to (23km) **Acquasparta**, another spa town (3-star hotel 'Villa Stella'). It preserves remains of its walls and in the pretty garden outside them there is a little aviary. In the centre is the fine *Palazzo Cesi (now owned by the University of Perugia; admission by previous appointment) built by Giovanni Domenico Bianchi in 1564. Here in 1624 Galileo stayed for a month as a guest of Federico Cesi. It has a lovely interior courtyard. In the loggia in the piazza are preserved interesting Roman cippi and inscriptions. Corso dei Lincei (named to commemorate the refoundation here in 1609 of the Accademia dei Lincei by Federico Cesi) leads along the garden wall of the Palace out of the village to the church of *San Francesco* (1290; kept locked; ask at

Santa Cecilia for the key). It contains a 15C Crucifix. On the other side of Palazzo Cesi a road leads to the church of *Santa Cecilia*. In the third domed chapel off the S side, built in 1581, are the tomb of Federico Cesi, reliquaries and cupboards containing vestments. Outside the walls is the church of the *Crocifisso* with a façade dating from 1606. The main road continues towards Massa Martana (see Rte 7) and Todi (Rte 8).

NARNI is situated on a hill (244m) 12km W of Terni. It is a pleasant old town (20,600 inhab.) which preserves many interesting medieval buildings along its nicely paved streets. It has fine views over the plain of Terni and the deep wooded gorge of the Nera river.

Information Office. 'Pro Loco', Palazzo Comunale.

Railway Station at Narni Scalo at the foot of the hill, on the Ancona–Rome line (slow trains only).

Buses ('ATC') to Terni.

Car Parking near Via Roma, or in Piazza Garibaldi (limited space).

Hotels and Restaurants. 4-star: 'Dei Priori' (with 'La Loggia' restaurant), 4 Vicolo del Comune: 3-star: 'Il Minareto', 32 Via dei Cappuccini Nuovi (also with a first-class restaurant). Trattorie and Pizzerie: 'Il Grifo', 3 Via Roma; 'La Cappuccina', Via Garibaldi. 2km outside on the Via Flaminia, Trattoria 'Del Cavallino'. **Camping site** (2-star) at Monte del Sole. Good places to **picnic** in the garden behind San Domenico, or around the Rocca.

Annual Festival. On the second Sunday in May a medieval tournament, the 'Corsa all'Anello' is held, preceded by two weeks of festivities.

History. Originally called 'Nequinum', it changed its name to *Narnia* (after the river) when it became a Roman colony in 299 BC. It was the birthplace of the emperor Nerva (AD 32), of John XIII (pope, 965–972), and of Erasmo da Narni, called Gattamelata, the Venetian condottiere (died 1443). Virgil, followed by Macaulay ('the pale waves of Nar'), refers to the whitish turbidity (due to its content of sulphur and lime) of the stream washing the foot of the hill.

The main road from Perugia and Terni runs through the modern suburb of *Narni Scalo* and then begins to climb before crossing the Nera river. From the bridge there is a brief glimpse of the monumental ruined ***Ponte d'Augusto**, which was built by Augustus to carry the Via Flaminia across the river gorge. The bridge, 30m high, had a span of 160m and was built of concrete faced with blocks of white travertine. One arch survives, but it is extremely difficult to see as there is nowhere to stop on the road bridge, and it can no longer be seen from the road beyond. There is a famous painting by Corot of the bridge. The Narni road then diverges left and climbs up round the hill through the *Porta Ternana*, commissioned by Pope Sixtus IV. Via Roma continues past a War Memorial (1927, by Pietro Lombardi) in the form of a lighthouse, and runs through the middle of **Piazza Garibaldi**. This is the unusual main square of the town, with a fountain above a huge cistern, a quaint neo-classical palace, a clock tower and the side door of the Duomo. On the right side of the square is the most interesting part of the town, regularly laid out on the site of the Roman Narnia; on the left some medieval streets survive and the hill-top is crowned by the Rocca (see below).

A road leads up under an archway to the main entrance of the ***Duomo** preceded by a fine PORTICO, a Lombard work of 1490. The main 12C portal has classical carvings. The INTERIOR, consecrated in 1145, has an outer S aisle added in the 15C, fine Corinthian columns, and two pretty pulpits (1490) on either side of the nave. On the W wall, in a niche, is a fresco of the Madonna and Child by a local painter. SOUTH AISLE. The third chapel has a fine carved Renaissance entrance arch (1490), a decorated barrel vault and a lovely tabernacle for the Host. In the nave here can be seen remains of the Cosmatesque pavement. Beyond is the ORATORIO DI SAN CASSIO where in 376 St Giovenale was buried. It is preceded by an old marble screen with Cosmatesque decoration and a relief above the door with two Lambs adoring the Cross. In the two niches are a 13C terracotta Pietà and a 13C statue of St Giovenale. High up on an inner wall (very difficult to see; the sacristan turns on a light on request) is a ruined 10C mosaic of the Redeemer, and remains of Roman masonry. Inside the oratory, with its old pavement, there is an interesting bas-relief and Cosmatesque fragments, and, in the inner cell, the open sacrcophagus (6C) of St Giovenale. On the last S pilaster of the nave is a painting of St Giovenale attributed to Vecchietta. In the SOUTH TRANSEPT the Cappella della Beata Lucia was built in 1710 and decorated with paintings by Francesco Trevisani. The PRESBYTERY dates from 1669–1714. In the apse, which retains its French Gothic form, are choir stalls of 1474. NORTH AISLE. Beyond a chapel with a 15C Madonna and Child and a funerary monument of Bishop Pietro Gormaz (1515) is the wall monument of Pietro Cesi, attributed to Bernardo da Settignano (1470). At the W end of the aisle is a wood statue of St Anthony Abbot enthroned, signed and dated 1475 by Vecchietta.

Outside the Duomo, in the little Piazza Cavour, is a house partly built with Roman blocks of stone, once belonging to the town walls. Just out of the piazza, off Vicolo Belvedere, is Via Arco Romano (right) with the *Porta Superior*, a Roman arch restored in the Middle Ages. The straight Via Garibaldi, with fine paving, on the line of the Roman Cardo Maximus, leads towards Piazza dei Priori. It passes (left) the pretty arched Via del Campanile with a view of the *Campanile* of the Duomo, constructed on a Roman base. It was completed in the 15C and is decorated with majolica plaques. Beyond the 19C *Teatro Comunale* the road widens to form **Piazza dei Priori** with its interesting medieval buildings. On the right is *Palazzo Sacripante* with fine medieval bas-reliefs on its façade, next to the *****Loggia dei Priori**, attributed to Gattapone, with two very tall arches and a Roman inscription. Next to the little pulpit used for reading public proclamations is a tall tower.

Opposite is **Palazzo dei Podestà** (now **Palazzo Comunale**) with more interesting Romanesque *reliefs, especially above the door into the 'Pro Loco' tourist office (which has a fresco by Torresani inside). In the courtyard are numerous Roman and medieval architectural fragments including columns, sarcophaghi, and a lion from a funerary monument. Upstairs (admission on request) some restored works of art are temporarily displayed in a small room (they belong to the PINACOTECA, formerly exhibited in San Domenico and eventually to be rehoused in Palazzo Eroli). These are: Annunciation by Benozzo Gozzoli, and a Standard of 1409 with the Dormition and Coronation of the Virgin (and, on the back, the Madonna enthroned), by the 'Maestro di Narni'. An Egyptian mummy (thought to date from the 4C BC) is also kept here. Among sculptures at present not on view are a bust in terracotta of St Bernardine by Lorenzo Vecchietta and a wooden Romanesque statue of the Madonna and Child. The SALA DEL CONSIGLIO is also shown: it is dominated by the *Coronation of the Virgin, a beautiful altarpiece by Domenico Ghirlandaio.

Beyond the lovely circular 14C fountain, with a bronze basin (1303), Via Mazzini continues gently downhill past the church of **Santa Maria in Pensole** (1175; usually closed) preceded by a Romanesque portico and three doors surrounded by fine (if worn) carving. The arches in the interior are similar to those in the Duomo, and the high altar is interesting. On the walls are remains of 14–15C frescoes. Various rooms beneath the church, with Roman fragments, can sometimes be visited. Opposite is the 17C Palazzo Bocciarelli next to the 16C *Palazzo Scotti*, with a fine loggia in the courtyard. Beyond can be seen the tall campanile of the 12C former church of **San Domenico**, now the seat of the Public Library and Archives (admission during office hours). The FAÇADE has a portal with interesting, if worn, decorations including medallions with busts of the twelve Apostles and, higher up, a cornice with animal and human heads as brackets. The INTERIOR contains numerous 13–16C fresco fragments. Opposite a marble tabarnacle by the school of Agostino di Duccio, is the fine wall monument of Gabriele Massei (1494). In a chapel off the left side (where exhibitions are held) are very worn frescoes by the Zuccari. Here is temporarily displayed the tusk of an elephant dating from the Pleistocene era, found in 1988 near Taizzano above the Nera river.

Behind the church (left) is a little public garden with remains of two sides of a very tall tower. There is a remarkable view over the deep Nera gorge to the wooded cliffs beyond. The Abbey of San Cassiano (see below) is conspicuous. The road and railway to Rome run on either side of the river.

From Piazza dei Priori (see above) roads descend right and left to the two churches of Sant'Agostino and San Francesco. Via dei Nobili and Via XIII Giugno lead down to **Sant'Agostino** with an unusual massive plain portal and a worn fresco attributed to Antoniazzo Romano on the façade. The INTERIOR has an exceptionally high nave with a 16C painting in the carved ceiling by the local artist Carlo Federico Benincasa. The first S altar has four saints and a predella by a follower of Antoniazzo Romano. A 16C carved wood Crucifix has been removed. In the apse is a massive 14C stone altar. Off the W end of the N aisle is a chapel (usually closed) with 16C frescoes by Lorenzo Torresani. On the right of the main door is a fresco attributed to Pier Matteo d'Amelia. Near the church, Via Gattamelata leads N past some old houses (including No. 70, traditionally supposed to be the birthplace of Gattamelata, the condottiere), to *Porta della Fiera* (or Porta Nuova) attributed to Vignola.

Off the other side of Piazza dei Priori is the church of *San Francesco* (usually closed) with a very worn carved portal. It contains interesting 14–15C frescoes on the columns and in the Cappella Eroli. In the sacristy are 16C frescoes by Alessandro Torresani.

From the S side of Piazza Garibaldi (see above) Via del Monte leads up through another part of the town which has a number of medieval streets. On the left Via Nerva leads to the 17C church of *Santa Margherita* whose walls are frescoed with stories from the life of St Margaret by the Zuccari. From here roads lead on up to the **Rocca**, a huge square-towered castle, very conspicuous above Narni from the plain of Terni. It was built for Cardinal Albornoz in the mid 14C and is attributed to Gattapone. It is being restored.

Just outside Narni (approached from a road near the bridge over the Nera, from which it is clearly seen) is the 12C Benedictine abbey of *San Cassiano*. Recently restored, it is open on Sundays.

The road from Narni towards Rome ascends the Nera valley. It passes near (4km) *Taizzano* with the abbey of Sant'Angelo in Massa (10C; now privately owned), and the ruined church of San Martino. 6km. Turning (right) for *Visciano*, near which is the quaint church of *Santa Pudenziana*, probably dating from the 11C, with a very tall campanile, and preceded by a primitive portico with two Roman columns. At Ponte

Sanguinaro this road joins the old road from Narni. 16km **Otricoli** is an old walled village on the site of the first settlement of Ocriculum (which later moved down to the banks of the Tiber). In the Middle Ages the inhabitants returned to this hill-top site to avoid the floods of the river. It has an attractive main street with porticoes and the church of Santa Maria, founded in the 6C or 7C with a neo-classical façade. The interior has remains of frescoes and medieval sculptural fragments. Off the main road, just beyond Otricoli, a road on the right leads in c 1km to the remains of the first church of Otricoli, San Vittore, and the old Roman Flaminia, lined with ruined funerary monuments. Here is the (unenclosed) site of the Roman *Ocriculum on the Tiber. The romantic overgrown ruins of the theatre, baths, and amphitheatre survive. Excavations here in 1776–84 by order of Pius VI resulted in numerous finds, now in the Vatican Museum (including a beautiful mosaic and the colossal head of Jupiter both in the Sala Rotonda). The site, of the greatest interest, is now semi-abandoned, and in need of protection, although excavations continue. The main road descends steeply to enter Lazio and cross the motorway and Tiber just below the village of Magliano Sabina (see *Blue Guide Northern Italy*).

A road winds SE of Narni to (14km) the *Speco di San Francesco* (568m), a picturesque Franciscan convent isolated in woods, founded by St Francis in 1213. St Bernardine built the present building in the 14C.

Another road (18km) winds due S from Narni to *Calvi dell'Umbria*, a medieval village (401m). In the church of Sant'Antonio is a crib of more than 30 large terracotta figures (1546). The church of San Paolo was designed in 1744 by Ferdinando Fuga (who also built the façade of Sant'Antonio).

From Narni N205 leads W, and beyond the Nera bridge, passes the *Madonna del Ponte* (rebuilt, after having been blown up along with the medieval road bridge in 1944) and ascends to (12km) **AMELIA**. This is a beautifully sited hill-top town (406m) above the Tiber surrounded by spectacular countryside. Its splendid polygonal walls are a remarkable survival from around the fifth century BC. The peaceful old town has interesting buildings of several different periods.

Information Office. 'APT dell'Amerino', 1 Via Orvieto (outside Porta Romana); Tel. 0744/981453.

Railway Stations. The nearest stations are Narni (on the Ancona–Rome line), 11km E, and Orte (on the Florence–Rome line), 15km S (bus services to both stations).

Buses ('ATC') to Terni, Orte, and Orvieto, as well as Alviano, Avigliano Umbro, Attigliano, Lugnano in Teverina, etc.

Car parking. Outside Porta Romana (mini-bus service up to the centre).

Hotels outside the old centre. 3-star: 'Scoglio dell'Aquilone', 23 Via Orvieto. 2-star: 'Anita', 31 Via Roma (on the Narni road).

Restaurants. 1st class: 'Anita' (see above); 'La Gabelletta', 3.5km away in Località La Gabelletta. Pizzeria in the old centre: 'La Tavernetta', Via della Repubblica. Good places to **picnic** outside the walls near Porta Romana.

History. This was the ancient *Ameria*, said by Pliny to have been founded three centuries before Rome. It became a Roman Municipium in 90 BC on the Via Amerina from Nepi to Chiusi. Virgil and Cicero mention the fertile countryside surrounding the town, noted especially for its vineyards. A remarkable bronze head of a statue of Germanicus, father of Caligula, was found here in 1963; it has been taken to Perugia for restoration. The native painter Pier Matteo d'Amelia (Manfredi; 1440–1509) has recently been identified with the anonymous painter up to now known as the 'Maestro dell'Annunciazione Gardner'. Alessandro Geraldini (1455–1525) was born here: he helped obtain the approval at the court of Spain for Columbus' expedition, and later travelled as bishop to Santo Domingo.

The main entrance to the town is through the 16C *Porta Romana*, outside which can be seen the best stretches of the polygonal (Pelasgic) *walls thought to date from the 5C BC. They are now c 8m high and 3.5m thick.

They can also be seen from a pretty garden to the left of the gate. Via della Repubblica leads up towards the centre of the old town. On the right is a piazza with a War Memorial (1923, by Angelo Guazzaroni) and the church of **San Francesco** (or Santi Filippo e Giacomo), with a rose window in its façade of 1401. In the chapel of Sant'Antonio on the right are six funerary *monuments of the Geraldini family. The one on the right above is by Agostino di Duccio (1477). Via della Repubblica continues for some way before reaching (left) the stepped Via Antonio da Sangallo which descends to the handsome *Palazzo Farrattini* with a fine long inscription dividing the first and second floors. Modelled on Palazzo Farnese in Rome, it was built in 1520 by Antonio da Sangallo the Younger. Inside is preserved a restored Roman mosaic. In front of the palace, beneath an arch, is a public fountain. Via della Repubblica now winds uphill past a fork with Via Assettati (which leads right through a medieval district to *Porta Leone* in the walls). Beyond several flying arches, it tunnels under the *Arco di Piazza* an impressive medieval gate made up from Roman materials, to emerge in the delightful old **Piazza Marconi**, once the centre of the city. Here is a little medieval pulpit for public proclamations, the 16C *Palazzo Petrignani* and the 15C *Palazzo Nacci.*

The stepped Via del Duomo leads steeply up out of the square (keep right) to the **Duomo**, rebuilt in 1640–80. The fine 12-sided CAMPANILE, which incorporates Roman fragments, was built as the Torre Civica in 1050. The INTERIOR was decorated with frescoes and stuccoes in the 19C by Luigi Fontana. There is a little Romanesque column by the door. On either side of the entrance to the second S chapel are two Turkish flags, thought to have been captured at the battle of Lepanto. The octagonal chapel (attributed to Antonio da Sangallo the Younger) contains two Farrattini funerary monuments by Ippolito Scalza. In the S transept, in a pretty frame, is a Last Supper by the local painter Gian Francesco Perini (1538; in a very ruined condition, but restored in 1989). In the N transept chapel is a 15–16C wood Crucifix. In the first chapel in the N aisle is the recomposed tomb of Bishop Giovanni Geraldini (1476) by Agostino di Duccio and assistants. The two organs are interesting. In the Oratorio del Sacramento (locked) are two paintings by Nicolò Pomarancio. Other paintings which belong to the church but which are normally kept locked, include a beautiful painting of the Madonna and angels, a Madonna and Child attributed to Antoniazzo Romano, and a painting of Salomé with the head of the Baptist.

Outside the Duomo there is a fine view from a little garden. A road continues round the Duomo and Via Alessandro Geraldini descends past the red church of *Santa Caterina* to Via Cavour. Here is the church of **Sant'Agostino**. In the façade (1477) is a handsome portal with a very worn fresco. The interior was decorated in 1747 by Francesco Appiani. The Vision of St John at Patmos is by Pomarancio. In the sacristy, interesting frescoes and sinopie have recently been uncovered, thought to date from c 1000: there is a red star decoration on the vault, unusual floral motifs and four standing figures of saints. To the left Via Garibaldi continues past Via Posterla which descends (right; with a view of a wooded landscape beyond the path which leads out of the 13C Porta Posterola) to the church of *San Magno* beside its unusual little tower, which contains a precious organ of 1680 with two keyboards, and a painting of the Death of St Benedict by Antonio Viviani. Via Garibaldi emerges in Piazza Matteotti, a pleasant little square with a few trees. Beneath it is a remarkable huge *Roman Cistern* divided into ten vaulted reservoirs built in the 2C AD. The rainwater collected here provided the town with water. *Palazzo Comunale*, with a

The Collegiata di Santa Maria Assunta, Lugnano in Teverina

clock, is a quaint building; on the left (No. 3) is the entrance to the courtyard which contains numerous Roman sculptural fragments, including several carved altars. In the Sala Consigliare (admission on request) is a Madonna with saints by Pier Matteo d'Amelia and a Crucifix with two saints by Livio Agresti. Via Garibaldi continues, passing (right) Via del Teatro with the charming *Theatre*, built in 1783 (and frescoed in 1880 by Domenico Bruschi). It is undergoing a lengthy restoration. A short way farther on Via Garibaldi regains Piazza Marconi (see above).

Amelia is in the centre of a beautiful district at the SW corner of Umbria between the Tiber and the Nera rivers. Here little medieval villages and castles are dotted among wooded hills (noted for their chestnuts) and fields of vineyards and olive groves. N205 leads W from Amelia across the high Ponte sul Rio Grande, a pretty bridge, to **Lugnano in Teverina** (7km), an interesting old hill town with fine views (2-star hotel and restaurant 'La Rocca'). Just below the narrow main street is a little piazza in front of the *Collegiata di Santa Maria Assunta*, a beautiful 12C church. The delightful façade (covered for restoration), with interesting carving, is preceded by a pronaos of 1230. The beautifully proportioned interior has carved capitals and a Cosmatesque pavement. The 'schola cantorum' has been recom-posed and includes two interesting bas-reliefs. In the apse is a triptych by Alunno. The crypt has graceful columns. At the top of the left flight of steps is a painting of St Jerome by Leandro da Bassano, and at the top of the right flight of steps, a Crucifix of the 13C (a fresco transferred to canvas). In the chapel on the right, Livio Agresti, Beheading of the Baptist (1571).

The road goes on, with superb views, to a turning which leads down to **Alviano** (13km). Its splendid square *castle* can be seen on a spur with the village behind it. The first castle on this site dated from 933; the present building was begun in 1495 by the condottiere Bartolomeo d'Alviano, and incorporates a cylindrical tower of the earlier castle (the three others were added at this time). The piano nobile has handsome windows. Beside the bridge at the entrance is a lion with an iron collar, and on the round tower to the left can be seen a Medusa's head. Inside is a Renaissance courtyard with a well. The castle was bought by Donna Olimpia Pamphili in 1651 and the Doria Pamphili left it to the Comune in 1920. It has recently been restored and on the upper floor is the town hall, and on the ground floor, in fine vaulted rooms, a local ethnographical museum. On the left of the courtyard is a chapel with frescoes illustrating a miracle of St Francis who in 1212 stilled the song of the swallows who were disturbing his preaching outside the castle. In front of the castle, Via Umberto I (and steps down left) lead to the 15C *parish church* with a pleasant interior with old columns and capitals and wood roof. Here is a *fresco by Pordenone of the Madonna and saints with a striking portrait of Pentesilea Baglione, the old widow of Bartolomeo d'Alviano (on the right, protected by St Anthony), who com-missioned the fresco. At the end of the right aisle is a painting of the Madonna in Glory by Alunno.

The road continues from Alviano above the Tiber, and the OASI DI ALVIANO, a lake created in 1963, which since 1978 has been a protected area, interesting for its birdlife in early spring, autumn and winter (red herons, bitterns, reed warblers, cormorants, wild geese, etc). Seven bird-watching stations have been built here (information from the Comune of Alviano). The road passes the ruins (right) of Guardea Vecchia (Guardege), once an important stronghold acquired in 1158 by Pope Hadrian IV, before reaching **Guardea** (18km). Here the 15C Castello del Poggio (recently restored) has an interesting 11C stair. This road winds on N to Todi (see Rte 8).

N205 leads E out of Amelia and beside the huge monumental gateway and cypress avenue leading to Villa dell'Aspreta is a turning (left) signposted for Montecastrilli and Avigliano Umbro. This road leads through thick ilex woods and open farming country and then branches left towards Avigliano past *Sambucetole*, with a bright coral-coloured church, and *Castel dell'Aquila* (11km) with a very tall tower. *Avigliano Umbro* (14km), became a Comune in 1975. It has an original castellated water tower. Its little theatre dates from 1928. *Dunarobba*, 3km N of Avigliano, has a massive 15–16C castle. Just outside the village, 1km along the Montecastrilli road, is the FOSSIL FOREST OF DUNAROBBA, one of the most important palaeontological sites in central Italy. Here in 1983–87, during work in a clay quarry, a group of some 40 fossilised tree trunks were found, particularly remarkable since they were still in an upright position. They grew on the SW shores of the huge 'Lago Tiberino' which in the Pleistocene era occupied a large part of Umbria. Some of them are 1.5m in diameter and 8m high: they date from the Villafranchian or Pliocene era and are similar to the present-day

Sequoia. For admission ask at the Comune of Avigliano Umbro: in the school next door is a research centre with documents and exhibitions relating to the fossils. On the Todi road 2km N of Dunarobba is *Sismano*, a tiny village in beautiful country at the foot of a medieval castle owned by the Corsini since 1607. The parish church has a painting of St Andrea Corsini by Andrea Polinori. In the Arnata valley, in an isolated locality known as 'Molinella', are three 18C water mills. The road continues down to Todi (see Rte 8).

Montecastrilli is 5km E of Avigliano in lovely country. Of Roman origin, it was important from 962 onwards as part of the 'Terre Arnolfe'. The parish church, with a tall brick campanile rebult in 1952, contains a 15C wood Crucifix. The convent of the Clarisse also dates from the 15C. The Romanesque churches in the district include the tiny *San Lorenzo in Nifili*, dating from the 11C.

A road leads W from Avigliano to the tiny village of *Santa Restituta* (10km) surrounded by chestnut woods, near which, on Monte l'Aiola, is the 'Grotta Bella' where excavations in the early 1970s yielded finds from the Neolithic to Roman era including small bronzes of the 5C BC. Beyond is *Toscolano* (13km), another charming small village in beautiful countryside amidst chestnut woods, with wide views. It is built on a circular plan. Ouside, at the beginning of an avenue (left) is the peach-coloured chapel of Santissimo Annunziata (ask for the key in the village), with frescoes (restored in 1987) attributed to Pier Matteo d'Amelia. The village is entered by a gate above which is the eagle of Todi and the campanile of Sant'Apollinare (key at the bar to the right of the gate) which contains a Crucifix and saints by Andrea Polinori (recently restored).

From Amelia a road runs SW downhill towards Attigliano in the Tiber valley. 9km. Road left for **Penna in Teverina** (3km), a little medieval borgo on a terrrace overlooking the Tiber. It has a quaint little central piazza. The Palazzo Orsini has a 19C garden with 18C busts of the Four Seasons outside the main gate, and monumental carved herms known as the 'Mammalocchi' at another gateway. A Roman villa has recently been discovered at Penna Vecchia. The view from the fields outside of the houses built into the walls is remarkable.

Giove (13km) has medieval walls. The huge Palazzo Ducale (now owned by the Dukes of Acquarone), was begun in the 16C by Duke Ciriaco Mattei and incorporated a pre-existing castle. There is a spiral staircase up to the piano nobile, and the rooms were decorated by the school of Domenichino. Beside it is the parish church with a painting of the Assumption by the school of Alunno. In the chapel of San Rocco is a fresco of the Crucifixion by the Foligno school. *Attigliano* (18km), now virtually abandoned, is on an Etruscan site. The inhabitants have moved to houses nearer the station. Hotels at *Pantaniccio*, including 'Umbria' (3-star). Four kilometres away, on the other side of the Tiber and across the motorway, is the famous park of *Bomarzo* in Lazio, described in *Blue Guide Northern Italy*.

11

Spoleto

SPOLETO is a beautiful old town (36,000 inhab.) on the Via Flaminia, with Roman and medieval monuments of the highest interest. It lies on a hill (317m) in a charming landscape of high and thickly wooded hills, but the plain to the N has been spoilt by untidy suburbs. It has become famous for its music and drama festival held here in June and July.

Information Office. 'APT', 7 Piazza della Libertà, Tel. 0743/220311.

Railway Station, Viale Trento e Trieste, reached from Piazza della Vittoria. Services on the Ancona–Rome line to Terni (25min) and to Foligno (15min).

Buses from the station ('Circolare B') every 10min through the town to Piazza Carducci.
   Country Buses from Piazza Garibaldi to Monteluco, Campello sul Clitunno; to Perugia, Foligno, Terni, Norcia, Cascia, Montefalco; and to Rome, Florence, Siena, and Urbino.

Car parking is extremely difficult in the old town. Most car parks charge an hourly tariff. Long-term car parking in Viale Cappuccini or near the Stadium.

Hotels. 4-star: 'Gattapone', 6 Via del Ponte; 'Dei Duchi', 4 Viale Matteotti; 3-star: 'Charleston', 10 Piazza Collicola; 'Nuovo Clitunno', 6 Piazza Sordini. 2-star: 'Aurora', 3 Via Apollinare; 'Anfiteatro', 14 Via Anfiteatro; 'Dell'Angelo', 25 Via Arco di Druso. At *Monteluco*: 'Ferretti' (2-star hotel with restaurant). **Camping site** (2-star) open in summer at Monteluco.

Restaurants. Luxury-class: 'Il Tartufo', 24 Piazza Garibaldi; 'Gulliver Atelier', 43 Via Porta Fuga. 1st class: 'Sabatini', 56 Corso Mazzini; 'del Mercato', Piazza del Mercato; 'Del Quarto', 1 Via Cattaneo; 'Il Panciolle', 3 Via del Duomo; 'La Lanterna', 6 Via Trattoria; 'Pentagramma', Via Martani. Trattorie: 'Del Festival', 8 Via Brignone; 'Sportellino', 2 Via Cerquiglia; 'Tre Fontane', 15 Via Egio; 'La Barcaccia', Piazza Fratelli Bandiera; 'Pecchiarda', Vicolo San Giovanni. In the environs: 1st class: 'Antica Posta Fabria', Località Fabreria 15, and 'Ferretti' at Monteluco. Good places to **picnic** near the Rocca and Ponte delle Torri, and at Monteluco.

Theatres. 'Teatro Nuovo', Via Vaita Sant'Andrea; 'Teatro Caio Melisso', Piazza Duomo. The renowned **Festival dei Due Mondi** has been held annually in the town since 1958 (at the end of June and beginning of July). Theatre, ballet, and opera performances are given in the Teatro Nuovo, Teatro Caio Melisso, the Roman theatre, and the former church and cloister of San Nicolò. Open-air concerts are given in Piazza Duomo.

History. Numerous Bronze Age finds have been made in the town and surrounding territory. The Umbrian 'Spoletium' was colonised by the Romans in 241 BC, and survived an attack by Hannibal in 217. It suffered serverely in the conflict between Marius and Sulla. In 576 Spoleto became the seat of a Lombard (and later Frankish) duchy which ruled over a large area of Umbria and the Marches during the Middle Ages. In 1354 it was incorporated in the States of the church. It was the birthplace of the painter Lo Spagna (died 1528).

In Piazza della Libertà is the entrance to the **Roman Theatre** and **Museo Archeologico** (9–13, 15–19; fest. 9–13). The THEATRE dates from the Imperial era; it was damaged by landslides and built over in the Middle Ages. The ruins were drawn in the 16C by Baldassare Peruzzi, and were rediscovered by Giuseppe Sordini in 1891. Since 1954 they have been uncovered and heavily restored. A remarkable barrel-vaulted passageway survives beneath the cavea. Behind the scena is the apse of the former church of *Sant'Agata* (now used as a restoration centre). In the conventual buildings is the MUSEO ARCHEOLOGICO. On the ground floor are two rooms with

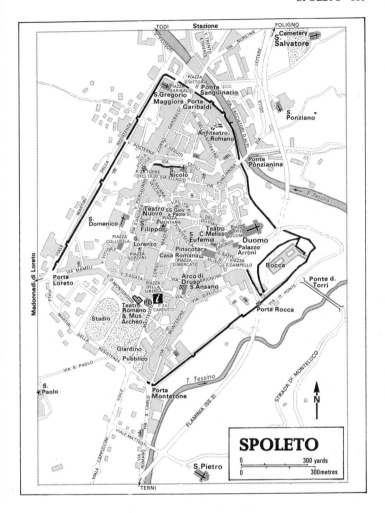

well-labelled finds from the town and surrounding territory. These date
from the Bronze Age to the Middle Ages and include material from the
tomb of a warrior found in Piazza d'Armi, and jewellery and pottery (7C–4C
BC) found, part of it by Giuseppe Bellucci, at the end of the last century.
More recent excavations in various parts of the city have yielded Bronze
Age material. In the hall beyond is a fine display of Roman epigraphs and
sculpture and, at the end, two remarkable *inscriptions of the 3C BC
forbidding the cutting of timber in a sacred grove. On the floor above,
diagrams and plans explain the history of the occupation of the Colle
Sant'Elia following excavations during the restoration of the Rocca Albornoz in 1983–86.

The steep Via Brignone leads uphill through Piazza Fontana with an elegant little fountain and *Palazzo Mauri* (16C–17C; being restored), seat of the Accademia Spoletina founded in the 17C, and of the Biblioteca Comunale. The church of **Sant'Ansano** was built in the Middle Ages above the foundations of a Roman temple. It was redesigned in the 18C by Antonio Dotti, and contains a fresco fragment of the Madonna and Child by Lo Spagna. Remains of the Roman temple (1C AD) have been exposed around the altar. Steps lead down (light on left) to the ancient CRIPTA DI SANT'ISACCO with primitive (11C–12C) frescoes (detached and restored). Outside can be seen the foundations of the cella of the Roman temple and Roman shops (for admission, enquire at the Museo Archeologico). These abut the **Arco di Druso**, dedicated in AD 23 to Drusus and Germanicus (the lower part of the arch is buried). Opposite is a 15C palace with the Albergo dell'Angelo where Gioacchino Rossini used to stay. Next to it is a large 16C palace. The Arco di Druso leads into **Piazza del Mercato** on the site of the Roman Forum. The huge and abundant wall fountain by Costantino Fiaschetti (1746) incorporates a monument to Urban VII by Carlo Maderno (1626; restored).

Via del Municipio leads up to Piazza del Comune (being repaved). Here is *Palazzo Comunale* with a tall tower, begun in the 13C but transformed in the 18C (and with a left wing of 1913). It faces a pretty row of old houses (being restored). The **Pinacoteca Comunale** is open 10–13, 15–18 (except Tuesday). A hand-list is lent to visitors. R1. Guercino, Mary Magdalene. R2 (with a view of the Duomo). Detached frescoes by Lo Spagna including a Madonna and Child with saints; *Reliquary Cross with miniature paintings (1200), two 13C painted Crucifixes. The interesting frescoes (late 12C or early 13C) of scenes of the Martyrdom of Saints John and Paul are attributed to 'Alberto Sotio' (they were detached from the ex-church of Santi Giovanni e Paolo). R3. Detached frescoes and a Madonna by Antonello de Saliba; 14–15C paintings including a triptych by Nicolò l'Alunno.

Beneath the left wing of Palazzo Comunale (entrance beneath the piazza in Via Visiale) are remains of a **Roman House** (admission 10–13, 15–18 except Tuesday), supposed to have belonged to Vespasia Polla (1C AD), mother of Vespasian, found and excavated in 1885–1912 by Giuseppe Sordini. It has very fine black-and-white geometric mosaic pavements (being restored in situ). In the large atrium is a beautiful well-head and impulvium. On the right is a case of finds supported on two handsome Roman marble pedestals. The tablinum, triclinium and peristyle have been identified and a fragment of red wall painting survives. The walls and vaults are medieval or modern.

Uphill to the east is *Piazza Campello*. Here is Palazzo Campello (transformed in the 18C) and the former church of Santi Simone e Giuda (13C). The colossal mask serving as a wall fountain (1624; restored in 1736) marks the end of the Roman (and medieval) aqueduct. The monument dedicated to those who fell in the struggle to liberate Spoleto from the Papal States is by Cesare Bazzani (1910). Here is the entrance gate to the huge *Rocca Albornoz** which was used as a prison up until 1982. It is undergoing a lengthy restoration and is expected to reopen in 1993 as a museum relating to the medieval Duchy of Spoleto, a restoration laboratory, and an exhibition centre. It was erected in 1359–64 by Gattapone for Cardinal Albornoz and still dominates the town. A long climb leads uphill to the main building with the Cortile d'Onore. Here is a well by Bernardo Rossellino, added when Nicholas V enlarged the castle. A number of frescoes have been uncovered here. Interesting remains of the 7C church of Sant'Elia have been found on the hillside (where excavations are in progress). The delightful view to the S takes in the Ponte delle Torri, the unspoilt valley of the Flaminia, and the walls which descend the hillside enclosing old houses with their orchards. To the N, the view extends over new buldings on the plain towards Assisi.

To the S is the Porta della Rocca and outside the gate are further remains of the old wall and the splendid *Ponte delle Torri, a bridge and aqueduct also probably built by Gattapone, but possibly on Roman foundations. It spans a deep ravine amidst ilex groves, and is 230m long and 80m high; it is one of the most remarkable sights in Italy (and was greatly admired by Goethe in 1786). A path on the far side leads across to the Monteluco road (see below); while another beautiful path leads right round the castle hill.

Via Saffi leads from Piazza Campello back towards the centre of the town. On the right is the stepped Via dell'Arringo (opened in the 13C), from the top of which there is a remarkable *view of the cathedral and the green hillside behind it crowned by the Rocca. The worn brick steps descend past the pretty apse of Sant'Eufemia (see below) and a sculpture by Lynn Chadwick (1962). On the right the 16C *Palazzo Arroni* has very worn graffiti decoration in great need of restoration. **Piazza del Duomo** (where concerts are held during the Festival) has brick paving in a herring-bone pattern. At the foot of the steps is a Roman sarcophagus (3C AD) set into the wall to serve as a wall fountain. Opposite is the pink-and-white building of the Opera del Duomo, the **Teatro Caio Melisso**, a little chamber theatre (at No. 3–5) built by Giovanni Montiroli (1877; restored for the festival) and decorated by Domenico Bruschi, and the church of Santa Maria della Manna d'Oro, with an octagonal top (described below).

The *Duomo (closed 13–15) was consecrated by Innocent III in 1198 and later much altered. The FAÇADE is preceded by an elegant Renaissance portico (1491) by Ambrogio da Milano and Pippo di Antonio da Firenze, incorporating two pulpits. Above are eight rose windows, and a mosaic signed by Solsternus (1207). The main portal is a fine 12C Romanesque work. The CAMPANILE (12C, with additions from 1416 and 1518) incorporates Roman fragments. The INTERIOR was transformed in 1634–44 for Urban VIII whose bust, by Bernini, surmounts the central door. The marble pavement dates in part from the 12C. SOUTH SIDE. The first chapel, the Cappella Eroli (light; fee) has frescoes by Pinturicchio (Madonna and Child with two saints, and the Eternal Father). In the adjoining Cappella dell'Assunta are early 16C frescoes. The first two 18C altarpieces are by Domenico Corvi (Deposition) and Antonio Concioli (Death of St Andrea Avellino). The third altarpiece of the Visitation is by Giovanni Alberti (16C). SOUTH TRANSEPT. On the right wall, recomposed funerary monument of Giovanni Francesco Orsini by Ambrogio da Milano (1499). The altarpiece of the Madonna and Child with saints is by Annibale Carracci. On the left wall is the tomb of Fra Filippo Lippi (see below) erected by Florentine artists at the order of Lorenzo il Magnifico, with a fine bust, and an inscription by Politian. Beneath the organ is the CAPPELLA DELLA SANTISSIMA ICONE rebuilt in 1626 by Giovanni Battista Mola. On the altar is a venerated 12C Madonna, two paintings by Cavalier d'Arpino, and two statues of Prophets attributed to Alessandro Algardi.

In the 12C APSE are *frescoes of the Life of the Virgin by Fra Filippo Lippi, perhaps his best work, and one of the masterpieces of the Renaissance (beautifully restored in 1987–90). He worked on them from 1467 until his death in 1469 (when he was buried in the neighbouring chapel, see above). The scenes, with monumental figures (larger than life-size), which cover

The Duomo, Spoleto

the vast space of the semicircular walls are divided by painted columns and friezes, the classical motifs of which are copied from buildings in Spoleto (including San Salvatore). In the central scene of the Transition of the Virgin, the group on the right includes Fra Filippo's self-portrait (in a white monk's habit over a black tunic, and with a black hat), a portrait of his son Filippino, then ten or twelve years old (the angel in front), and portraits of Fra Diamante and Pier Matteo d'Amelia, who were his assistants and who painted the Nativity scene. In the half-dome is the splendid Coronation of the Virgin, the best preserved fresco in the cycle, rich in blue and gold. The numerous figures include the sibyls, Eve, and other female personalities from the Old Testament, and angels with a great variety of musical instruments. Above, God the Father takes the place of Christ. No evidence of cartoons was found during restoration work on the figurative scenes. Many of the details (some of which have been lost) were added in tempera and highlighted with gilded wax roundels.

The fine CAPPELLA DEL SACRAMENTO was built in the early 17C: the 17–18C paintings are by Francesco Refini, Pietro Labruzzi and Liborio Coccetti. In the NORTH TRANSEPT is a good 16C painting of the Madonna and Child with two saints, and on the altar, St Ponziano among lions by Cristoforo Unterberger. NORTH AISLE. The CAPPELLA DELLE RELIQUIE is closed for restoration (and the stalls are temporarily exhibited in the church of Santa Maria della Manna d'Oro, see below). Third altar, Antonio Cavallucci (18C), Presentation in the Temple; second altar, Etienne Parrocel (attributed), Madonna and Child with saints; first altar, brightly coloured *Crucifix, signed and dated 1187 by 'Alberto So(tio)', the earliest known Umbrian painter. It was in the church of Santi Giovanni e Paolo until 1877, and was restored in 1991. A 14C wood statue of the Madonna and Child which also belongs to the church has been removed for restoration.

In the piazza is the church of **Santa Maria della Manna d'Oro** (unlocked on request at the Duomo), built as an ex-voto after the Sack of Rome in 1527. The octagonal drum was probably added later. In the 17C interior are a 16C font and paintings by Sebastiano Conca (Rest on the Flight, and Birth of the Virgin), and his pupil Nicola Costantini. Here have been temporarily placed the carved and inlaid stalls (1548–54) from the Cappella delle Reliquie in the Duomo, since their restoration. They are the work of Giovanni Andrea di Ser Moscato and Damiano di Mariotto (the paintings of Prophets and sibyls are by Francesco Nardini). Above the door are the remains of a funerary monument of Bishop Bernardino Lauri (died c 1516). Steps beside the campanile lead down to Piazza della Signoria where the 14C arcade of *Palazzo della Signoria* can be seen. The palace, which was never completed, adjoins the Teatro Caio Melisso (see above).

In Via Saffi, at the top of Via dell'Arringo (right) is *Palazzo Arcivescovile* with a small collection of works of art, including a fresco by the 'Maestro di Fossa' (not on view). In the courtyard is the 12C church of *Sant'Eufemia. The beautiful plain Romanesque interior (usually unlocked) has a matroneum, interesting capitals, and some 15C frescoes on the columns. The 15C triptych, behind the 13C Cosmatesque altar, has been removed for many years.

Via Saffi and Via Fontesecca continue downhill to a monumental flight of steps built in 1923 which descend to Piazza Pianciani. On the left is the church of **San Filippo**. The impressive façade (recently cleaned) dates from 1640 (by the local architect Loreto Scelli). Inside, on the S side, is a Presentation of the Virgin in the temple and a Crucifixion by Gaetano Lapis da Cagli. The altar in the N transept has columns in verde antico and a Holy Family by Sebastiano Conca. On the first N altar, Descent of the Holy Spirit by Lazzaro Baldi. In the elegant panelled 18C Sacristy is a marble *Bust of St Filippo Neri by Alessandro Algardi. In the piazza is the little medieval church of *Sant'Angelo* (now used as a parish office) with 16C frescoes. Corso Mazzini, the main street of the town, leads from here to Piazza della Libertà (see above). It passes Via delle Terme in which is Palazzo Rosari-Spada which houses the GALLERIA COMUNALE D'ARTE MODERNA (open 9–13, 15–19.30; fest. 10–13, 15–18; Tuesday morning closed).

Via Tobagi leads from San Filippo to the former church of **Santi Giovanni** e **Paolo** (left), consecrated in 1174. It is open in summer (10–12); at other times on request at the Pinacoteca. The frescoes inside are particularly interesting, and include a contemporary scene of the Martyrdom of St Thomas Becket (died 1170) and a figure of St Nicolò, both attributed to 'Alberto Sotio' (late 12C or early 13C). The other votive frescoes date from the 14C and 15C. Farther downhill is the **Teatro Nuovo** built by Ireneo Aleandri (1854–64). It is decorated inside by Giuseppe Masella and Vincenzo Gaiassi, with a back-cloth by Francesco Coghetti. Beside it is a hall decorated by Cesare Bazzani (1910). Nearby is the grand *Palazzo Collicola* (1737, by Sebastiano Cipriani) and the tiny 12C church of *San Lorenzo*.

The 13C church of **San Domenico** has a pleasant pink-and-white banded exterior. INTERIOR. The first S altar has an early 15C fresco of the Triumph of St Thomas Aquinas (detached and restored). In the S transept, Madonna and four saints by Giovanni Lanfranco. To the right of the presbytery a barrel-vaulted chapel is entirely covered with frescoes by a 15C artist. On the E wall of the church (below Gothic windows with 20C stained glass) are more frescoes. Above the altar hangs a 14C painted Crucifix. In the chapel to the left of the presbytery, with a dome decorated by Liborio Coccetti, Christ in the Garden by Cesare Nebbia. On the N wall of the nave is a touching fresco of the Pietà, a 14C painting of St Peter Martyr, and a striking polychrome wood Crucifix (recently restored). The crypt has further remains of frescoes.

Via Pierleone Leoni leads down to Piazza Torre dell'Olio which takes its name from the tall thin tower beyond *Porta Fuga* (12C?) or *di Annibale*, beneath which Via Porta Fuga descends to join Corso Garibaldi. The busy Via Cecili skirts the best section of **walls**. The polygonal masonry dates from the end of the 4C BC; the walls were consolidated by the Romans and in subsequent centuries up to the 15C. They are interrupted by the 14C apse of **San Nicolò**. The church, together with the former convent, have been restored as a cultural and congress centre. The Cloister may be visited (10–13, 15–18 except Tuesday). Excavations during restoration work here bought to light Bronze Age material. The ruins of the *Amphitheatre*, farther on, are within the ex-conventual barracks and difficult of access.

Corso Garibaldi and Via dell'Anfiteatro meet at the unattractive Piazza Garibaldi where the church of SAN GREGORIO was well restored in 1949. In the good Romanesque interior is a tabernacle attributed to Benedetto da Rovezzano (chapel to the left). Outside Porta Garibaldi (rebuilt since the War) are the remains (below ground level) of the *Ponte Sanguinario*, a Roman bridge, abandoned when the river was diverted in the 14C and rediscovered in 1817 when the existing bridge was built. From Piazza della Vittoria, a busy road junction, Viale Trento e Trieste leads to the *Station*, outside which is a huge iron sculpture by Alexander Calder (1962).

From Piazza della Vittoria a road (signposted; not a pretty walk) leads beneath the Flaminia superstrada to (c 1km) the cemetery. Here is the remarkable church of •**San Salvatore** (or *Il Crocifisso*), a palaeo-Christian church of the late 4C or early 5C of the greatest interest for its numerous classical elements. The damaged façade has fine portals and three unusual windows showing Oriental influence. The interior (open 7–17; 7–19 in summer) has Corinthian columns and a Roman architrave. Remarkable acanthus leaf capitals at the four corners of the presbytery stand out above the classical cornice.

A side road off Via di San Salvatore leads to the 12C church of **San Ponziano** (shown by a custodian, 8–12, 15–18), dedicated to the patron saint of Spoleto. It has a fine façade. The interior was remodelled by Giuseppe

Valadier in 1788. The crypt has two conical pillars, thought to be *metae* from a Roman circus, serving as columns; 14C and 15C fresco fragments; and a palaeo-Christian sarcophagus.

Outside the town to the S (c 1km from the centre) is the ancient church of **San Pietro** (reached on foot from Piazza del Mercato by the steep old Via Monterone, Via San Carlo, and then left across the Flaminia 'superstrada'; or by a pretty walk across Ponte della Torre by the Strada di Monteluco). The church, reconstructed in the 13C, has a Lombard *FAÇADE with a magnificent variety of large 12C reliefs, among the most important Romanesque sculptures in Umbria. On the upper part are statues of Saints Peter and Andrea above two bulls looking down. Around the central oculus are symbols of the Evangelists. The central door is surmounted by an Oriental lunette with Cosmatesque decoration and two eagles. On either side of the classical decoration around the door, in between panels of blind arcading, are paired reliefs representing allegories of work and Eternal Life (a farmer with two bullocks and a dog, a deer feeding its offspring and eating a serpent, and two peacocks pecking at grapes). The ten larger reliefs flanking the door represent (right) Christ washing St Peter's feet, the Calling of Saints Peter and Andrew, and three symbolic scenes relating to animal fables. On the left side: Death and Judgement of the Just, and Death and Judgement of Sinners, and three scenes showing struggles between lions and men. The INTERIOR was remodelled in 1699. On the W wall are 16C votive frescoes. The stoups date from the 15C. On the third S altar, Adoration of the Magi by a 16C Umbrian painter. The font dates from 1487. The *Canonica* outside has antique fragments in its façade. A path leads to the little church of *San Silvestro*, behind San Pietro, with a 14C fresco of the Calvary.

The church of **San Paolo Intervineas**, c 1km SW of the town (reached from Piazza della Libertà by Viale Matteotti and Viale Martiri della Resistenza) was mentioned by St Gregory the Great. It was rebuilt in the 10C and again in the 13C. It has a fine façade with a rose window. In the interior (for admission ring at the old people's home next door, 9–14) there are early 13C frescoes of prophets and the Creation, and an old altar. Also on the W side of the town, beyond Porta Loreto, a straight road lined with a long portico leads to the church of the *Madonna di Loreto*, begun in 1572 by Annibale Lippi on a Greek-cross plan with three paintings by Giovanni Baglione (1609).

A winding road (8km) ascends from San Pietro to **Monteluco** via the 12C church of *San Giuliano*, incorporating fragments of its 6C predecessor. The frescoes in the apse are by the 'Maestro di Eggi' (1442). The road climbs through the ilex woods of Monteluco (804m), occupied from the 7C by anchorites, to the convent of San Francesco (belvedere). The slopes are now a summer resort.

A pretty road (N395) from Spoleto climbs across the hills to Piediparterno (19km) in the Valnerina, described in Rte 12.

The main road (N3) which leads N to Foligno passes close to *Eggi* (5km) with frescoes by the 'Maestro di Eggi' in the church of San Michele Archangelo. San Giacomo (8km), Campello sul Clitunno, and the famous spring and temple of Clitunno (12km) are all described in Rte 6.

Another road leads NW towards Montefalco (23km: see Rte 7) via *San Brizio* (8km) with its 13C walls and an interesting parish church, and *Bruna* (11km), with a sanctuary of 1510. Castel Ritaldi (12km) is also described in Rte 7.

The road (N 418) which leads across the hills from Spoleto to Acquasparta (12km; see Rte 10) passes close to the pretty village of *Sant'Angelo in Mercole* (6km from Spoleto).

12

Foligno to Norcia, Cascia, and the Valnerina

This route covers a beautiful remote part of Umbria at its SE corner. Numerous earthquakes over the centuries have shaken its towns and villages, but they have always been carefully reconstructed and well restored. Work is still in progress in numerous localities to repair the damage wrought in 1979. Nearly all the monuments of interest are well signposted, but many churches in the remoter villages are kept locked for safety (the key can sometimes be found by asking locally; otherwise they are open only for services).

Road. N77.—16km *Casenove*. N319. 19km *Rasiglia*—32km *Sellano*—42km *Borgo Cerreto*—62km **Norcia**—80km **Cascia**—92km *Monteleone di Spoleto*—119km S. Anatolia di Narco in the **Valnerina**—153km **Terni**, see Rte 10.

Beautiful **walks** can be taken in this area: information with printed guide and map from the 'APT della Valnerina' in Cascia (Tel. 0743/71401).

From the N and Perugia, Norcia and Cascia are best reached by road from Foligno (described below), whereas the Valnerina, traversed by N209, can also be approached from Terni (see Rte 10). The Colfiorito road (N77) from Foligno, which passes close to the Abbazia di Sassovivo, is described in Rte 6 as far as (16km) *Casenove*. Here N319 diverges right for Norcia. At 19km *Rasiglia*, the road passes beside the Sanctuary of the *Madonna delle Grazie* (right; well signposted), which dates from 1450 (altered at the beginning of this century). In the interior, the walls have very interesting votive frescoes by the 15C Foligno school, including an unusual representation of an angel pacifying two warriors, St Anthony Abbot enthroned, and a Crucifixion. In the apse, designed at the beginning of this century, are numerous ex-votos. In the crypt (1947) is a recomposed and restored 15C sculptural group of the Madonna in Adoration.

The road now climbs gently up, winding through wooded hills to a summit level of 800m at the Valico del Soglio. It then descends through Villamagina to (32km) *Sellano*, founded by the Romans in 84 BC, in a lovely position with views of the wooded hills dotted with little hamlets. The main road passes the elegant octagonal church of the Madonna della Croce (1538). An avenue leads across a bridge to the church of Santa Maria (13C; enlarged in the 16C), with a coral-and-white façade. The interesting interior is being restored. The road descends into another deserted wooded valley. 42km **Borgo Cerreto** is situated at a T-junction with the VALNERINA road (N209), off which to the left of this junction (2km) the road for Norcia diverges (right) SE.

A road (signposted) leads across the river to the church of *San Lorenzo* whose 14C façade holds a rose window. The interior, with 15C votive frescoes, is only open for services. This by-road continues up to **Ponte** (1km), in a fine position between the valleys of the Nera and Tissino, beneath its ruined castle. There is a view of Cerreto di Spoleto (see below) across the Nera valley. The unusually tall rectangular façade of Santa Maria Assunta (1201) has recently been radically restored. The splendid rose window above a telamone is surrounded by symbols of the Evangelists. The exterior of the apse is also interesting. The beautiful interior has a fine dome and crossing. The

14C and 15C Umbrian frescoes include a detached Crucifixion. The altarpiece attributed to the 'Maestro di Cesi' was removed to Spoleto many years ago. The fine painting of the Deposition dates from the 17C.

The main road continues N towards Triponzo. Just before a tunnel a by-road leads left to **Cerreto di Spoleto** (2km), high up (558m) on a rock face above Borgo Cerreto. The piazza has a pretty fountain and lamp-posts. The 15C former Palazzo Comunale, with coats of arms on its façade, has recently been heavily restored. Also here is a 17C palace. Just outside the square is the church of the *Annunziata*. In the interior, at the W end, is an unusual octagonal font carved in local stone by Lombard sculptors in 1546. On the third right altar, Madonna of the Rosary, signed and dated 1583 by Felice Damiani. On the first left altar is a seated statue of the Madonna and Child in gilded wood. Beyond the church is the 15C *Torre Civica* (covered for restoration). At the other end of the piazza a road descends left past a public garden and, above (right), the church of *Santa Maria Delibera* (closed) with 16C altarpieces, beside a gate in the walls. It ends just before the 14C church of *San Giacomo* (locked; the key is kept at the Comune). Right on the edge of the hill (with a view beyond an arch of the valley), it is reached by steps. The interior (restored in 1974) contains important 15C frescoes (some attributed to the 'Maestro di Eggi'). The high altarpiece of the Visitation is signed and dated 1573 by Camillo Angelucci.

The main road to Triponzo traverses a tunnel, outside which is a Roman inscription (signposted) recording work carried out here by the Romans. *Triponzo* (3km) has been all but abandoned since the earthquake of 1979. This road continues up the Nera valley to cross the border into the Marches (6km) and continue to Visso, a lovely little town, see *Blue Guide Northern Italy*.

The Valnerina S of Borgo Cerreto is described at the end of this route. From the Valnerina road N396 leads SE towards Norcia through a series of tunnels along a narrow gorge of the river Corno. At (55km) *Serravalle di Norcia* (3-star hotel 'Italia'), the road for Cascia diverges right (see below). The Norcia road continues through the valley which widens out with lovely hills ahead and soon Norcia comes into view.

62km **NORCIA** is a delightful little town (5400 inhab.), situated in a fertile basin surrounded by a wide amphitheatre of hills. Over the centuries local architects have carefully reconstructed the principal monuments of the town damaged by a series of destructive earthquakes, and, since 1979 many churches and palaces are again in restoration and not at present accessible. It has particularly attractive buildings whose height was regulated to two storeys in 1859, and the lower walls of its palaces and churches are often buttressed for added solidity. Norcia has a notably cheerful atmosphere with numerous excellent food shops and restaurants, specialising in local delicacies (including black truffles and cured hams and salami). It has a number of pretty fountains and its 14C walls survive intact.

Information Office. 'Pro Nursia', Piazza San Benedetto.

Buses to Cascia, Borgo Cerreto, Spoleto, Foligno, Perugia, and Rome.

Hotels. 3-star: 'Posta', 12 Via Battisti; 'Garden', 12 Viale XX Settembre; 'Grotta Azzurra', 10 Via Alfieri.

Numerous good **restaurants** including 'Dal Francese', 16 Via Riguardati, and 'Grotta Azzurra' (see above). There are good places to **picnic** outside the walls.

History. On a site occupied in prehistoric times, Norcia came under Roman influence from 290 BC and was called 'frigida Nursia' by Virgil. It was the birthplace of St Benedict (480–550) and of his twin sister St Scholastica. It was a powerful free commune in the 13–15C. The first public service of steam carriages in Italy was inaugurated from Spoleto to Norcia in 1926. The town has suffered from terrible earthquakes throughout its history, particularly in 1703, 1730, 1859, and last, in 1979.

The main entrance to the town is through Porta Romana which leads in to Corso Sertorio, opened at the end of the 19C, which ends in the charming *Piazza San Benedetto, centre of the town, surrounded by handsome buildings. It has an attractive circular pavement with a monument to St Benedict (1880). The **Basilica of San Benedetto** has a fine 14C *FAÇADE with statues of Saints Benedict and Scolastica in two tabernacles, and in the lunette above the portal a fine relief of the Madonna and Child with two angels. On the right side is a portico, added c 1570, beneath which are interesting old stone measures for corn. Beyond the campanile of 1388 (restored in 1635) is a little tabernacle with a 15C fresco of the Madonna and Child. The INTERIOR was remodelled in the 18C. On the left of the entrance is a 16C fresco of the Madonna with Saints Barbara and Michael Archangel (being restored). On the second N altar, Resurrection of Lazarus, by the local painter Michelangelo Carducci (1560). In the N transept, Filippo Napoletano, St Benedict and Totila (1621). In the apse is a 16C wood Crucifix and choir stalls by local craftsmen (1515). In the S transept, Vincenzo Manenti, Madonna and St Scolastica and other saints. Off the S side, stairs descend to the CRYPT with remains of a late Roman house.

The delightful **Palazzo Comunale** (being restored) has a portico (1492) on the ground floor and a handsome enclosed loggia above (rebuilt in 1876 by Domenico Mollaioli). Steps (flanked by two lions, also by Mollaioli) lead up to the main portal (late 16C) at the base of the bell tower (1703). In the Sala del Consiglio is a painting of the Coronation of the Virgin by Jacopo Siculo (1541). In the 18C Cappella dei Priori is a reliquary of St Benedict in gilded silver by the local goldsmith Giovanni di Giovanni di Antonio (1450). Opposite is the handsome fortified palace, with four angle towers, called **'La Castellina'** (also being restored, and not at present open to the public), commissioned from Vignola by Julius III in 1554. Outside are two lions (formerly outside San Benedetto). In the courtyard are Roman fragments of statues and inscriptions. On the upper floor (reconstructed in 1779) is the **Museo Civico Diocesano** which has been closed indefinitely. The works of art include: Giovanni della Robbia (attributed), Annunciation (two glazed terracotta statues); 13C stone and polychrome wood statues of the Madonna and Child; a 13C *Deposition group of five wood statues; 15C wood statues including a German Pietà, and St Sebastian. The paintings include: a 12C Cross, a Madonna and Child with saints by Antonio da Faenza, a Risen Christ by Nicola da Siena (c 1460), and a 15C Sienese painting of St Francis in glory. An interesting old ballot box dates from the 15C.

Beside the Castellina, just off the piazza, is the **Duomo** (Santa Maria Argentea), built in 1560 by Lombard artists working with Vignola. The two statues in niches date from 1935, and the campanile was rebuilt in 1869. The INTERIOR was designed c 1755 by Cesare Maggi. S Side. First altar, Giuseppe Paladini, St Vincent Ferrer (1756); second altar, Pomarancio, Madonna and saints. On the third pilaster is a bust of Pius VII (1825). At the end of the N aisle, in the Cappella della Madonna della Misericordia, Madonna with Saints Benedict and Scolastica, with a view of Norcia, dating from the early 16C (restored in 1988). The beautiful altar in coloured marbles and intarsia is attributed to Francesco Duquesnoy (1640–41). On the first altar in the N aisle, wood Crucifix of 1494 by Giovanni Tedesco. The organ dates from the 18C.

The other churches in the town are all, at present, closed, and some are being restored. A road on the left side of the Duomo leads to *San Lorenzo*, a palaeo-Christian church rebuilt in the Middle Ages. It has Roman fragments on its exterior. It preserves a wood ceiling and stalls. From Piazza San Benedetto Via Battisti leads past *San Francesco* (restored in 1978) a fine 14C Gothic church with a portal and rose window. It contains early 16C frescoes. Opposite is the Monte di Pietà (1585). Across Piazza Garibaldi, with a round fountain, is the *Chiesa della Misericordia* with an 18C façade. At No. 12 Via Cavour is Palazzo Accica with another 18C façade. Via Marconi leads across Corso Sertorio, the main street of the town, to Piazza Vittorio Veneto. Here the *Teatro Civico*, on the site of an 18C theatre, was rebuilt by Domenico Mollaioli in 1876, but destroyed by fire in 1952. It is still closed for restoration, although work on the exterior is completed.

Via Colombo and (left) Via Anicia lead to the church of *Sant'Agostino* with a 14C portal and fresco in the lunette. It contains good early 16C frescoes and the wood altars, organ, and cantoria date from the 17C. The 17C altarpieces include a Pietà with saints by Gaspare Celio, and a Madonna and Child with Saints by Anastagio Fontebuoni. Opposite is the 17C Palazzo Bucchi-Corazzini. Nearby, in Via Amadio, is the church of the *Addolorata* (or San Filippo; awaiting restoration) with a 19C façade (with statues of 1935). The interior is decorated with stuccoes. In Via Manzoni is *Santa Caterina* with its campanile set into the walls. It has a 16C fresco of the Coronation of the Virgin. Beyond Sant'Agostino, is *Palazzo Colizzi* with a fine portal and windows of 1755, on the corner of Via Umberto, once the main street of the town. It leads left past the curious **'Tempietto'**, on a street corner, a very unusual edifice built in 1354 (and restored in 1975). It is a large tabernacle with classical elements and is thought to have been erected in connection with a Holy Week procession. Beyond is Piazza Carlo Alberto with a pretty fountain, and the church of *San Giovanni*, with its square campanile built into the walls. It is being restored. It has a fine wood ceiling (1713), and a fresco of the Madonna and Child with Saints Benedict and Scolastica (1520). The 'Madonna della Palla' is attributed to the sculptor Giovanni Dalmata. Via delle Vergine leads to the huge *Monastero della Pace* built behind a high wall in 1507, and abandoned after the earthquake of 1859 (and further ruined in 1979). Nearby, in Via delle Vergine, against the walls, is the monastery of *Sant'Antonio Abate* (being restored) with a conspicuous 18C campanile. The *Chiesa del Crocifisso* (covered with scaffolding) has a façade of 1747. Via Anicia leads back towards the centre past the *Oratorio di Sant'Agostinaccio* with a 17C interior with good local woodwork (including the ceiling and stalls). Near Piazza Palatina, with a fountain and trees, is the church of the *Madonna degli Angeli* with more good stalls. The 14C WALLS preserve numerous gateways. Outside Porta Palatina is a medieval public fountain.

FROM NORCIA TO PRECI, 18km. This is a beautiful road which passes a number of churches and small villages, nearly all of which were damaged in the earthquake of 1979. The road leads uphill to (6km) the *Forca d'Ancarano* (1008m) in pine forests, before descending into the *Valnido*, a lovely solitary valley. On the right is the church of **Santa Maria Bianca** (locked and covered with scaffolding since the earthquake), with a 15C loggia along the S side, a 16C portico at the W end, and an unusual campanile. On the left of the portal are worn frescoes in an edicola by a follower of Lo Spagna. The interior has fine columns and remains of 15C frescoes. The 'Madonna Bianca' is a high relief attributed to the Florentine artist Francesco di Simone Ferrucci (1511). The church also owns a wood Crucifix and statues of Saints Roch and Sebastian dating from the 16C. A short distance away can be seen the parish church of *San Benedetto* with a Madonna of the Rosary by Vincenzo Manenti. At (9km) *Ancarano* a road is signposted (right) for *Capo del Colle* (850m) with the 15C church of Sant'Antonio Abate, and high above, remains of the 14C Castelfranco. 11km. Another road right (signposted 'Sant'Andrea') leads up to the hamlet of **Campi Vecchio** which has been almost totally abandoned since the earthquake, but restoration work is in progress. Conspicuous from the plain below is the delightful *portico, with its well proportioned columns and arches, of the church of *Sant'Andrea*. On the façade, asymmetrically placed, is a Gothic portal with two charming lions. The square campanile has been rebuilt. In the interior (key at No. 1 Via Entedia) is a graceful 16C font and 16C gilded wood altars. Higher up the hill is *Santa Maria di Piazza* (closed) with a bell-cote, and 15C frescoes in the nave by the Sparapane. Still higher can be seen the tower of an old ruined castle. Works of art belonging to Campi (but not at present on view) include a painted Cross signed by 'Petrus pictor' (1242) and altarpieces by Antonio Sparapane.

The main road continues through the lower hamlet of Campi and beyond it, on the right of the road beside the cemetery, is the church of **San Salvatore** with a delightful primitive low *façade. Above two portals are two rose windows on slightly different levels, and the porch is supported by one column. The interesting interior (locked) contains frescoes by Giovanni and Antonio Sparapane and Nicola da Siena and a font for total immersion. 13km. A road leads left for **Todiano** (3km) and *Abeto* (4km) in the Valle Oblita, with a number of Florentine works of art. At Todiano the parish church has a Madonna with Saints Montano and Bartolomeo by Filippino Lippi and his bottega, a Crucifix between two angels, and St Bartholomew, John the Baptist, and Mary Magdalene, signed and dated 1623 by Francesco Furini. The collection of 15C Crosses, 17C copes and chasubles, and 18C silver belonging to the church further attest to its close connection with Florence over the centuries. At Abeto is the church of San Martino, rebuilt in the 18C. It contains the 'Madonna della Neve' and Saints Sebastian and Nicholas by Neri di Bicci, an Annunciation signed and dated 1603 by Pompeo Caccini, and a Madonna of the Rosary signed and dated 1641 by Matteo Rosselli.

The main road continues towards Preci through the sparsely populated green valley. Just beyond (15km) Piedivalle on the river is a road (right; signposted) for the former ***Abbey of Sant'Eutizio**, in the little side valley of Castoriana, just off the road, opposite its village. St Gregory the Great refers to the hermits St Spes and St Eutizio who lived in grottoes here in the 5C when they were visited by St Benedict. The Benedictine monastery was particularly important in the 12–14C. Giacomo Crescenzi, friend of St Philip Neri, took a special interest in the monastery in the late 16C, but the decorations of that date in the church were eliminated in 1956. Beside the entrance is the pentagonal E end of the church which was added in the 14C. The façade has a rose window (1236) with symbols of the Evangelists, and beside it, built on the top of an outcrop of rock is the 17C campanile. The beautiful interior (1190) has a single nave with a raised and vaulted apse. A painted Crucifix by Nicola da Siena (c 1460) has been removed for restoration. Behind the altar is an unusual funerary monument to St Eutizio, a fine work of 1514 attributed to Rocco da Vicenza. The stalls by Antonio Seneca (1516) are being restored. The interesting crypt has two huge sandstone columns. An archway leads into the former abbey with good two-light windows, and a fountain in the courtyard from which steps lead up to the grottoes in the rock face.

Numerous poplar trees grow along the river valley. A road left leads to

(18km) *Preci* a quiet little hamlet where restoration is in progress (2-star hotel 'Agli Scacchi', and 3-star camping site at Castelvecchio 'il Collaccio'). It was famous from the 14C to the 17C for its school of surgeons, who attended patients as illustrious as Sixtus V, Elizabeth I of England, the Sultan Mehjemed, and the empress Eleonora Gonzaga. Behind Piazza Municipio is the ruined church of Santa Caterina. The other church (Santa Maria) is closed: beside it is the 'palazzetto' with two very worn lions and a loggia of two arches. Two roads continue from here to join N209 in the Valnerina, on the border with the Marches close to Visso (see *Blue Guide Northern Italy*).

From Norcia a straight road leads due S across the beautiful plain called the Piano di Santa Scolastica past the cemetery and church of (3km) *Santa Scolastica*, a 17–18C building on the site of a very early church. During restoration work in 1978 an interesting fresco cycle with scenes from the life of St Benedict was discovered beneath the whitewash. These date from the late 14C and early 15C. Just beyond, a lovely road, with splendid views leads up towards the MONTI SIBILLINI and crosses the border into the Marches at (22km) the *Forca Canapine* (1541m). Another road branches off this road before reaching the summit, across the *Piano Grande, a remarkable lonely upland plain beneath Monte Vettore (2478m). The scenery is particularly beautiful here and in the *Piani di Castelluccio*, a huge carsic basin on the site of a glacial lake, which is also of great botanical interest. 30km *Castelluccio* (1452m), is famous for its lentils, and a centre for excursions on foot in the Monti Sibillini (also visited by hang-gliders). It has a centrally-planned parish church (recalling the Madonna della Neve, see below) which contains a wood statue of the Madonna (c 1530).

From Santa Scolastica (see above) the road in the valley continues through Savelli to the site of the **Madonna della Neve**, 15km from Norcia, a beautiful Renaissance octagonal church (1565–71) on a design by Bramante which was totally ruined in the earthquake of 1979. A concrete band inserted into the drum during recent restoration work may have caused its destruction.

The road for Cascia from Norcia follows the N396 as far as (68km) *Serravalle* (see above) and then diverges S (N320) through a beautiful uninhabited and wooded valley. At *Logna* the parish church of San Giovenale has 16C votive frescoes and a wood statue of the Madonna and Child. The painting of the Madonna of Loreto with Saints Paul and Francis is by Francesco Vanni. 80km **CASCIA** (4000 inhab.), is famous for its sanctuary of St Rita, the 'Saint of impossibilities', who lived and died here in 1457. Built on the side of a hill it has been disfigured in recent years by new high buildings. It has all the usual characteristics of important pilgrimage shrines.

Information Office. 'APT della Valnerina-Cascia', Piazza Garibaldi (Tel. 0743/71147).

Buses to Norcia, Roccaporena, Monteleone di Spoleto, Foligno, Perugia, Terni, Rome, and Rieti.

Hotels and **Restaurants**. 3-star: 'Delle Rose', Via Teresa Fasce; 'Cursula', 3 Via Cavour; 'Monte Meraviglia', 15 Via Roma.

Annual Festival. 'Festa di Santa Rita' on 22 May. Good Friday procession.

History. The Roman municipium of Cursula was destroyed by earthquake and a new city founded on the side of the hill. By 553 it was known as Cascia. It has had a tumultuous history and has also been frequently devastated by earthquakes (especially in 1599, 1703, and 1979). St Rita was born in 1381 at Roccaporena 5 km W of Cascia. An Agostinian nun, she was canonised in 1900. Giovanni da Cascia, the musician, was also born here in the 14C.

At the entrance to the town is Piazza Garibaldi, with the church of **San Francesco**, built in 1424, with a fine portal and rose window. The interior, redesigned in the 17C and in 1925, has white stucco decoration. Trees can

Archangel Raphael with Tobias, attributed to the bottega of Antonio Rizzo, Pinacoteca, Cascia

be seen outside the E window. In a niche on the W wall, fresco of the Madonna and Child with two saints, and three saints by the Umbrian school (1443). S side, first altar, pavement tomb of Bishop Antonio Elemosina, who ordered the building of the church. On the third altar, Madonna and Child enthroned with two saints. In the nave are Roman fragments. Near the finely carved 17C wood pulpit are more frescoes including a Trinity, attributed to Bartolomeo di Tommaso da Foligno (c 1440). The S transept is covered for restoration. In the apse are 14C stalls and worn 15C frescoes. In the N transept is a beautiful large gilded wood altar by Fiorenzo di Giuliano incorporating an *Ascension by Nicolò Pomarancio (signed and dated 1596), and on either side, Noli me Tangere and Christ appearing to the Apostles, attributed to Pierino Cesarei. The church also owns a 15C wood statue of St Bernardine.

At the other end of the piazza is the collegiata of **Santa Maria**, the oldest church in Cascia, founded in 856. It has two doorways (1535 and 1620) and a Romanesque lion (the other one is in the little garden in front of the church). S wall, Deposition, fresco fragment by Nicola da Siena (very ruined, but being restored). First altar, Gaspare and Camillo Angelucci, 'Pala della Pace' (1547). At the E end of the N aisle the 16C font is to be recomposed. At the beginning of the N aisle, Nicolò Frangipane, Mysteries of the Rosary, surrounding a 15C carved Crucifix. Other precious works of art owned by the church are to be exhibited in the Pinacoteca in Palazzo Santi (see below). Near the church is the *Oratorio della Confraternità del Sacramento* with a 16C Madonna and Child with saints.

From Piazza Garibaldi steps lead down through an old gate to a road which leads to the church of **Sant'Antonio Abate** (sometimes used for exhibitions) which has an interesting fresco cycle of the life of St Anthony Abbot in the apse, and an Annunciation on the E wall, by the 15C Umbrian school. In the monks' choir are frescoes of the Passion by Nicola da Siena, and over the altar a carved 16C tabernacle.

Above Piazza Garibaldi is the town hall in *Palazzo Frenfanelli*. Next to it is *Palazzo Santi*, where the Pinacoteca is due to be opened soon. The contents include: wood statues including two by the bottega of Antonio Rizzo of the *Archangel Raphael with Tobias, and St Sebastian; 16C paintings; and works of art from the church of Santa Maria. Steps continue up to the ugly white **Basilica di Santa Rita**, built in 1937–47 on the site of an earlier church which dominates the town. The interior, in an unsuccessful combination of styles, is lavishly decorated.

Above the town is the church and convent of **Sant'Agostino** (signposted off the Monteleone road), which is closed for restoration. It was built in 1380. It contains 15C frescoes and a Madonna and Saints Augustine and Rita by Virgilio Nucci (1590). Above are the remains of the **Rocca**, built in 1465 and destroyed by papal troops in 1517.

Roccaporena, 5km W of Cascia, was the birthplace of St Rita: her house was transformed into a church in 1630 (and restored in 1946). The parish church of San Montano here dates from the 14C. In the criptoporticus of the Sanctuary of Santa Rita, erected in 1948, is a statue of her by Venanzo Crocetti. The tall rock (827m) called the 'Scoglio della Preghiera' can be climbed to visit the chapel of the Saint, reconstructed in 1981.

A hilly road (N471; signposted Leonessa) leads S from Cascia traversing beautiful farming country with few houses. In the river valley N471 continues S towards Leonessa in Lazio (see *Blue Guide Northern Italy*) while this route diverges right to climb up to the remote little town of (92km) **Monteleone di Spoleto** (990m).

At the beginning of this century, late Bronze Age tombs were found in the vicinity and a remarkable wooden chariot decorated with bronze reliefs, thought to be an Etruscan work (which was sold to the Metropolitan Museum of New York). The castle of Brufa, erected here in 880, came under the control of Spoleto from 1265 until 1559. After that date the little town prospered until it was severely damaged by earthquake in 1703 (and again hit in 1979).

A garden with old stone medieval measurements and two columns slopes up to the 14C Torre dell'Orologio with an archway beneath. On the right is the impressive restored exterior of the huge convent and church of *San Francesco*, founded in 1290. The Gothic *portal has fine carving. The cloister and interesting interior are still closed. Beyond the tower, beside which is a picturesque ruined portico, is the former *Palazzo dei Priori* which has been partially restored. Inside is a theatre (in need of total reconstruction). From Piazza del Mercato, with a few trees, there is a fine view of the valley. The houses and churches (including San Nicola) further up the hill, were badly shaken in 1979. At the bottom of the garden is the Corso which leads straight down to Porta Spoletina through the San Giacomo district, laid out on a grid plan. On the right is Porta San Giorgio and at the beginning of the Corso is *Palazzo Bernabò* (covered for restoration) with a fine façade. Beyond a house built in 1517, is the 17C *Palazzo Rotondi*, now the town hall, and another *Palazzo Bernabò* dating from the 17C with balconies. Beside the 14C gate is the former church of San Giovanni.

From Monteleone the beautiful road leads across the hills towards the Valnerina. At first it descends into another deserted valley and at 101km passes a turning for *Usigni* (2km; 1000m), a remote little village. The Baroque church of San Salvatore (well signposted) is attributed to Bernini. It was commissioned by cardinal Fausto Poli who was born here and who was a member of the court of Urban VIII. It is open only on Sunday (the key is kept by the priest in Poggiodomo). The mountainous Valnerina road continues through woods above the tiny lonely village of *Gavelli* (being restored after earthquake damage) on a precipitous cliff. The coral-coloured church of San Michele has been restored but is kept locked. It has an interesting interior with early-16C frescoes, some by Lo Spagna. The road continues steeply down, with a view of the pretty village of *Caso* (728m), below the road. The Romanesque bell-cote of the church of *Santa Cristina* (signposted) can be seen in woods to the right: it contains 14–16C frescoes.

119km **Sant'Anatolia di Narco** is in the **VALNERINA**. Tucked in amongst the narrow streets is the church of Sant'Anatolia (awaiting restoration). Below the church, beyond an arch and outside Porta Castello is Santa Maria delle Grazie with a pleasant exterior (1572–75). In the interior (ring for the key at No. 12 near Sant'Anatolia) is a 15C fresco of the Madonna and Saints by the 'Maestro di Eggi' on the E wall, surrounded by later frescoes by Pier Matteo Piergili who also frescoed the vault. Just before reaching the main road (N209) a rough road (signposted) leads right for San Felice di Narco. It passes a medieval fountain, a small chapel (the former pieve di Santa Maria di Narco), and crosses a bridge to the delightful 12C church of *San Felice di Narco* with a lovely façade (being restored). The fine reliefs include the Lamb of God on the tympanum. The beautiful interior has massive red-and-white paving stones. The raised sanctuary is flanked by two transennae. On the left wall of the nave is an interesting 15C fresco of the Adoration of the Magi (among the elongated figures is that of a falconer). In the apse is an early 15C fresco of the Redeemer. The crypt preserves an old sarcophagus. The little medieval village of *Castel San Felice* (or San Felice di Narco) is on a hill in the middle of the valley. It is being restored. **Vallo di Nera** is 3km from Castel San Felice up the Valnerina. It is a carefully restored village with attractive roofs. The lower church of *Santa Maria* (if closed ring at No. 4) contains an apse frescoed by Cola di Pietro da Camerino and Francesco di Antonio (1383) and frescoes in the nave also by Cola di Pietro. Lovely old red and white marble steps lead up past a barrel-vaulted chapel to the 14C church of *San Giovanni Battista* at the top of the town (if closed, ring at the priest's house next door), with apse frescoes by Jacopo Siculo (1536). From Piedipaterno a winding road (N395; 19km) leads across hills to Spoleto (see Rte 11). The upper part of the valley is described above.

The Terni road descends the valley past the pretty village of *Scheggino* below its castle (2-star hotel, with restaurant, 'Del Ponte', and 2-star camping site at Valcasana). On the left bank of the Nera is the church of San Nicolò with frescoes by Lo Spagna and a Madonna of the Rosary signed and dated 1595 by Pierino Cesarei. The road continues through *Ceselli* with two interesting churches and a rough road (right) leads up to the hamlet of *San Valentino* with a 13C church. 130km *Sambucheto* is near the splendid abbey of San Pietro in Valle. This, together with the road from here to (153km) Terni, is described in Rte 10.

INDEX TO ARTISTS

INDEX

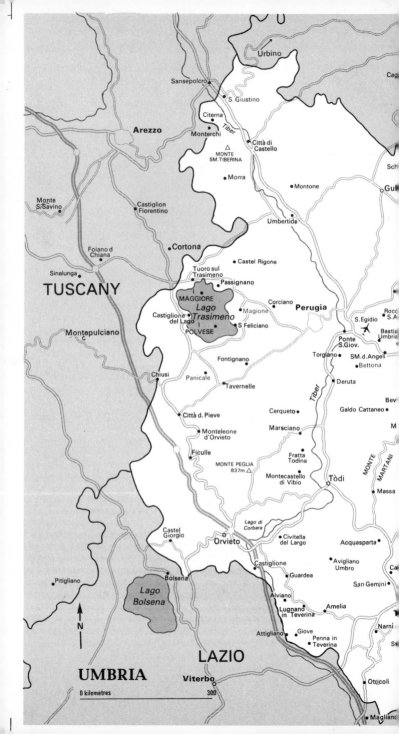

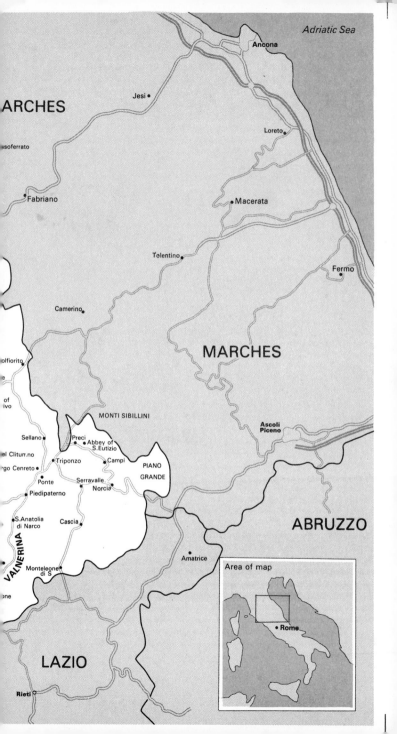

Adriatic Sea

MARCHES

asoferrato

Fabriano

Jesi •

Ancona

Loreto •

• Macerata

Tolentino •

Fermo •

Camerino •

MARCHES

olfiorito

of
ivo

Sellano •

el Clitur.no

rgo Cenreto •

Ponte •

Piedipaterno

S.Anatolia
di Narco

Preci
• Abbey of
S.Eutizio

• Triponzo • Campi

Serravalle
Norcia •

PIANO
GRANDE

Cascia •

MONTI SIBILLINI

Ascoli
Piceno

ABRUZZO

VALNERINA

Monteleone
di S

one

Amatrice •

LAZIO

Rieti ○

Area of map

• Rome